T0391263

Young Children's Language in Context

This book explores how young children's language development is intricately connected to the context in which it takes place. The term 'context' not only specifies a geographical location, but also encompasses notions of culture, community and activity. 'Context' also refers to discourse features and functions, and to the relationships between the speakers. Every context thus embodies specific practices, intentions and values which privilege particular words, phrases, meanings and communication conventions.

Each chapter highlights the dynamic, fluid and multifaceted interplays between language and context to illustrate how context, in every sense, is inextricably intertwined with young children's language and literacy learning opportunities. The chapters interrogate the topic of 'Young Children's Language in Context' by collectively exploring the multiple ways that context, broadly and variously conceptualised, intersects with language and literacy experiences. Authors examine how contexts shape language and literacy learning opportunities, how children's language shapes their social-interactive and relationship contexts, and how their language and literacy experiences are, themselves contexts which create socially and culturally endorsed ways to represent ideas, intentions and expectations. This book will be of interest to researchers and advanced students of early childhood education and language development. It was originally published as a special issue in the *International Journal of Early Years Education*.

Sheila Degotardi is Professor of early childhood education and the Director of the Centre for Research in Early Childhood Education at Macquarie University, Sydney Australia. Her research specialises in infant-toddler pedagogies, with a focus on language, social interactions and inter-personal relatedness.

Shelley Stagg Peterson is Professor of literacy education in the Department of Curriculum, Teaching and Learning at the Ontario Institute for Studies in Education of the University of Toronto (Canada). Her current project, Northern Oral language and Writing through Play (NOW Play), uses collaborative action research with teachers and early childhood educators to examine ways in which play and experiential learning can support young children's language and literacy.

Jiangbo Hu is Professor at Hangzhou College of Child Development and Education, Zhejiang Normal University (China), and an honorary research fellow at Macquarie School of Education, Macquarie University (Australia). Her research focuses on monolingual and bilingual children's early language experiences across different cultural settings.

Young Children's Language in Context

Edited by
Sheila Degotardi, Shelley Stagg Peterson and Jiangbo Hu

Routledge
Taylor & Francis Group

LONDON AND NEW YORK

First published 2023
by Routledge
4 Park Square, Milton Park, Abingdon, Oxon OX14 4RN

and by Routledge
605 Third Avenue, New York, NY 10158

Routledge is an imprint of the Taylor & Francis Group, an informa business

British Library Cataloguing in Publication Data
A catalogue record for this book is available from the British Library

ISBN13: 978-1-032-45997-4 (hbk)
ISBN13: 978-1-032-45998-1 (pbk)
ISBN13: 978-1-003-37962-1 (ebk)

DOI: 10.4324/9781003379621

Typeset in Minion Pro
by Newgen Publishing UK

Publisher's Note
The publisher accepts responsibility for any inconsistencies that may have arisen during the conversion of this book from journal articles to book chapters, namely the inclusion of journal terminology.

Disclaimer
Every effort has been made to contact copyright holders for their permission to reprint material in this book. The publishers would be grateful to hear from any copyright holder who is not here acknowledged and will undertake to rectify any errors or omissions in future editions of this book.

Contents

Citation Information   vii

Notes on Contributors   ix

Introduction—Language in context: positioning young children's language
and literacy learning within place, community and culture   1
Sheila Degotardi, Shelley Stagg Peterson and Jiangbo Hu

1   Mapping the literature on parent–child language across activity contexts: a
    scoping review   6
    Caitlin Holme, Sam Harding, Sue Roulstone, Patricia J. Lucas and Yvonne Wren

2   Language expansion in Chinese parent–child mealtime conversations:
    across different conversational types and initiators   25
    Ling Sheng, Wenming Dong, Feifei Han, Shiming Tong and Jiangbo Hu

3   'I'm a big boy, you're a baby': Negotiating labels, group boundaries and
    identities in an early childhood community of practice   41
    Anna Strycharz-Banaś, Carmen Dalli and Miriam Meyerhoff

4   Language as context: a case of early literacy practices in
    New Zealand and Sweden   55
    Amanda Bateman and Asta Cekaite

5   When and why do early childhood educators reminisce with children about
    their past experiences?   71
    Penny Van Bergen and Rebecca Andrews

6   Infant educators' use of mental-state talk in Australia and China: a
    cross-cultural comparative study   87
    Sheila Degotardi, Feifei Han and Jiangbo Hu

7 Viewing young children's drawing, talking, and writing through a
'language as context' lens: implications for literacy assessment 106
Shelley Stagg Peterson and Nicola Friedrich

Index 122

Citation Information

The chapters in this book were originally published in the *International Journal of Early Years Education*, volume 30, issue 1 (2022). When citing this material, please use the original page numbering for each article, as follows:

Introduction
Language in context: positioning young children's language and literacy learning within place, community and culture
Sheila Degotardi, Shelley Stagg Peterson and Jiangbo Hu
International Journal of Early Years Education, volume 30, issue 1 (2022), pp. 1–5

Chapter 1
Mapping the literature on parent-child language across activity contexts: a scoping review
Caitlin Holme, Sam Harding, Sue Roulstone, Patricia J. Lucas and Yvonne Wren
International Journal of Early Years Education, volume 30, issue 1 (2022), pp. 6–24

Chapter 2
Language expansion in Chinese parent–child mealtime conversations: across different conversational types and initiators
Ling Sheng, Wenming Dong, Feifei Han, Shiming Tong and Jiangbo Hu
International Journal of Early Years Education, volume 30, issue 1 (2022), pp. 25–40

Chapter 3
'I'm a big boy, you're a baby'. Negotiating labels, group boundaries and identities in an early childhood community of practice
Anna Strycharz-Banaś, Carmen Dalli and Miriam Meyerhoff
International Journal of Early Years Education, volume 30, issue 1 (2022), pp. 41–54

Chapter 4
Language as context: A case of early literacy practices in New Zealand and Sweden
Amanda Bateman and Asta Cekaite
International Journal of Early Years Education, volume 30, issue 1 (2022), pp. 55–70

Chapter 5

When and why do early childhood educators reminisce with children about their past experiences?
Penny Van Bergen and Rebecca Andrews
International Journal of Early Years Education, volume 30, issue 1 (2022), pp. 71–86

Chapter 6

Infant educators' use of mental-state talk in Australia and China: a cross-cultural comparative study
Sheila Degotardi, Feifei Han and Jiangbo Hu
International Journal of Early Years Education, volume 30, issue 1 (2022), pp. 87–105

Chapter 7

Viewing young children's drawing, talking, and writing through a 'language as context' lens: implications for literacy assessment
Shelley Stagg Peterson and Nicola Friedrich
International Journal of Early Years Education, volume 30, issue 1 (2022), pp. 106–121

For any permission-related enquiries please visit:
www.tandfonline.com/page/help/permissions

Notes on Contributors

Rebecca Andrews, School of Education, Macquarie University, Sydney Australia.

Amanda Bateman, Te Kura Toi Tangata - School of Education, University of Waikato, Hamilton, New Zealand.

Asta Cekaite, Department of Child Studies, Linköping University Linköping, Sweden.

Carmen Dalli, Faculty of Education, Victoria University of Wellington, Wellington, New Zealand.

Sheila Degotardi, Macquarie School of Education, Macquarie University, Sydney, Australia.

Wenming Dong, Hangzhou College of Preschool Education, Zhejiang Normal University, Xiaoshan District, People's Republic of China.

Nicola Friedrich, Department of Curriculum, Teaching, and Learning, OISE/University of Toronto, Toronto, Canada.

Feifei Han, Office of Pro-Vice-Chancellor (Arts, Education and Law), Griffith Institute for Educational Research, Griffith University, Brisbane, Australia.

Sam Harding, Bristol Speech and Language Therapy Research Unit, North Bristol NHS Trust, Bristol, UK.

Caitlin Holme, Bristol Speech and Language Therapy Research Unit, North Bristol NHS Trust, Bristol, UK; Faculty of Health Sciences, University of Bristol, Bristol, UK.

Jiangbo Hu, Hangzhou College of Child Development and Education, Zhejiang Normal University, Hangzhou, People's Republic of China.

Patricia J. Lucas, School for Policy Studies, University of Bristol, Bristol, UK.

Miriam Meyerhoff, All Souls College, University of Oxford, Oxford, UK.

Shelley Stagg Peterson, Department of Curriculum, Teaching and Learning, OISE/University of Toronto, Toronto, ON, Canada.

Sue Roulstone, Bristol Speech and Language Therapy Research Unit, North Bristol NHS Trust, Bristol, UK; Centre for Health and Applied Sciences, University of the West of England, Bristol, UK.

Ling Sheng, Hangzhou College of Preschool Education, Zhejiang Normal University, Xiaoshan District, People's Republic of China.

Anna Strycharz-Banaś, Faculty of Education, Victoria University of Wellington, Wellington, New Zealand.

Shiming Tong, Hangzhou College of Preschool Education, Zhejiang Normal University, Xiaoshan District, People's Republic of China.

Penny Van Bergen, School of Education, Macquarie University, Sydney Australia.

Yvonne Wren, Bristol Speech and Language Therapy Research Unit, North Bristol NHS Trust, Bristol, UK; Faculty of Health Sciences, University of Bristol, Bristol, UK.

Introduction—Language in context: positioning young children's language and literacy learning within place, community and culture

Sheila Degotardi, Shelley Stagg Peterson and Jiangbo Hu

The early childhood years are a critical period for the development of language and literacy skills. Not only do most children rapidly learn to understand and speak one or more languages, but they also learn to assign representational meaning to sounds and symbols. These skills allow young children to communicate with those around them, engage in conversations, share their ideas and information, and receive information from others. Children's engagement with language and literacy, and their subsequent language and literacy development therefore constitute a powerful and foundational tool for learning (Barnes 2011; Boyd and Galda 2011; Mercer and Littleton 2007; Zauch et al. 2016).

While human beings are born with innate neurological dispositions that enable the development of language and literacy skills, young children's language development cannot be divorced from the context in which it takes place. The term 'context' frequently specifies a geographical location, but the concept is much broader, encompassing notions of culture and community as well as the activity within which human behaviour occurs (Gruenewald 2003). When considering language and literacy learning, context also refers to discourse features and functions, and to the relationships between the speakers (Halliday 2003). Every context thus embodies specific practices, intentions and values, so each one privileges particular words, phrases, meanings and communication conventions (Montag, Jones, and Simit 2018).

Context, in every sense, is therefore inextricably intertwined with young children's language and literacy learning opportunities. The inter-relationships, however, are complex, consisting of dynamic, fluid and multifaceted interplays between language and context. At one level, context will influence, or even prescribe language and literacy learning opportunities. Specific activity contexts bring with them scripts and narratives that are structured by the function and nature of the activity itself (Nelson 1985, 2007). These 'interaction formats' (Bruner 1985) provide children with meaningful experiences with the words, language functions and conversational rituals which are particular that that context. The familiarity and predictability of these formats and scripts enable children to both participate in, and derive meaning from the language interactions that occur (LeMonda et al. 2019; Degotardi and Pearson 2017).

At another level, children's language shapes the context. The nature, content and intentionality of children's words and conversations establish relationship dynamics that may include or exclude others and other worldviews. Using language and nonverbal communication modes, children also establish roles and narratives that are part of the meaning-making process in interactional contexts. Through their intentional use of words and phrases, children create linguistic repertoires for constructing and negotiating social meanings and ideas. The resulting communities of practice (Wenger 1998) see children using language to reproduce, invent and transform their social-interactive and relationship contexts (Corsaro 2005).

A further level of complexity is seen when young children's language and literacy experiences are conceptualised *as* a context. On one hand, because language is firmly embedded within social and cultural knowledge and value systems, language experience reflects sociocultural identity and thus creates contexts of socially and culturally endorsed ways to represent ideas, intentions and expectations (Bornstein and Cheah 2006; Purcell-Gates 2007). On the other hand, language use itself may comprise a context in which children are presented with meaning-making opportunities that are available through the affordances of the language and discourse experiences that they themselves create (Eggins 2004).

The papers included in this special issue interrogate the topic of 'Young Children's Language in Context' by collectively exploring the multiple ways that context, broadly and variously conceptualised, intersects with language and literacy experiences. The first two papers draw attention to the ways in which young children's language experiences can be shaped by the situational and cultural context in which they occur. The question of how language experiences vary according to the activity in which they take place is addressed by Caitlin Holme, Sam Harding, Sue Roulstone, Patricia Lucas and Yvonne Wren. These authors conducted a comprehensive scoping review to summarise and synthesise the findings of 59 relevant studies that examined variation in parent and young children's talk across different activities, including play, book-reading, routine, caregiving contexts, and electronic media use. By noting that 'interactions do not occur in a vacuum but are embedded within the activity contexts in which children spend their daily lives,' their findings can inform those who wish to identify ways to foster early language learning in everyday contexts.

Also considering how language use can be shaped by culture, Ling Sheng, Wenming Dong, Feifei Han and Jiangbo Hu focused on the Chinese family's language expansion in mealtime conversations. Their study reveals dynamic interactions between different types of conversations and language functions, which were initiated by both Chinese parents and children in a culturally specific way. The characteristics of language expansion across the different types of conversations demonstrated how language use can be shaped by the context of communication conventions embedded in Chinese culture. The findings have the implication for promoting mealtime conversations as a language learning context for young children in terms of using expanded language for maintaining the coherence of conversations for meaning-making.

The next three papers in our special issue shine a spotlight on how the language used by young children shapes their social-interactive and learning contexts. In a longitudinal study which traced how children's language choices over the course of 18 months, Anna Strycharz-Banas, Carmel Dalli and Miriam Meyerhoff examine how these children's used labels like 'big boy' and 'baby' to establish and manage their peer relationship contexts. Through a series of conversation extracts, their papers demonstrate how children used these labels to establish and re-negotiate individual and collective identities and boundaries. Their study draws attention to how 'aspiring or "apprentice" members of a community of practice learned how to use the linguistic routines that characterised membership.' Findings speak to how young children recognise that language can establish power relationships, and how children's competency in using the linguistic routines that characterise particular relationship contexts is instrumental in cementing group membership.

By applying an ethno-methodological approach to child-educator interactions, Amanda Bateman and Aste Cekaite explored how literacy expectations in early childhood curricula in Sweden and New Zealand are implemented through talk-in-interaction between children and educators. This study moves away from the broader perspective of context being a static environmental space to context as co-constructed by the participants through their immediate interactions. The conversational analysis illustrates the different features of these children's literacy learning experiences, considering a variety of contextual resources involving the concrete social situations, the types of activities, the participants' knowledge about topics, and their interactional biographies.

The 229 Australian early childhood educators surveyed in Penny Van Bergen's and Rebecca Andrews' study explained that they engage in reminiscing conversations about shared past experiences with infants and three-to-five-year-old children multiple times on a daily basis in their long day care settings. Educator-child reminiscing is viewed as a context for engaging children 'in potentially rich, decontextualised conversations about their own past experiences.' Children construct new meanings of their experiences as they make connections between past experience and the new information that educators provide in mediation that is both spontaneous and relevant (Vygotsky 1978). In addition to supporting children's conceptual learning, the shared reminiscing interactions provide a context for children to develop language, as well as social and emotional competence. These interactions contribute to children's building of a sense of self, and to the creation of emotional bonds between children and educators.

The final two papers emphasise the positioning of language *as* context. Sheila Degotardi, Feifei Han and Jiangbo Hu present the first study to examine cross-cultural differences in the mental state talk used by infant-toddler educators in China and Australia. The authors note that caregivers' explicit references to desires, emotions, perceptions and cognitions form a critical aspect of the linguistic context which socialises young children into ways of talking and thinking about the mind (Degotardi 2015; Meins et al. 2003). The study uses naturally occurring educator talk to infants, and compares the frequency of different categories of mental state talk between the two cultural cohorts. The reported differences appear to reflect deep-rooted cultural philosophical approaches to child-rearing and education, with implications for understanding cultural differences in developmental trajectories of young children's understanding of the mind.

In the final article, Shelley Stagg Peterson and Nicola Friedrich conceptualise the assessment of five- to six-year-old children's writing and drawing, a familiar practice in Canadian kindergarten and Grade 1 classrooms, as an interaction context (Bruner 1985) in which roles taken up by children and a researcher can be examined through analysing the purposes and socio-cultural understandings communicated in children's self-talk and talk with the researcher, as well as in children's drawing and writing. Children's talk supported and at the same time, provided a window into the planning, revising, monitoring and consolidating processes of children's symbolic meaning-making. In this respect, the talk provided a context for children to meet the challenges of creating texts (Myhill and Jones 2009) and for the researcher to carry out the familiar assessment role of the teacher. In many respects, the roles taken up in the assessment context were consistent with socially expected roles of teacher and student. However, the talk in this child–adult interaction also created a context for the researcher and the children to co-construct meaning, transforming their expected roles. In some instances, the researchers took up roles as conversational partners who were interested in the stories and understandings that children were communicating in their texts.

This special issue aims to interrogate the many ways that 'context' is inextricably intertwined with young children's language- and literacy learning experiences. Collectively, the papers represent a multi-theoretical and multi-methodological approach to understanding and appreciated the situatedness and diversity of young children's language and literacy experiences. At a time when governments and policy-makers are increasingly seeking pedagogical methods that can be 'scaled up' and applied uniformly across a variety of contexts, these papers remind us that language, in all its forms and features, is inherently local.

Montag, Jones, and Simit (2018) have argued that any particular language learning experience is 'not merely a big bag of words, but a sequence of small bags of words encountered in time' (p. 401). Each context presents a unique bag of words, phrases and texts which will shape children's learning and identity. As Snow (2017) eloquently observes:

> Conversations constitute situations in which language is linked to context, in which knowledge structures and built and elaborated and in which, because they get answers to the questions they pose, children become increasingly curious. Those are the real mechanisms for building better brains (p. 8).

The papers in this special issue therefore collectively reject calls to decontextualise pedagogical approaches to language and literacy learning. Instead, they draw attention to the real-world, localised interactions that support young children as meaning-makers within their communities and cultures.

Disclosure statement

No potential conflict of interest was reported by the author(s).

References

Barnes, Douglas. 2011. "Exploratory Talk for Learning." In *Exploring Talk in School*, edited by Nancy Mercer, and Steve Hodgkinson, 1–15. Thousand Oaks, CA: Sage.

Bornstein, Marc H., and Charissa S. L. Cheah. 2006. "The Place of "Culture and Parenting" in the Ecological Contextual Perspective on Developmental Science." In *Parenting Beliefs, Behaviors, and Parent-Child Relations*, edited by Kenneth H. Rubin and Ock Boon Chung, 3–33. New York, NY: Psychology Press.

Boyd, Maureen P., and Lee Galda. 2011. *Real Talk in Elementary Classrooms: Effective Oral Language Practice*. New York, NY: Guilford.

Bruner, Jerome. 1985. "The Role of Interaction Formats in Language Acquisition." In *Language and Social Situations*, edited by J. P. Forgas, 31–46. Heidelburg, Germany: Springer.

Corsaro, William A. 2005. *The Sociology of Childhood*. 2nd ed. Thousand Oaks, CA: Pine Forge Press.

Degotardi, Sheila. 2015. "Mind Mindedness: Forms, Features and Implications for Infant-Toddler Pedagogy." In *Routledge International Handbook of Young Children's Thinking*, edited by S. Robson, and S. Flannery Quinn, 179–188. London: Routledge.

Degotardi, Sheila, and Emma Pearson. 2017. "Infant Play: How Interactions Build and Support Relationships." In *Play in Early Childhood Education: Learning in Diverse Contexts*, edited by Marjory Ebbeck, and Manjula Waniganayake, 76–96. Sydney: Oxford University Press.

Eggins, Suzanne. 2004. *An Introduction to Systemic Functional Linguistics*. 2nd ed. London: Continuum.

Gruenewald, David A. 2003. "Foundations of Place: A Multidisciplinary Framework for Place-Conscious Education." *American Educational Research Journal* 40 (3): 619–654. doi:10.3102/00028312040003619.

Halliday, M. A. K. 2003. *The Language of Early Childhood*, edited by Jonathan J. Webster. London: Continuum.

LeMonda, Tamis, S. Catherine, Stephanie Custode, Yana Kuchiro, Kelly Escobar, and Tiffany Lo. 2019. "Routine Language: Speech Directed to Infants During Home Activities." *Child Development* 90 (6): 2135–2152. doi:10.1111/cdev.1308.

Meins, E., Charles Fernyhough, Rachel Wainwright, David Clark-Carter, Mani Das Gupta, Emma Fradley, and Michelle Tuckey. 2003. "Pathways to Understanding Mind: Construct Validity and Predictive Validity of Maternal Mind-Mindedness." *Child Development* 74 (4): 1194–1211. doi:10.1111/1467-8624.00601.

Mercer, Nancy, and Karen Littleton. 2007. *Dialogue and the Development of Children's Thinking: A Sociocultural Approach*. New York, NY: Routledge.

Montag, Jessica L., Michael N. Jones, and Linda B. Simit. 2018. "Quantity and Diversity: Stimulating Early Word Learning Environments." *Cognitive Science* 42 (2): 375–412. doi:10.1111/cogs.12592.

Myhill, Debra, and Susan Jones. 2009. "How Talk Becomes Text: Investigating the Concept of Oral Rehearsal in Early Years' Classrooms." *British Journal of Educational Studies* 57 (3): 265–284.

Nelson, Katherine. 1985. *Making Sense: The Acquisition of Shared Meaning*. New York, NY: Academic Press.

Nelson, Katherine. 2007. *Young Minds in Social Worlds: Experience, Meaning, and Memory*. Cambridge, MA: Harvard University Press.

Purcell-Gates, Victoria. 2007. "Complicating the Complex." In *Cultural Practices of Literacy: Case Studies of Language, Literacy, Social Practices, and Power*, edited by V. Purcell-Gates, 1–22. New York, NY: Routledge.

Snow, Catherine E. 2017. "The Role of Vocabulary Versus Knowledge in Children's Language Learning: A Fifty Year Perspective." *Infancia y Aprendizaje* 40 (1): 1–18. doi:10.1080/02103702.2016.1263449.

Vygotsky, Lev. 1978. *Mind in Society: The Development of Higher Psychological Processes*. Cambridge, MA: Harvard University Press.

Wenger, Etienne. 1998. *Communities of Practice: Learning, Meaning, and Identity*. Cambridge, UK: Cambridge University Press.

Zauch, Lauren Head, Taylor A. Thul, Ashley E. Darcey Mahoney, and Jennifer L. Stapel-Wax. 2016. "Influence of Language Nutrition on Children's Language and Cognitive Development: An Integrated Review." *Early Childhood Research Quarterly* 36: 318–333. doi:10.1016/j.ecresq.2016.01.015.

ORCID

Sheila Degotardi ⓘ http://orcid.org/0000-0003-2066-2223
Shelley Stagg Peterson ⓘ http://orcid.org/0000-0001-6985-5603
Jiangbo Hu ⓘ http://orcid.org/0000-0001-5471-7689

Mapping the literature on parent–child language across activity contexts: a scoping review

Caitlin Holme ⓘ, Sam Harding ⓘ, Sue Roulstone ⓘ, Patricia J. Lucas ⓘ and Yvonne Wren ⓘ

ABSTRACT

Linguistic interactions between parents and their children are frequently studied to investigate how children acquire language. From observations, researchers have identified interaction strategies that foster children's language development. In turn, interventions to support children's early language skills employ styles of interaction derived from these observations. However, researchers have not often considered how the activity context selected for observation may affect the language used, or whether these contexts reflect children's diverse experiences.

The aim of this scoping review was to explore the breadth of literature about language use across a range of activities. Included studies described linguistic outputs of parents and typically developing children (aged 1;0–5;11 years) and activity context(s). Searches were conducted in PsycInfo, Medline, CINAHL, ERIC-ProQuest and Google Scholar.

From 16,718 records, 59 studies were retained. Studies were charted according to the population included, linguistic outputs recorded, activity contexts studied and the methodological design. To allow for comparison of results across activity contexts, five thematic categories were identified: play activities, book reading, naturalistic routines, media and methodological implications. Challenges for future research are discussed, including ways to ensure the ecological validity of findings by coupling naturalistic language recordings with data collected during diverse everyday activity contexts.

1. Introduction

For decades, researchers have employed various methods to observe language used during social interactions between parents and children (Bergelson et al. 2019; Nyberg et al. 2020). Data from these observations have been used to construct theories about

ⓑ Supplemental data for this article can be accessed https://doi.org/10.1080/09669760.2021.2002135.

how children acquire language and to highlight how participation in communicative exchanges predicts children's vocabulary development (Zimmerman et al. 2009). Critical to these theories is the understanding that language acquisition is a mutual process (Donnelly and Kidd 2021), with linguistic outputs from both caregiver and child contributing to later lexical development. Theories have in turn been vital in informing early intervention for children who are struggling to acquire language (van Kleeck 1994).

1.1. Methods for studying parent–child language

Historically, psycholinguistic studies have been based on observations of infants and their parents in laboratory settings, engaging in activities selected by researchers for ease of eliciting and recording child language (Yont, Snow, and Vernon-Feagans 2003). While these approaches might be methodologically attractive in reducing potential confounders or distractions, they may not capture children's everyday interactions as they occur at home (Wang et al. 2020). Indeed, Casillas, Brown, and Levinson (2020) note that children's exposure to language ebbs and flows throughout the day during different daily activities.

In recent years, new technologies have been developed to record naturalistic observations in the home using automated recording devices (Bergelson et al. 2019). These methods do not require the researcher to be present, thereby avoiding risks to ecological validity caused by power asymmetries and potential impact on caregiver behaviours (Paugh and Riley 2019; Dudley-Marling and Lucas 2009). These naturalistic recordings are less labour intensive and also provide a large amount of linguistic data which is more reflective of children's day to day experiences (Greenwood et al. 2011).

However, researchers have found that without context, data from naturalistic recordings can be difficult to interpret (d'Apice, Latham, and von Stumm 2019). Kuchirko (2019) argues that for researchers to understand how children acquire language, they must consider naturalistic linguistic interactions in real time and across diverse everyday activities.

1.2. Activity contexts in early intervention

Knowledge of how activity contexts relate to differences in language is vital to speech and language therapists and early years practitioners, who often use interventions based on parent–child interaction (PCI) when working with children with developmental language delays (Roulstone et al. 2015). The evidence suggests that parents are more likely to find PCI interventions acceptable when they are oriented to their family's routines and activities, and consistent with their wider belief systems (O'Toole, Lyons, and Houghton 2021). As Crago (1992, 34) comments, 'without knowing the cultural situations, interactions and interactants in a child's life, the clinician may not be able to structure the situation and the participants in the language-sampling process in an effective way'.

Gaining an understanding of how linguistic outputs vary across activities and interactions can inform intervention. However, reviews to date have focussed on PCI in clinical populations (Blackwell et al. 2014) or how children's home environments and parent behaviours affect language outcomes (Topping, Dekhinet, and Zeedyk 2011). Reviews have only considered the impact of specific activities like book reading (Manz et al. 2010) or screen time (Madigan et al. 2020). In a recent meta-analysis about the effects of quantity and quality of parental linguistic input on child language skills, Anderson et al. (2021) charted data about the location and context of observations. However, they did not consider potential differences between specific activity contexts, or their effect on child language outputs.

In summary, it is important to understand the current evidence regarding variation in parent and child language use across activities in order to consider how methodological choices could influence findings. Moreover, for interventions to be tailored to individual families, it is important that practitioners understand the range of activities and interactions that children take part in at home. Following the 'Population, Concept, Context' framework recommended for scoping reviews (Peters et al. 2020), we defined the 'population' of interest as parents and preschool-aged children, the 'concept' as their linguistic outputs across different situations, and the 'context' as the activities that have been studied. Therefore our research objective was to explore the range of existing literature about variation in linguistic outputs of parents and their preschool children across different activity contexts.

2. Methods

A scoping review methodology was appropriate for our exploratory research objective. Unlike a systematic review, scoping reviews typically do not include quality appraisal or formal synthesis and do not attempt to determine whether study findings are robust or generalisable (Arksey and O'Malley 2005). Instead, scoping reviews ask broad questions to examine the range of available evidence, and to synthesise findings from a body of knowledge that is heterogeneous in methods and discipline (Tricco et al. 2018). The scoping review was conducted in accordance with the Joanna Briggs Institute (JBI) methodology (Peters et al. 2020).

2.1. Eligibility criteria

2.1.1. Population
Study participants were parents/carers with a preschool-age child with typically developing language ability. Preschool age was defined as 1;0–5;11 years, to include an age range at which children have begun to produce identifiable words, but most children globally have not yet started formal schooling (World Bank Group 2020). Studies were excluded if children were bilingual, had an identified speech and language disorder/delay, a history of hearing difficulties, a chronic health condition, other developmental conditions or a congenital birth anomaly.

2.1.2. Concept
Studies were required to record interactions between parents and children and analyse an aspect of the linguistic output. Given that Blackwell et al.'s (2014) systematic review focussed on parent–child interaction literature within a similar age range, accepted outputs were adapted from their findings. These included: quantity of language, for example counts of adult or child words; complexity of language, for example lexical

diversity or mean length of utterance (MLU); dialogue participation, for example number of conversational turns; and syntactic features, such as counts of nouns or verbs.

2.1.3. Context

We included studies that compared language outputs across two or more activity contexts. A comparison could be 'within-activity', for example two book reading contexts that differed by book genre, or 'across-activity', for example a comparison of play and bath time. Studies were excluded if interactions took place between non-parental caregivers and children in early years settings.

2.1.4. Methodological approaches

We considered any study using a within-group design, to ensure that findings reflected variation in language use by the same participants across different activity contexts. To maintain a minimum standard of studies, papers were only included if they had been published within peer reviewed journals.

2.2. Search strategy

The full search strategy was developed with support from a clinical librarian, optimised in PsycInfo and then adapted for further databases (Supplementary Material 1). Studies published in languages other than English were excluded due to limited resources for translation.

2.2.1. Information sources

The following databases were searched: PsycInfo, Ovid Medline, CINAHL, ERIC-ProQuest and Google Scholar.

2.2.2. Source of evidence screening and selection

Search results were collated, uploaded to EndNote and deduplicated. Titles of studies clearly unrelated to the concept being studied were removed at this point. The first and second authors (CH and SH) independently reviewed 10% of the remaining abstracts to ensure consensus about inclusion, after which CH reviewed all remaining titles and abstracts. At full-text screening, a random sample of 20% of texts were reviewed by SH, with 100% agreement with CH on inclusion or exclusion of the sample. CH was sole reviewer for the remaining full text manuscripts, with consultation with SH for any cases where CH was unclear.

2.2.3. Data extraction

Data were extracted and charted from relevant papers using an extraction form developed according to JBI guidance (Peters et al. 2020), and piloted by CH and SH on four studies (Supplementary Material 2). Thematic categories were developed in advance and then amended iteratively during the charting process, for example additional activity categories were added to better reflect data from the studies.

2.2.4. Analysis and presentation of results

Data were calculated and presented in tables according to the population (participant characteristics), concept (linguistic outputs) and context (activities studied). In most cases a simple binary count was used to calculate the overall frequency of measures. For the population data, where studies had multiple participants who fell into different categories, calculations were made as a proportion of total participants across studies.

Data were also collated according to the methodology, methods of observation and setting that were used. Methodology was categorised as structured (specific instructions or tasks were given), semi-naturalistic (specific activities were selected but participants were free to act as they wished) or naturalistic (participants went about their routines free of constraints).

To present results, studies were first organised into themes. A narrative synthesis approach was then used to collate and describe the main findings of included studies.

3. Results

3.1. Overview of included studies

The PRISMA flowchart in Figure 1 illustrates the full screening process. Of 12,469 unique records, 816 were selected for full text screening. After searching university and clinical library databases and contacting authors via Research Gate, 15 studies could not be retrieved. Of the 801 manuscripts that were screened in full, 59 were selected for inclusion. Reasons for exclusion at full-text level are displayed in Figure 1.

3.2. Review findings

A table with individual details of included studies is provided in Supplementary Material 3. A total of 60 studies were charted, as one article reported two separate studies (Gelman, Chesnick, and Waxman 2005).

3.2.1. Population

Children were evenly split by gender (50.5% were boys). Studies most frequently included children within the 12–23 month age range (31 studies) and 24–35 month age range (29 studies). While 31 studies did not give an explanation of how children were defined as typically developing, 14 studies used a defined language measure such as the Peabody Picture Vocabulary Test. The remainder relied on parent report, general measures of health or researcher screening (five studies each). English was the home language of participants in 31 studies while 13 articles represented participants who spoke additional languages. The child's language was not listed in 17 studies but was also presumed to be English due to university affiliation of authors or location of the study.

Of the parent participants, 89.2% (n=1735) were mothers. In 29 studies all participants were from mid-high socioeconomic status (SES), while 22 studies gave no information about SES. Overall 56.6% (n=747) of participants were from the USA and from Caucasian or European American ethnicities (n=1006, 84.7%). Nine studies did not provide information about ethnicity or cultural background of participants. Full details about child and parent participants can be found in Supplementary Material 4.

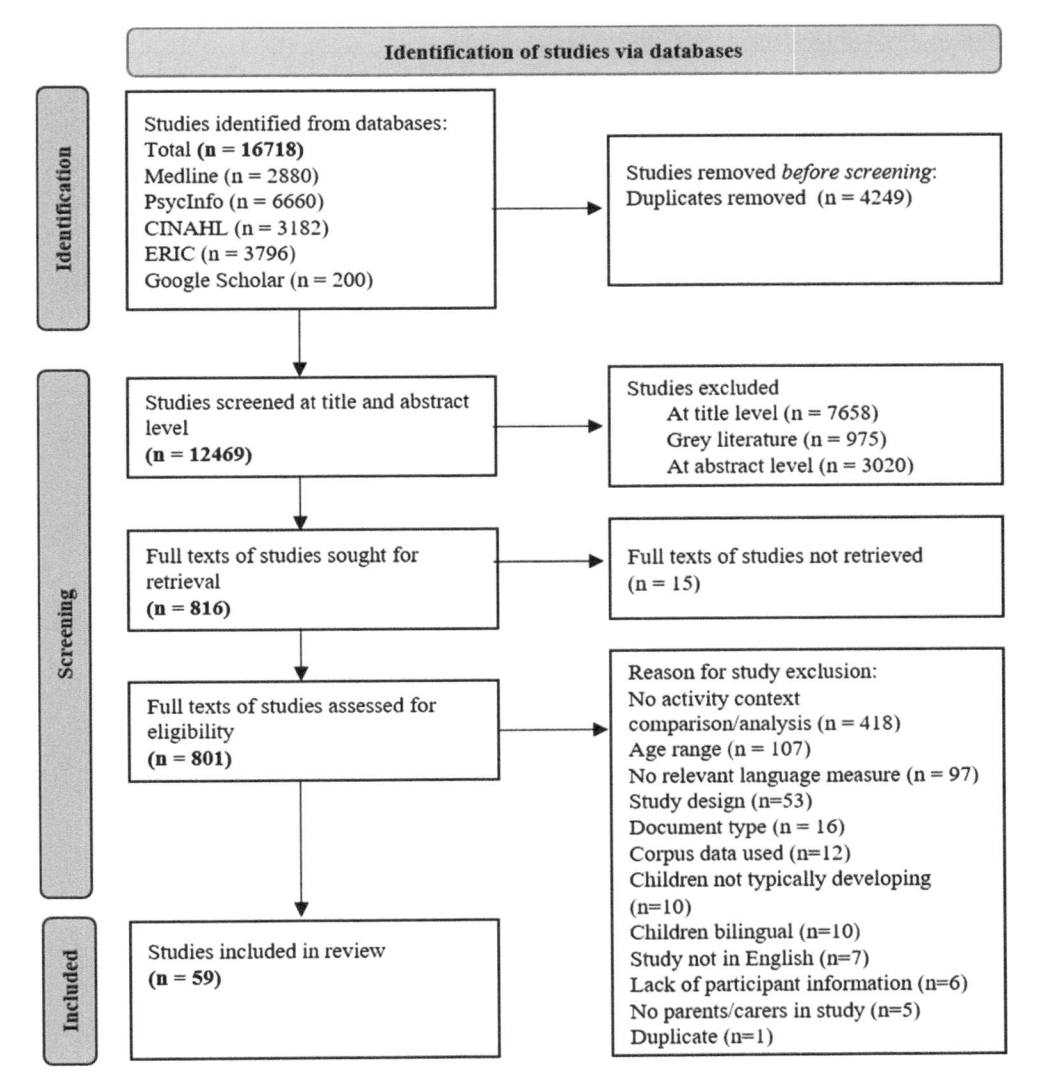

Figure 1. PRISMA flow diagram for article selection.

3.2.2. Concept

Table 1 illustrates the overall frequency of linguistic outputs reported in studies.

Quantity of language was the most frequent linguistic output reported, with 37 studies including a count of words or utterances. Another frequently reported measure was the purpose of language (32 studies), for example whether parents used language to elaborate or direct. Syntactic variation was less frequently reported, although within this category 13 studies provided a count of syntactic features, most frequently nouns and verbs.

3.2.3. Context

Distribution of activity contexts by frequency is presented in Figure 2. The most frequently studied activity contexts were play (36 studies) and book reading (32 studies).

Table 1. Table of language output measures.

	Count of articles	Percentage of total articles
Participant that measures related to		
Parent	21	35.0%
Child	3	5.0%
Both parent and child	36	60.0%
Quantity of language		
Total words/utterances	37	61.7%
Words/utterances per minute	11	18.3%
Count type/token or type-token ratio (TTR)	26	43.3%
Complexity of language		
Lexical diversity	13	21.7%
Mean length of utterance (MLU)	25	41.7%
Use of abstract language	4	6.7%
Dialogue participation		
Conversational turns/topic continuation	10	16.7%
Purpose of language (describe, elaborate, request etc.)	32	53.3%
Type of communicative act (question, label, etc.)	22	36.7%
Syntax		
Count of syntactic features (e.g. nouns/verbs)	13	21.7%
Grammatical complexity	4	6.7%

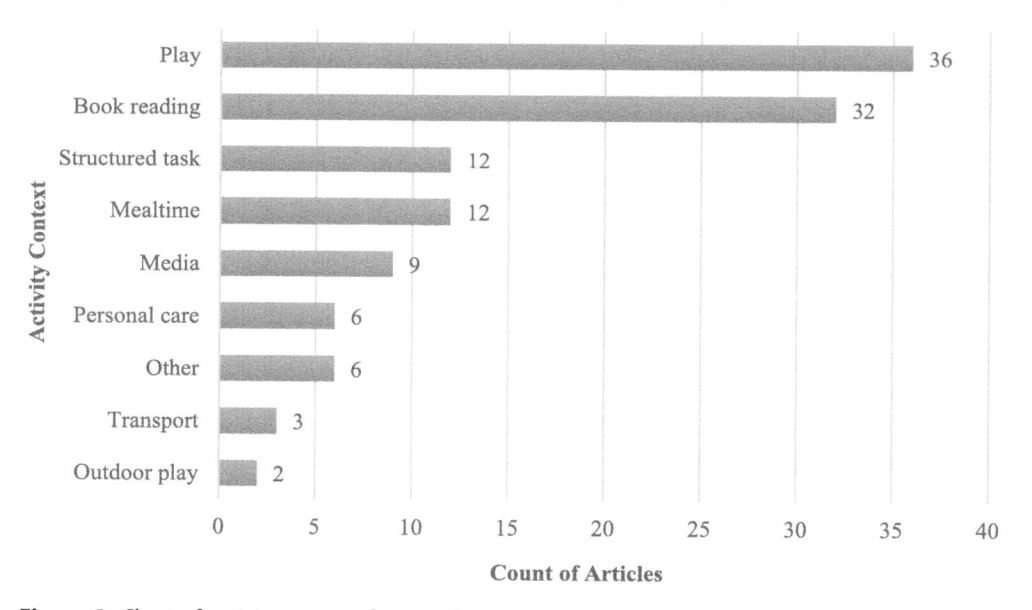

Figure 2. Chart of activity context frequencies.

Daily routine activities such as mealtime (12 studies) and personal care (six studies), for example dressing or bath time, were less commonly studied than play or structured activities.

3.2.4. Methodological approaches

Overall 34 studies used a structured design. Semi-naturalistic contexts were used in 17 studies and naturalistic designs for six. In addition three studies compared structured and naturalistic study designs to illustrate differences in linguistic outputs across contexts. Observations were most frequently recorded in children's homes (29 studies), followed by university laboratories (18 studies) or in more than one location (seven studies). One study took place in a nursery and five studies did not provide information about location.

The method most frequently used to record parents and children was via videotape (38 studies), while audio-recording was used in eight studies and a combination of video and audio in seven. LENA™ (The LENA Research Foundation 2021) digital language processors were used in three studies and head-mounted cameras in one study. The researcher was present for the observation in 30 studies, absent in 16 studies and this information was not specified in 14 studies. Where the researcher was absent from the observation, this was either because a remote recording device was used, the equipment was set up by caregivers, or because researchers recorded the interaction from an adjacent room.

3.3. Narrative summary

To compare findings, studies were organised into themes, identified according to the study objectives and main activity contexts included. Details of quantitative results and statistics are included in Supplementary Material 3. A table providing further contextual detail about activities included within studies is displayed in Supplementary Material 5.

3.3.1. Play activities

Play was the most frequently studied activity context. Studies that compared play with book reading activities found that play was associated with fewer overall utterances (Jones and Adamson 1987), and shorter utterances (Poulain and Brauer 2018). In contrast, Doering, Schluter, and von Suchodoletz (2020) saw the opposite effect for US mothers, who used more complex utterances during play than book reading. The authors suggest that linguistic outputs may depend on whether parents view play as an educational opportunity, or a chance to passively observe their child. Crain-Thoreson, Dahlin, and Powell (2001) also saw linguistic variation according to how an activity was structured by parents. In their study, children were exposed to more lexically diverse language during book reading, but there was a more even ratio of parent to child utterances in play, suggesting that during this activity parents gave children more opportunities to participate in the conversation. In Kertoy and Vetter's (1995) study, mothers also incorporated children into the conversation more during play than while completing a structured cooking activity. However, Kaye and Charney (1981) found that turn-taking behaviours remained consistent across book reading and play contexts.

Studies also examined noun and verb use in play and reading across multiple languages. Results suggested that the proportion of nouns used by parents is higher during book reading, while verb use is greater during play (Tardif, Gelman, and Xu 1999; Ogura et al. 2006; Altinkamiş, Kern, and Sofu 2014). In contrast Choi (2000) found that English-speaking mothers emphasised nouns in both book reading and play contexts. Goldfield (1993) studied the influence of different types of play on noun and verb use, and found that while noun types and tokens were more frequent in toy-play, verb types and tokens were more frequent in non-toy-play.

Researchers also considered how the type of toy may influence opportunities for language, finding that toys which promoted engagement in role play activities, such as toy shops or dolls, were associated with more verbal interaction and co-operative communication (Leaper and Gleason 1996) and overall number and length of utterances (O'Brien and Nagle 1987). In contrast, Ryckebusch and Marcos (2004) found that parents used more action requests during structured 'building' play with construction toys than during play with other toys. Studies also considered the representational status of toys or other objects in relation to language. In a study by Gelman, Chesnick, and Waxman (2005), overall amounts of language were higher when talking about objects as compared to pictures, while Jipson, Gülgöz, and Gelman (2016) found that talk about a living creature elicited more gendered pronouns and proper names.

Finally, studies considered how the familiarity of toys may impact the language that parents and children use. Lucariello and Nelson (1986) found that during general play contexts, children used more basic level tokens as compared with novel and unfamiliar contexts. In contrast, in Farrar, Friend, and Forbes' (1993) study, children used more lexical types when playing with toys that represented familiar events, as compared with unfamiliar events. Studies investigating how parents scaffold language when discussing unfamiliar objects found that parents produced new nouns in more salient utterance positions (Cleave and Bird 2006) and were less likely to label objects that were unfamiliar to them or their child (Henderson and Sabbagh 2010).

3.3.2. Book reading

Contexts in which parents read books or tell stories to children were frequently highlighted as opportunities for children to receive rich and complex linguistic input. All-day recordings of parent–child interaction showed that, when compared with naturally occurring non-book reading interactions, book reading utterances had greater lexical diversity and syntactic complexity (Ece Demir-Lira et al. 2019) and involved a higher proportion of adult word counts and conversational turns (Gilkerson, Richards, and Topping 2017).

Results varied according to the method researchers used to structure reading activities, and the language included within their analyses. For example Sorsby and Martlew (1991) found that parents used a greater number of utterances in a structured task than during book reading, however they only counted extra-textual utterances in the book reading task. Using a different approach, Fraser and Roberts's (1975) structured task was compared with a 'story-telling' activity in which mothers were given picture prompts and allowed to construct the narrative themselves; in their study, story-telling was associated with significantly more utterances.

Studies also investigated how diverse forms of book reading or story telling might influence language outputs. Torr and Clugston (1999) found that compared with narrative books, while reading informational books parents used more extra-textual utterances and more questions requiring reasoning language. In contrast, Nyhout and O'Neill (2013) reported more complex language during narrative than didactic books. Variation has also been found in relation to the overall linguistic complexity of book text. Compared with simple picture books, books with more grammatical complexity within the text and chapter books were associated with less complex language from parents (Noble, Cameron-Faulkner, and Lieven 2018) and children (Leech and Rowe 2014). Noble, Cameron-Faulkner, and Lieven (2018) suggested this may be because parents rely more on the text to deliver the story in more complex narratives. In contrast, Muhinyi et al. (2020) found that books with more complex text facilitated extratextual talk, abstract language and elaboration by mothers, while Muhinyi and Hesketh (2017) found no significant differences in the amount of maternal talk and MLU when reading low text or high text books. Finally, Riordan et al. (2018) considered the influence of rhyme and found that parental reading styles were different during non-rhyme books, with more language incorporating inferences and predictions.

3.3.3. Naturalistic routines

Several studies found that routine contexts, such as mealtime and bath time, are associated with fewer utterances and less complex language from parents and children than either play or book reading (Rondal 1980; Camaioni and Longobardi 1995; Bornstein, Tamis-LeMonda, and Haynes 1999; Masur and Rodemaker 1999; Tulviste 2003; Flynn and Masur 2007; Hoff 2010). In contrast, others have found that mealtimes favoured more complex language from parents than play, with longer MLU (Lawrence and Shipley 1996), more sophisticated words (Weizman and Snow 2001) and more conversation-eliciting utterances (Hoff-Ginsberg 1991). Lawrence and Shipley (1996) and Tulviste and Raudsepp (1997) both compared use of directive language during mealtimes and structured tasks. Lawrence and Shipley (1996) found that parents used more directives during mealtimes, while Tulviste and Raudsepp's (1997) data showed that more language was used to direct physical activity or attention during the structured task.

Naturalistic recording methods allowed researchers to follow parents and children during their daily routines and document naturally occurring activities. The all-day recordings from Soderstrom and Wittebolle's (2013) study showed that book reading and organised playtime contexts (for example singing or painting activities) were associated with greater quantities of language, although these were also the activities that occurred least frequently. Lower levels of parental talk were found for mealtimes and travel, although child vocalizations were comparatively high during personal care. Soderstrom and Wittebolle (2013) found lower quantities of language when children were outdoors at the park, while Cameron-Faulkner, Melville, and Gattis (2018) showed that children were more talkative and engaged in more connected communication with parents in a natural outdoor environment as compared with an indoor activity. In Tamis-LeMonda et al.'s (2019) study, children were exposed to more words and more tokens per minute during book reading and personal care contexts than play or mealtime.

3.3.4. Media

With children's increasing exposure to electronic devices, studies have begun to investigate the influence of media on children's interactions. Pempek, Kirkorian, and Anderson (2014) and Ewin et al. (2021) found that presence of background television and parents' independent mobile phone use were associated with fewer utterances from parents.

Compared with independent mobile phone use, during joint engagement with devices parents used more utterances, although still fewer overall than during non-digital toy play. (Ewin et al. 2021) Lavigne, Hanson, and Anderson (2015) found that compared with free play, parents' total utterances decreased during joint television viewing, although their use of new words per utterance increased. Stoneman and Brody (1982) considered the influence of the genre of television, and found that mothers talked more and asked more questions about the programme content while watching an educational programme as compared with a sitcom.

Studies also considered the role of media in book reading by comparing digital books with print books. Print books were associated with more language (Worden, Kee, and Ingle 1987), increased dialogic practices (Munzer et al. 2019) and more expansions (Ozturk and Hill 2020), although Lauricella, Barr, and Calvert (2014) found that children verbalised more during electronic book reading.

3.3.5. Methodological implications

A small number of studies aimed to inform methodological approaches for recording parent and child language by considering the effect of changing the observational context. Kwon et al. (2013) found that language used by parents and children was more complex during free play as compared with a structured task, while Bornstein, Painter, and Park (2002) showed that children's utterances increased in frequency and length when in direct interaction with their mothers as compared to free play while close to their mothers. Stevenson et al. (1986) found no significant differences in the amount or complexity of parent and child language when comparing a home and laboratory setting. Data from Tamis-LeMonda et al. (2017) showed that while short, structured tasks were associated with consistently high amounts of complex language from parents, in real-life naturalistic routines language fluctuated across time, interspersed with periods of silence. Finally, studies considered the effect of time spent in a preschool setting on the language that parents and children use. Larson, Barrett, and McConnell (2020) found that adult word counts were slightly higher before taking children to child-care and after picking them up, as compared with days when children were at home all day. Marvin and Privratsky (1999) found no difference in the amount of talk that children used after preschool when they were given after school materials to take home.

4. Discussion

4.1. Summary of evidence

The primary aim of this scoping review was to explore the range of existing literature about variation in linguistic outputs of parents and their preschool children during different activity contexts.

Findings suggested that play activities provide opportunities for co-operative inter-action, while book reading is a context in which children are exposed to complex linguistic input. Results for routine activities like mealtime and personal care exhibited large variation, while interaction in infrequently studied activity contexts such as outdoor play merit further study. When remote recording methods were used to document children' daily routines, results confirmed that book reading and organised play contexts provided rich linguistic input (Soderstrom and Wittebolle 2013). However, these were also the activities that parents and children engaged in together least frequently. It is therefore interesting to consider whether the reliance on these contexts reflects children's real-life experiences.

The predominance of play and book reading contexts may also reflect a cultural bias among researchers. While play is seen as integral to children's development in many Western countries, Roopnarine (2011) reports that in many parts of the world, play is viewed as simply an activity that keeps children occupied. Book reading also reflects a cultural tradition which varies in frequency across cultures, as well as according to levels of parental literacy. Avineri et al. (2015) argue that our understanding of literacy events could be expanded by including a wider range of culturally relevant activities such as playing word games, singing songs or reciting prayers. The meaning that an activity holds may vary across families and their contexts, a finding that was also reflected in the studies presented here. For example, Doering, Schluter, and von Suchodoletz (2020) argued that differences in the language used during play may depend on whether parents view the activity as an educational opportunity. Similarly, Flynn and Masur (2007) state that given the 'goal-directed agenda' of a bath time context, language use depended on whether mothers were more focussed on interaction or on the task of bathing. For this reason, Tamis-LeMonda (2003) argues that studies should incorporate parents' views to better understand variation in how parents structure their child's activities and interactions.

We were also interested in understanding the range and diversity of participants that have been included in studies. Although our inclusion criteria focussed on parents and carers, 90% of participants were mothers. This is reflective of a general trend in parenting research that has largely focussed on maternal influences on development and neglected to include fathers or indeed any other type of carer (Cabrera, Volling, and Barr 2018). In addition, results from this review primarily represented participants who were of Caucasian or European American ethnicity and middle-class, in line with the participant sampling bias reported in developmental research (Nielsen et al. 2017). The prevalence of English-speaking participants from the USA is in line with reports that PCI interventions for speech and language are based on evidence about typical speech and language development in English, gathered from participants within the 'dominant' US culture (Leadbeater and Litosseliti 2014).

Finally, we considered how the range of methodological approaches used may affect study findings. Although most studies took place in children's homes, the majority of articles used a structured, researcher-directed design. Studies recognised potential limitations to ecological validity as a result of this methodological approach, given that interactions are recorded for a limited time only (Kwon et al. 2013) and the situational context was prompted by researchers (Doering, Schluter, and von Suchodoletz 2020). In addition, when studies compared naturalistic and structured interactions, they found that structured tasks typically led to more complex and dense language from parents, while quantity of language was more dispersed during naturalistic routines (Tamis-LeMonda et al. 2017). The predominant method for data collection was video recording. Some studies described how researchers attempted to be as 'unobtrusive' (Flynn and Masur 2007) or 'discreet' (Rondal 1980) as possible, while another study claimed that subjects 'seemed unaffected' by the presence of recording equipment (Worden, Kee, and Ingle 1987). In contrast, some did acknowledge how recording equipment (Ozturk and Hill 2020) and the presence of the researcher (Tamis-LeMonda et al. 2017) might have influenced the way that parents and children interacted in their data.

4.2. Future directions

By considering how parent–child language varies across activity contexts, this scoping review aimed to inform researchers' methodological choices and also consider the evidence base that informs early interventions for speech and language.

Given that ecological validity is limited when observations take place in laboratories (Wang et al. 2020) or with a researcher present (Dudley-Marling and Lucas 2009), the use of non-obtrusive observation to record naturalistic language is important. Despite increasing prevalence of naturalistic recording methods, many studies did not meet the inclusion criteria for this scoping review (for example Bergelson et al. 2019) due to a lack of detail about individual activity contexts that took place during the recording. It is therefore important that future studies consider ways to combine the detailed activity context data of structured tasks with naturalistic language recordings. The scoping review also found that there was a lack of diversity in participant groups that have been studied, therefore it is pertinent that researchers reflect on potential biases in study design and make efforts to recruit beyond traditional participant groups.

With regard to practitioners working in early years education and speech and language therapy, parent–child interaction is a frequent focus for intervention. Yet as Gallimore, Goldenberg, and Weisner (1993) note, interactions do not occur in a vacuum but are embedded within the activity contexts in which children spend their daily lives. To provide effective intervention, it is important that practitioners consider how activities might be structured to best fit each family's individual circumstances.

4.3. Limitations

A possible limitation of our scoping review is publication bias, as we only included peer-reviewed journal articles. In addition, our review was limited to studies written in English and with monolingual participants. Therefore findings may have been skewed towards research based in English-speaking countries and with participants who represented limited cultural and linguistic diversity.

4.4. Conclusion

This scoping review demonstrated that much of the current evidence on parent–child interaction across activity contexts is based on structured, researcher-directed tasks, most frequently centred around play and book reading. It is important to consider how research might better reflect the diversity present in our communities, both in terms of participants and children's real everyday routines. A more culturally competent approach to research and intervention might involve consultation with individual families to consider how different daily activities present naturally occurring communication opportunities.

Acknowledgments

The first author gratefully acknowledges funding from the Heather van der Lely foundation for her PhD study. The authors would like to thank Sarah Rudd at North Bristol NHS Trust for her input in developing the search strings.

Data availability statement

This scoping review has been registered on Figshare at the following link: https://figshare.com/projects/The_Effect_of_Activity_Context_on_the_Language_used_by_Parents_and_Children_A_Scoping_Review_Protocol/99182

Disclosure statement

No potential conflict of interest was reported by the author(s).

Funding

This review protocol forms part of the first author's PhD project. This work was supported by the Heather van der Lely Foundation (registered charity number: 1168658): [grant number No official grant number - PhD stipend funding].

ORCID

Caitlin Holme ⓘ http://orcid.org/0000-0003-4214-112X
Sam Harding ⓘ http://orcid.org/0000-0002-5870-2094
Sue Roulstone ⓘ http://orcid.org/0000-0002-9052-1330
Patricia J. Lucas ⓘ http://orcid.org/0000-0002-0469-8085
Yvonne Wren ⓘ http://orcid.org/0000-0002-1575-453X

References

*Denotes articles included in the scoping review

*Altinkamiş, N. Feyza, Sophie Kern, and Hatice Sofu. 2014. "When Context Matters More Than Language: Verb or Noun in French and Turkish Caregiver Speech." *First Language* 34 (6): 537–550.

Anderson, Nina J., Susan A. Graham, Heather Prime, Jennifer M. Jenkins, and Sheri Madigan. 2021. "Linking Quality and Quantity of Parental Linguistic Input to Child Language Skills: A Meta-Analysis." *Child Development* 92 (2): 484–501.

Arksey, Hilary, and Lisa O'Malley. 2005. "Scoping Studies: Towards a Methodological Framework." *International Journal of Social Research Methodology: Theory and Practice* 8 (1): 19–32.

Avineri, Netta, Susan Blum, Eric Johnson, Ana Celia Zentella, Shirley Brice-Heath, Teresa McCarty, Nelson Flores, Elinor Ochs, Tamar Kremer-Sadlik, and Django Paris. 2015. "Invited Forum : Bridging the Language Gap." *Journal of Linguistic Anthropology* 25 (1): 66–86.

Bergelson, Elika, Andrei Amatuni, Shannon Dailey, Sharath Koorathota, and Shaelise Tor. 2019. "Day by Day, Hour by Hour: Naturalistic Language Input to Infants." *Developmental Science* 22 (1): 1–10.

Bergelson, Elika, Marisa Casillas, Melanie Soderstrom, Amanda Seidl, Anne S. Warlaumont, and Andrei Amatuni. 2019. "What Do North American Babies Hear? A Large-Scale Cross-Corpus Analysis." *Developmental Science* 22 (1): 1–12.

Blackwell, Anna K.M., Sam Harding, Selma Babayiṇit, and Sue Roulstone. 2014. "Characteristics of Parent-Child Interactions: A Systematic Review of Studies Comparing Children with Primary Language Impairment and Their Typically Developing Peers." *Communication Disorders Quarterly* 36 (2): 67–78.

*Bornstein, Marc H., Kathleen M. Painter, and Jaihyun Park. 2002. "Naturalistic Language Sampling in Typically Developing Children." *Journal of Child Language* 29 (3): 687–699.

*Bornstein, Marc H., Catherine S. Tamis-LeMonda, and O. Maurice Haynes. 1999. "First Words in the Second Year: Continuity, Stability, and Models of Concurrent and Predictive Correspondence in Vocabulary and Verbal Responsiveness Across Age and Context." *Infant Behavior and Development* 22 (1): 65–85.

Cabrera, Natasha J., Brenda L. Volling, and Rachel Barr. 2018. "Fathers Are Parents, Too! Widening the Lens on Parenting for Children's Development." *Child Development Perspectives* 12 (3): 152–157.

*Camaioni, Luigia, and Emiddia Longobardi. 1995. "Nature and Stability of Individual Differences in Early Lexical Development of Italian-Speaking Children." *First Language* 15 (44, Pt.2): 203–218.

*Cameron-Faulkner, Thea, Joanna Melville, and Merideth Gattis. 2018. "Responding to Nature: Natural Environments Improve Parent-Child Communication." *Journal of Environmental Psychology* 59 (February): 9–15.

Casillas, Marisa, Penelope Brown, and Stephen C. Levinson. 2020. "Early Language Experience in a Tseltal Mayan Village." *Child Development* 91 (5): 1819–1835.

*Choi, Soonja. 2000. "Caregiver Input in English and Korean: Use of Nouns and Verbs in Book-Reading and Toy-Play Contexts." *Journal of Child Language* 27 (1): 69–96.

*Cleave, Patricia L., and Elizabeth Kay-Raining Bird. 2006. "Effects of Familiarity on Mothers' Talk About Nouns and Verbs." *Journal of Child Language* 33 (3): 661–676.

Crago, Martha B. 1992. "Ethnography and Language Socialization: A Cross–Cultural Perspective." *Topics in Language Disorders* 12 (3): 28–39.

*Crain-Thoreson, C., M. P. Dahlin, and T. A. Powell. 2001. "Parent-Child Interaction in Three Conversational Contexts: Variations in Style and Strategy." *New Directions for Child and Adolescent Development* 2001 (92): 23–38.

d'Apice, Katrina, Rachel M Latham, and Sophie von Stumm. 2019. "A Naturalistic Home Observational Approach to Children's Language, Cognition, and Behavior." *Developmental Psychology* 55 (7): 1414–1427.

*Doering, Elena, Kevin Schluter, and Antje von Suchodoletz. 2020. "Features of Speech in German and US-American Mother-Toddler Dyads During Toy Play and Book-Reading." *Journal of Child Language* 47 (1): 112–131.

Donnelly, Seamus, and Evan Kidd. 2021. "The Longitudinal Relationship Between Conversational Turn-Taking and Vocabulary Growth in Early Language Development." *Child Development* 92 (2): 609–625.

Dudley-Marling, Curt, and Krista Lucas. 2009. "Pathologizing the Language and Culture of Poor Children." *Language Arts* 86 (5): 362–371.

*Ece Demir-Lira, Ö., Lauren R. Applebaum, Susan Goldin-Meadow, and Susan C. Levine. 2019. "Parents' Early Book Reading to Children: Relation to Children's Later Language and Literacy Outcomes Controlling for Other Parent Language Input." Developmental Science 22 (3): 1–16.

*Ewin, Carrie A., Andrea Reupert, Louise A. McLean, and Christopher J. Ewin. 2021. "Mobile Devices Compared to Non-Digital Toy Play: The Impact of Activity Type on the Quality and Quantity of Parent Language." *Computers in Human Behavior* 118: 106669.

*Farrar, Michael Jeffrey, Margaret J. Friend, and James N. Forbes. 1993. "Event Knowledge and Early Language Acquisition." *Journal of Child Language* 20 (3): 591–606.

*Flynn, Valerie, and Elise Frank Masur. 2007. "Characteristics of Maternal Verbal Style: Responsiveness and Directiveness in Two Natural Contexts." *Journal of Child Language* 34 (3): 519–543.

*Fraser, Colin, and Naomi Roberts. 1975. "Mothers' Speech to Children of Four Different Ages." *Journal of Psycholinguistic Research* 4 (1): 9–16.

Gallimore, Ronald, Claude N. Goldenberg, and Thomas S. Weisner. 1993. "The Social Construction and Subjective Reality of Activity Settings: Implications for Community Psychology." *American Journal of Community Psychology* 21 (4): 537–560.

*Gelman, Susan A., Robert J. Chesnick, and Sandra R. Waxman. 2005. "Mother-Child Conversations About Pictures and Objects: Referring to Categories and Individuals." *Child Development* 76 (6): 1129–1143.

*Gilkerson, Jill, Jeffrey A. Richards, and Keith J. Topping. 2017. "The Impact of Book Reading in the Early Years on Parent–Child Language Interaction." *Journal of Early Childhood Literacy* 17 (1): 92–110.

*Goldfield, Beverly A. 1993. "Noun Bias in Maternal Speech to One-Year-Olds." *Journal of Child Language* 20 (1): 85–99.

Greenwood, Charles R., Kathy Thiemann-Bourque, Dale Walker, Jay Buzhardt, and Jill Gilkerson. 2011. "Assessing Children's Home Language Environments Using Automatic Speech Recognition Technology." *Communication Disorders Quarterly* 32 (2): 83–92.

*Henderson, Annette M.E., and Mark A. Sabbagh. 2010. "Parents' Use of Conventional and Unconventional Labels in Conversations with Their Preschoolers." *Journal of Child Language* 37 (4): 793–816.

*Hoff-Ginsberg, Erika. 1991. "Mother-Child Conversation in Different Social Classes and Communicative Settings." *Child Development* 62 (4): 782–796.

*Hoff, Erika. 2010. "Context Effects on Young Children's Language Use: The Influence of Conversational Setting and Partner." *First Language* 30 (3–4): 461–472.

*Jipson, Jennifer L., Selin Gülgöz, and Susan A. Gelman. 2016. "Parent-Child Conversations Regarding the Ontological Status of a Robotic Dog." *Cognitive Development* 39: 21–35.

*Jones, Celeste Pappas, and Lauren B Adamson. 1987. "Language Use in Mother-Child and Mother-Child-Sibling Interactions." *Child Development* 55 (4): 1278–1289.

*Kaye, Kenneth, and Rosalind Charney. 1981. "Conversational Asymmetry Between Mothers and Children." *Journal of Child Language* 8 (1): 35–49.

*Kertoy, Marilyn K., and Dolores Kluppel Vetter. 1995. "The Effect of Conversational Setting on Topic Continuation in Mother-Child Dyads." *Journal of Child Language* 22 (1): 73–88.

Kuchirko, Yana. 2019. "On Differences and Deficits: A Critique of the Theoretical and Methodological Underpinnings of the Word Gap." *Journal of Early Childhood Literacy* 19 (4): 533–562.

*Kwon, Kyong Ah, Gary Bingham, Joellen Lewsader, Hyun Joo Jeon, and James Elicker. 2013. "Structured Task Versus Free Play: The Influence of Social Context on Parenting Quality, Toddlers' Engagement with Parents and Play Behaviors, and Parent-Toddler Language Use." *Child and Youth Care Forum* 42 (3): 207–224.

*Larson, Anne L., Tyson S. Barrett, and Scott R. McConnell. 2020. "Exploring Early Childhood Language Environments: A Comparison of Language Use, Exposure and Interactions in the Home and Childcare Settings." *Language, Speech and Hearing Services in Schools* 51 (3): 706–719.

*Lauricella, Alexis R., Rachel Barr, and Sandra L. Calvert. 2014. "Parent-Child Interactions During Traditional and Computer Storybook Reading for Children's Comprehension: Implications for Electronic Storybook Design." *International Journal of Child-Computer Interaction* 2 (1): 17–25.

*Lavigne, Heather J., Katherine G. Hanson, and Daniel R. Anderson. 2015. "The Influence of Television Coviewing on Parent Language Directed at Toddlers." *Journal of Applied Developmental Psychology* 36: 1–10.

*Lawrence, Valerie W., and Elizabeth F. Shipley. 1996. "Parental Speech to Middle- and Working-Class Children from Two Racial Groups in Three Settings." *Applied Psycholinguistics* 17: 233–255.

Leadbeater, C., and L. Litosseliti. 2014. "The Importance of Cultural Competence for Speech and Language Therapists." *Journal of Interactional Research in Communication Disorders* 5: 1–26.

*Leaper, Campbell, and Jean Berko Gleason. 1996. "The Relationship of Play Activity and Gender to Parent and Child Sex-Typed Communication." *International Journal of Behavioral Development* 19 (4): 689–703.

*Leech, Kathryn A., and Meredith L. Rowe. 2014. "A Comparison of Preschool Children's Discussions with Parents During Picture Book and Chapter Book Reading." *First Language* 34 (3): 205–226.

The LENA Research Foundation. 2021. "Research Studies Conducted Using LENA Technology." 2021. Accessed online 14/10/2021 at: https://www.lena.org/research/.

*Lucariello, Joan, and Katherine Nelson. 1986. "Context Effects on Lexical Specificity in Maternal and Child Discourse." *Journal of Child Language* 13 (3): 507–522.

Madigan, Sheri, Brae Anne McArthur, Ciana Anhorn, Rachel Eirich, and Dimitri A. Christakis. 2020. "Associations Between Screen Use and Child Language Skills: A Systematic Review and Meta-Analysis." *JAMA Pediatrics* 174 (7): 665–675.

Manz, Patricia H., Cheyenne Hughes, Ernesto Barnabas, Catherine Bracaliello, and Marika Ginsburg-Block. 2010. "A Descriptive Review and Meta-Analysis of Family-Based Emergent Literacy Interventions: To What Extent Is the Research Applicable to Low-Income, Ethnic-Minority or Linguistically-Diverse Young Children?" *Early Childhood Research Quarterly* 25 (4): 409–431.

*Marvin, Christine A., and Amy J. Privratsky. 1999. "After-School Talk: The Effects of Materials Sent Home from Preschool." *American Journal of Speech-Language Pathology* 8 (3): 231–240.

*Masur, Elise Frank, and Jennifer E. Rodemaker. 1999. "Mothers ' and Infants ' Spontaneous Vocal, Verbal, and Action Imitation During the Second Year." *Merrill-Palmer Quarterly* 45 (3): 392–412.

*Muhinyi, Amber, and Anne Hesketh. 2017. "Low- and High-Text Books Facilitate the Same Amount and Quality of Extratextual Talk." *First Language* 37 (4): 410–427.

*Muhinyi, Amber, Anne Hesketh, Andrew J. Stewart, and Caroline F. Rowland. 2020. "Story Choice Matters for Caregiver Extra-Textual Talk During Shared Reading with Preschoolers." *Journal of Child Language* 47 (3): 633–654.

*Munzer, Tiffany G., Alison L. Miller, Heidi M. Weeks, Niko Kaciroti, and Jenny Radesky. 2019. "Differences in Parent-Toddler Interactions with Electronic Versus Print Books." *Pediatrics* 143 (4): e20182012.

Nielsen, Mark, Daniel Haun, Joscha Kärtner, and Cristine H. Legare. 2017. "The Persistent Sampling Bias in Developmental Psychology: A Call to Action." *Journal of Experimental Child Psychology* 162: 31–38.

*Noble, Claire H., Thea Cameron-Faulkner, and Elena Lieven. 2018. "Keeping It Simple: The Grammatical Properties of Shared Book Reading." *Journal of Child Language* 45 (3): 753–766.

Nyberg, S., M. Rudner, Birberg Birberg Thornberg, U. Koch, F.-S. Barr, R. Heimann, and M. Sundqvist. 2020. "The Natural Language Environment of 9-Month-Old Infants in Sweden and Concurrent Association With Early Language Development." *Frontiers in Psychology* 11: 1981.

*Nyhout, Angela, and Daniela K. O'Neill. 2013. "Mothers' Complex Talk When Sharing Books with Their Toddlers: Book Genre Matters." *First Language* 33 (2): 115–131.

*O'Brien, Marion, and Keith J. Nagle. 1987. "Parents' Speech to Toddlers: The Effect of Play Context." *Journal of Child Language* 14 (2): 269–279.

*Ogura, Tamiko, Philip S. Dale, Yukie Yamashita, Toshiki Murase, and Aki Mahieu. 2006. "The Use of Nouns and Verbs by Japanese Children and Their Caregivers in Book-Reading and Toy-Playing Contexts." *Journal of Child Language* 33 (1): 1–29.

O'Toole, Ciara, Rena Lyons, and Catherine Houghton. 2021. "A Qualitative Evidence Synthesis of Parental Experiences and Perceptions of Parent–Child Interaction Therapy for Preschool Children With Communication Difficulties." *Journal of Speech, Language, and Hearing Research* 64: 3159–3185.

*Ozturk, Gulsah, and Susan Hill. 2020. "Mother–Child Interactions During Shared Reading with Digital and Print Books." *Early Child Development and Care* 190 (9): 1425–1440.

Paugh, Amy L., and Kathleen C. Riley. 2019. "Poverty and Children's Language in Anthropolitical Perspective." *Annual Review of Anthropology* 48: 297–315.

*Pempek, Tiffany A., Heather L. Kirkorian, and Daniel R. Anderson. 2014. "The Effects of Background Television on the Quantity and Quality of Child-Directed Speech by Parents." *Journal of Children and Media* 8 (3): 211–222.

Peters, M. D. J., C. Godfrey, P. McInerney, Z. Munn, A. C. Tricco, and H. Khalil. 2020. Chapter 11: Scoping Reviews (2020 Version)." In *JBI Manual for Evidence Synthesis*, edited by Edoardo Aromataris, and Zachary Munn. Online : JBI. Available from: https://synthesismanual.jbi.global. Accessed 03/02/2021

*Poulain, Tanja, and Jens Brauer. 2018. "The Changing Role of Mothers' Verbal and Nonverbal Behavior in Children's Language Acquisition." *First Language* 38 (2): 129–146.

*Riordan, Jessica, Elaine Reese, Sarah Rouse, and Elizabeth Schaughency. 2018. "Promoting Code-Focused Talk: The Rhyme and Reason for Why Book Style Matters." *Early Childhood Research Quarterly* 45: 69–80.

*Rondal, J. A. 1980. "Fathers' and Mothers' Speech in Early Language Development." *Journal of Child Language* 7 (2): 353–369.

Roopnarine, Jaipaul L. 2011. "Cultural Variations in Beliefs About Play, Parent-Child Play, and Children's Play: Meaning for Childhood Development." In *The Oxford Handbook of the Development of Play*, edited by Peter Nathan, and Anthony D. Pellegrini, 19–37. New York/Oxford: Oxford University Press.

Roulstone, S. E., J. E. Marshall, G. G. Powell, J. Goldbart, Y. E. Wren, J. Coad, N. Daykin, et al. 2015. "Evidence-Based Intervention for Preschool Children with Primary Speech and Language Impairments: Child Talk – an Exploratory Mixed-Methods Study." *Programme Grants for Applied Research* 3 (5): 1–408.

*Ryckebusch, Céline, and Haydée Marcos. 2004. "Speech Acts, Social Context and Parent-Toddler Play Between the Ages of 1;5 and 2;3." *Journal of Pragmatics* 36 (5): 883–897.

*Soderstrom, Melanie, and Kelsey Wittebolle. 2013. "When Do Caregivers Talk? The Influences of Activity and Time of Day on Caregiver Speech and Child Vocalizations in Two Childcare Environments." *PLoS ONE* 8 (11): e80646.

*Sorsby, Angela J., and Margaret Martlew. 1991. "Representational Demands in Mothers Talk to Preschool Children in Two Contexts: Picture Book Reading and a Modelling Task." *Journal of Child Language* 18 (2): 373–395.

*Stevenson, Marguerite B., Lewis A. Leavitt, Mary A. Roach, Robin S. Chapman, and Jon F. Miller. 1986. "Mothers' Speech to Their 1-Year-Old Infants in Home and Laboratory Settings." *Journal of Psycholinguistic Research* 15 (5): 451–461.

*Stoneman, Zolinda, and Gene H. Brody. 1982. "An In-Home Investigation of Maternal Teaching Strategies During Sesame Street and a Popular Situation Comedy." *Journal of Applied Developmental Psychology* 3 (3): 275–284.

Tamis-LeMonda, Catherine S. 2003. "Cultural Perspectives on the 'Whats?' and 'Whys?' of Parenting." *Human Development* 46 (5): 319–327.

*Tamis-LeMonda, Catherine S., Stephanie Custode, Yana Kuchirko, Kelly Escobar, and Tiffany Lo. 2019. "Routine Language: Speech Directed to Infants During Home Activities." *Child Development* 90 (6): 2135–2152.

*Tamis-LeMonda, Catherine S., Yana Kuchirko, Rufan Luo, Kelly Escobar, and Marc H. Bornstein. 2017. "Power in Methods: Language to Infants in Structured and Naturalistic Contexts." *Developmental Science* 20 (6): ePub 2017.

*Tardif, Twila, Susan A. Gelman, and Fan Xu. 1999. "Putting the 'Noun Bias' in Context: A Comparison of English and Mandarin." *Child Development* 70 (3): 620–635.

Topping, Keith, Rayenne Dekhinet, and Suzanne Zeedyk. 2011. "*Hindrances for Parents in Enhancing Child Language.*" *Educational Psychology Review* 23 (3): 413–455.

*Torr, Jane, and Lynn Clugston. 1999. "A Comparison Between Informational and Narrative Picture Books as a Context for Reasoning Between Caregivers and 4-Year-Old Children." *Early Child Development and Care* 159 (1): 25–41.

Tricco, A. C., E. Lillie, W. Zarin, K. K. O'Brien, H. Colquhoun, D. Levac, D. Moher, et al. 2018. "PRISMA Extension for Scoping Reviews (PRISMA-ScR): Checklist and Explanation." *Annals of Internal Medicine* 169 (7): 467–473.

*Tulviste, Tiia. 2003. "Contextual Variability in Interactions Between Mothers and 2-Year-Olds." *First Language* 23 (3): 311–325.

*Tulviste, Tiia, and Margit Raudsepp. 1997. "The Conversational Style of Estonian Mothers." *First Language* 17 (50, Pt 2): 151–163.

van Kleeck, Anne. 1994. "Potential Cultural Bias in Training Parents as Conversational Partners With Their Children Who Have Delays in Language Development." *American Journal of Speech-Language Pathology* 3 (1): 67–78.

Wang, Yuanyuan, Rondeline Williams, Laura Dilley, and Derek M. Houston. 2020. "A Meta-Analysis of the Predictability of LENA^{TM} Automated Measures for Child Language Development." *Developmental Review* 57 (May): 100921.

*Weizman, Zehava Oz, and Catherine E. Snow. 2001. "Lexical Input as Related to Children's Vocabulary Acquisition: Effects of Sophisticated Exposure and Support for Meaning." *Developmental Psychology* 37 (2): 265–279.

*Worden, Patricia E., Daniel W. Kee, and Melanie J. Ingle. 1987. "Parental Teaching Strategies with Preschoolers: A Comparison of Mothers and Fathers Within Different Alphabet Tasks." *Contemporary Educational Psychology* 12: 95–109.

World Bank Group. 2020. "Primary School Starting Age (Years)." 2020. Accessed online 21/07/21 at: https://data.worldbank.org/indicator/SE.PRM.AGES?view=map.

Yont, Kristine M., Catherine E. Snow, and Lynne Vernon-Feagans. 2003. "The Role of Context in Mother-Child Interactions: An Analysis of Communicative Intents Expressed During Toy Play and Book Reading with 12-Month-Olds." *Journal of Pragmatics* 35 (3): 435–454.

Zimmerman, Frederick J., Jill Gilkerson, Jeffrey A. Richards, Dimitri A. Christakis, Dongxin Xu, Sharmistha Gray, and Umit Yapanel. 2009. "Teaching by Listening: The Importance of Adult-Child Conversations to Language Development." *Pediatrics* 124 (1): 342–349.

Language expansion in Chinese parent–child mealtime conversations: across different conversational types and initiators

Ling Sheng ⓘ, Wenming Dong, Feifei Han ⓘ, Shiming Tong and Jiangbo Hu ⓘ

ABSTRACT

This study examined the distribution of language expansion in parent–child (preschool aged) mealtime conversations in 30 Chinese middle-class families. The conversations were categorised into four types: *contextualised & conflicted, contextualised & non-conflicted, decontextualised & conflicted,* and *decontextualised & non-conflicted.* The language expansions were analysed using the systemic functional linguistic theory related to cohesive patterns in language expansion: *elaborations, extensions,* and *enhancements.* While the parents dominated the conversations generally, the children were active contributors, initiating over one-quarter of the conversations. Initiation had an impact on the distribution of the conversational types: the proportions of *contextualised & non-conflicted conversations* was significantly higher in child-initiated conversations. The *contextualised & conflicted* conversations accounted for a higher proportion in parent-initiated conversations. It was the conversational type rather than initiation, which had an effect on the distribution of language expansion patterns. The least occurring *decontextualised & conflicted* conversations generated the most *extensions.* The frequently appeared *contextualised & non-conflicted* conversations, however, produced the fewest expanded messages. The implications from the findings for promoting high-quality mealtime conversations conducive to children's language learning are discussed.

Introduction

Research suggests that family mealtime conversations can be regarded as a critical context for children's language learning and social progress (Bova and Arcidiacono 2013; Ferdous et al. 2016; Fruh et al. 2011; Hu et al. 2019). Mealtime talk includes both adult–adult and adult–child conversations in which the richness of topics and the complexity of language use may be different from the instance of adult–child interactions in other situations. Parents as skilful language users can create extensive opportunities for children's language learning with sophisticated vocabularies and complex syntactic structures in their dinner table talk (Snow and Beals 2006; Busch 2017). The well-timed turn-taking, the maintenance of one's turn and the cohesive links with previous talk presented in the family members' talk facilitate children's language practices and improve children's language expression as well as social-cognitive abilities (Arcidiacono and Bova 2015; Busch 2017).

Socioeconomic status (SES) and cultural background of families are widely acknowledged as an important factor affecting the style of dinner table conversations. In mealtime talk, middle-class parents are more likely to use expanded genres (e.g. narrative, explanatory, or argumentative talk) to discuss decontextualised topics at the dinner table compared to those from a disadvantaged background. These expanded discourses are often characterised by having low-frequency words, decontextualised topics, and justification discourses, which are conducive to children's language development (Arcidiacono and Bova 2015; Demir et al. 2015; Rowe 2013). Middle-class parents in these studies refer to parents who obtained university degrees or have a professional job. Apart from SES, cultural background has also been shown to influence mealtime talk regarding communication roles and conversational topics and styles (Aronsson and GottAzén 2011; Galatolo and Caronia 2018). In Western culture, children are typically encouraged to join the conversations with adults, whereas in some other cultures, children are expected to keep quiet while adults talk (Rydstrom 2003; Fiese, Foley, and Spagnola 2006). Even within Western cultures, the features of mealtime talk differ from culture to culture. For instance, Aukrust (2002) reported that the genres of mealtime conversations in Norwegian families were different from that in American families. Norwegian families produced more narrative talk on social practices and events at school whilst American families generated more explanatory talk for reasoning social affairs. These studies indicate that mealtime conversations vary individually by socioeconomic status and by culture.

To date, most mealtime talk research is undertaken in Western cultures and little has been done in Chinese families, especially the families in Mainland China. It is widely acknowledged that the manners of Chinese adult–child interactions differ substantially from those of Western cultures (Dai, McMahon, and Lim 2020; Doan and Wang 2010). In addition, much of the existing research predominantly focuses on adult language use in mealtime talk, with children's language use at the dinner table being largely ignored. However, children are not merely passively affected by the language environment but are active contributors to the social interactions they are involved in (Halliday [1980] 2004). To address these less researched areas, this study examines language use of both parents and children in Mainland Chinese families who speak Mandarin (Chinese families hereafter) in their mealtime conversations. Specifically, we focus on language expansions in expanded genres (e.g. narrative or explanatory talk) that regards the feature of ideas being exchanged spontaneously and cohesively in conversations, as they have extensive pedagogical functions for children's language learning (Bohanek et al. 2009; Busch 2017; Snow and Beals 2006). Results of this study would increase the cultural diversity in the mealtime research field and enhance our understanding about the language environment of Chinese families that is established by both parents and children.

Learning opportunities in mealtime conversations for children

Adopting a sociolinguistic perspective, research that investigates the pedagogical functions of mealtime conversations emphasises the influence of language interactions on children's learning experiences (Halliday [1980] 2004). In particular, the expanded genres in mealtime conversations (e.g. narratives, explanations, or arguments) containing decontextualised information, are said to be favourable, as they create substantial language learning occasions for children to develop vocabulary knowledge, expressive discourses, and early literacy skills. (Aukrust 2002; Fruh et al. 2011; Rowe 2013). Snow and Beals (2006) examined the proportion of parents' narrative and explanatory talk in their interactions with their preschool children (four or five years) at the dinner table and identified positive correlations between the quantity of the talk and their children's performance in The Peabody Picture Vocabulary Test in grade six. Bohanek et al. (2009), however, explored the influence of parents' narrative talk at the dinner table on children's social-cognitive learning experiences. The researchers found that mothers and fathers play different roles in supporting their children to gain understanding in life events of remote and recent. The fathers' narrative talk focused on day-to-day problem solving whereas the mothers' talk paid attention to shared family history or rationale of social affairs, all of which assisted the children to create coherence over their experiences relating to their emotional bond, self-awareness, social understanding and logical thinking.

A handful of studies also revealed the potential benefit of arguments in mealtime conversations for children's language and social-cognitive development (Arcidiacono and Bova 2015; Bova and Arcidiacono 2014; Busch 2017). This type of expanded talk drives children to react quickly to address their parents' challenging proposals for defending their own viewpoints, during which their expressive language and the social-cognitive skills for providing appropriate negotiations are practised and strengthened. In dinner table arguments, conflicting parent–child conversations are frequently observed (Bova 2019; Bova and Arcidiacono 2014). These conflicting conversations initiated by parents tend to relate to contextualised issues, such as children's table manners or food intake; whereas the conflicts initiated by children are more likely to involve decontextualised questions, like information seeking outside family issues, which has been highlighted to be important in children's language and social development (Bova 2019). These studies suggest that children are active participants in mealtime conversations and are able to enrich the content of mealtime conversations significantly.

Much of the existing research examines the pedagogical functions of parent–child mealtime conversations separately in two dimensions: (1) whether the mealtime conversation has contextualised information and (2) whether the conversation involves a conflict or not. The present study sets to investigate the parent–child conversations considering the interaction between the two dimensions, which forms four types of conversations: namely *contextualised & conflicted, contextualised & non-conflicted, decontextualised & conflicted, and decontextualised & non-conflicted*. This kind of categorisation extends the existing research through the examination of the nuances of parent–child mealtime conversations in the specific conversational types that were rarely reported.

Parent–child communication in Chinese families

Although there is little research on parent–child mealtime talk in Chinese families, a number of studies have investigated communication styles in Chinese families (from Mainland China to overseas Chinese communities). Inconclusive results have been reported with regard to the levels of parental authoritativeness and child-centeredness in Chinese parents' interactions with children (Guo 2015; Luo, Catherine, and Song 2013). Such mixed results may well reflect the sociocultural change in China shifting from traditional Chinese morals (e.g. Confucianism) to a mixture with Western values due to globalisation (Guo 2015; Luo, Catherine , and Song 2013). Earlier studies of the communication styles in older generation Chinese families tend to report the predominate 'Jiazhang' role (the leading role) of Chinese parents in a family. For instance, in an earlier study, Wang (2001) compared the discussion of Chinese mothers and American mothers with their children about past emotional events. Chinese parents were found to use much more directive language with less emotional expressions compared to their Western counterparts. In more recent studies, however, the younger generation of Chinese parents was reported to show active and open styles in their interactions with their young children for promoting children's autonomy and agency (Li 2020; Hu and Torr 2016).

Apart from parent–child communication styles, research has also been conducted to examine the impact of Chinese parent–child communication on children's cognitive and socio-emotional development based on the notion that language plays a vital role in fulfilling individual's social and cognitive developmental progress (Halliday [1980] 2004). Zhang (2018) investigated 51 Chinese mothers' interactions with their three-year-old children and found that the mothers' interactional behaviours (e.g. language use in praise or criticism) were not only associated with children's language performance but also their emotional understanding. From the perspective of language functions, Hu and Torr (2016) explored the use of reasoning talk in Chinese mother–child daily conversations. The researchers reported that when explaining affairs or directing children's behaviours, Chinese mothers' reasoning talk with logical and cooperative principles may foster children's understanding of the natural laws of physical world and the social rules in Chinese society. These studies demonstrate that through spontaneous daily conversations, parents may significantly shape their children's way of thinking and manner of social interactions.

Like the mealtime talk research, the existing studies of Chinese parent–child communication extensively discussed parents' communication styles or parents' language use, yet little attention was paid to children's language contribution to the communication. In some socioeconomically disadvantaged Chinese families where parents have few conversations with children, the children play active roles in initiating conversations (Ji and Zhang 2020). The relations between children and adult–child communication are bi-directional. Hence, studies neglecting children's role in the interactions could only reveal an incomplete picture of the complexity of parent–child interactions. To address this issue, the present study adopted a dual perspective by including both the Chinese parents and children's language use.

A theoretical framework for analysing language expansion in parent–child conversations

This study focuses on expanded genres in parent–child conversations that contain extensive language expansions. The analysis of the language expansion reveals the flow of informational exchange between parents and children that reflects the speakers' metalinguistic sense in maintaining the cohesion of the conversation for 'meaning making' in collaboration (Eggins 2004). Halliday ([1980] 2004) argues that language learning includes three levels: learning language that refers to language knowledge (e.g. lexicon and syntactic knowledge); learning through language that concerns the interpersonal social roles in an interaction (e.g. modality); and learning about learning that relates the use of language appropriating for the specific instance in interactional contexts (e.g. theme choice or cohesion maintenance). The analysis of language expansion enables identification of language learning opportunities embedded in mealtime conversations from perspectives of 'learning about language'.

The present study draws on the theory of 'mode' in Systemic Functional Linguistics (SFL). Mode concerns the cohesion of language that is suited in an instance of social interaction (Halliday and Matthiessen 2004). According to Halliday and Matthiessen, there are three main conjunctive relations (expansion patterns, which is used hereafter) for maintaining the coherence in language use: *elaboration, extension*, and *enhancement*. Table 1 displays the descriptor, representative lexical expressions, and the example sentences of the three expansion patterns. To some extent, the expansion patterns are associated with conversational genres (Eggins 2004). For example, *extensions* are widely used in a narrative talk whereas *enhancements* are more likely to appear in argumentative discourse.

The present study

Because of the pedagogical functions of mealtime conversations, in particular, the expanded genres of mealtime talk, the present study aimed to examine: (1) the distribution patterns of different types of Chinese parent–child mealtime conversations; and (2) the distribution patterns of language expansions in Chinese parent–child mealtime conversations. This study is significant in three aspects. Firstly, the present study will include both parents' and children's language in the mealtime conversations. This

Table 1. The three expansion patterns.

Expansion patterns	Descriptors	Representative lexical expressions	Examples
Elaboration	A message restates or clarifies the previous message in the text	in other words, I mean, for instance, to illustrate, in fact, actually …	*Today is a special day, <u>actually, it is the day for eating Zhongzi</u> (a special food for a Chinese traditional festival).*
Extension	A message adds new information to or changes the meaning of the previous message	and, also, moreover, in addition, nor, but, yet, instead …	*You said Dingding snatched your toy, <u>and you told your teacher, right?</u>*
Enhancement	A message extends the previous message in terms of dimensions including time, comparison, cause, condition, or concession	then, next, afterwards, just then, soon, until, because, therefore, otherwise, despite …	*I like doing math <u>because I need to calculate many things in the future.</u>*

study will make distinction as to whether the conversation is initiated by parents or children, and to see the extent to which differences in the initiation influence the distribution patterns of conversations and language expansions in the conversations. Secondly, as different types of conversations may be affected by the initiator, and language expansion patterns may also appear differently in different types of conversations and by initiator. Hence, the present study will examine the effect of conversational types on the language expansion patterns that is rarely explored in the existing research. Thirdly, as culture has been shown to be an influential factor impacting parent–child conversational styles, the present study will examine parent–child mealtime conversations in Chinese families, as the majority of research has been conducted in Western countries, which differ from China in terms of culture. Specifically, the following research questions are addressed:

1. What are the distribution patterns of: (a) the four types of conversations; and (b) the four types of conversations by initiation; in Chinese parent–child mealtime conversations?
2. What are the distribution patterns of language expansions: (a) in the total conversations; and (b) by initiation, conversational types, and the interaction between initiation × conversational types; in Chinese parent–child mealtime conversations?

Materials and methods

Participants and data generation

The study is part of a larger project investigating Chinese children's early language experiences (CCELE) at home and in childcare centres. The participants of the study were 30 Chinese middle-class families recruited from a local preschool in Deqing, Zhejiang Province, China. The focus on middle-class families is based on the consideration that the main objective of this study is to reveal pedagogical functions in expanded genres in mealtime talk. Previous research suggests that this type of language is more likely to appear in middle-class families (Bohanek et al. 2009; Bova and Arcidiacono 2013). The recruitment of the participants was targeted on those parents who (1) had professional jobs; (2) at least one of the parents had received university education; (3) had only one preschool-aged child; and (4) speaking Mandarin at home. This group of families also represents the fast-growing group of population in Chinese small cities/towns. Ethical approval for the larger project was obtained from Zhejiang Normal University and the signed written consent forms were collected from the participating preschools and families. The parents were informed about the nature of the study and were told to record their dinner table interactions with their children using a mobile phone by themselves at any time. The parents were encouraged to discuss with their children about this video recording meal in advance and anecdotal data showed that the children were aware of this event. The recorded video clips were sent to the preschool and then collected by the research assistant.

The original clips were between 20 and 35 min. As the study targeted the mealtime conversations of all the family members (mother, father, and the child), the parts of table setting or without the participation of all the family members, or the parents not sitting with their children were excluded. The exclusion resulted in approximately a 15-minute video for each family.

Coding of the data

The selected video clips were transcribed verbatim and were coded using a five-step scheme as shown below. The development of the coding scheme was grounded on the relevant theories of SFL that have been widely adopted in language studies in early childhood education, including studies with Mandarin-speaking Chinese parents, like the current participants (Hu et al. 2019; Hu and Torr 2016).

- (1) Identification of messages: The sentences were broken into messages. One message is defined as the smallest semantic unit, which includes an implicate or explicate subject and a verb (Hasan 1996).
- (2) Identification of conversations: In this study, one conversation was defined as the parents' and the child' turn takings which focused on one topic and lasted at least four turns.
- (3) Classification of conversations into four types, namely *contextualised & conflicted, contextualised & non-conflicted, decontextualised & conflicted, and decontextualised & non-conflicted* conversations: The information of a conversation was examined on: (1) whether it was contextualised with here-and-now food eating issues or decontextualised information away from the dinner table; and (2) whether it had conflicts between the parents and the children on the topic or not. The examples of the four types of conversations are listed in Table 2.
- (4) Identification of language expansions: The messages in each conversation were examined one by one to identify whether they belonged to language expansions, which were defined as a message expanding the meaning of the previous messages.
- (5) Categorisation of expansion patterns: Each identified expanded message was categorised as one of the three expansion types, namely *elaboration, extension* or *enhancement*.

Inter-coder reliability

The data coding was processed by one researcher independently in Excel. To ensure the reliability of the coding, a second coder randomly selected and coded the data of six

Table 2. Four types of conversations.

Types of conversations	Examples
Contextualised & conflicted	Child: *I cannot eat any more* Mother: *Just little bit rice and dishes* Child: *I really cannot eat any more* Mother: *It is not good if you don't eat the food.*
Contextualised & non-conflicted	Mother: *Hi, can I give a fish? Mind the small bones.* Child: *Ok, I can see the small bones.* Mother: *OK* Child: *I find a big bone*
Decontextualised & conflicted	Mother: *I think dad can take you out to play when you come back (from the preschool).* Child: *We go to the Yager Zoo?* Mother: *It would be very hot if we go the the Yager Zoo. How about 'Sea World'?* Child: *No, I don't like there.*
Decontextualised & non-conflicted	Father: *Xiangru (the child's name) Do you want to eat fried dumpling for breakfast?* Mother: *Did you have fried dumpling in the morning?* Child: *Yishi Tample, we had it around Yishi Tample* Mother: *Wow, that is a famous restaurant.* Child: *It is delicious.*

families out of 30 families, representing 20.0% of the total data. The inter-coder reliability – Cohen's Kappa coefficients were calculated. The coefficients were .83 for initiation, .80 for conversational types, and .76 for expansions. According to McHugh (2012), all the values of the Cohen's Kappa coefficients showed substantial agreement.

Data analysis

Individual conversation rather than individual family was used as a case in the data analyses, because the main aim of the research was concerned with revealing the generic distribution patterns of language expansions in conversations across families rather than detecting variations of such patterns between families by their different characteristics. To minimise the impacts of individual differences of families, their SES background, location of the families, parents' education and jobs, language speaking at home, formation of the families were all controlled for in the participants recruitment (see Participants for details).

To answer research question (1a), a series of one-sample proportion tests were conducted for pairwise comparisons of the proportions of the four types of the conversations. For research question (1b), a 4 (conversational type) × 2 (initiation) cross-tabulation was conducted. Similarly, to provide an answer to research question (2a), one-sample proportion tests were performed for pairwise comparisons of the proportions of the three types of language expansions in total conversations. With regard to research question (2b), a 2 (initiation) × 4 (conversational type) MANOVA was used, with the three types of language expansions as dependent variables. The data analyses were carried out in IBM SPSS 25.

Results

Results of distribution patterns of the total and the four types of conversations by initiation

Table 3 presents the descriptive statistics of the total and the four types of conversations by initiation. Altogether 6,007 messages generated 633 conversations, of which parent-initiated conversations comprised 463 (73.1%) and child-initiated conversations comprised 170 (26.9%). A one-sample proportion test showed that parents initiated a significantly higher proportion than children ($z = 26.21, p < .01$). The results of the one-sample proportion tests for the pairwise comparison of the four types of conversations are displayed in Table 4. Viewed together, these results demonstrate that irrespective of the initiator, *decontextualised & non-conflicted* conversations (42.0%) accounted for the

Table 3. Descriptive statistics of the total and the four types of conversations by initiation.

Variables	parent-initiation		child-initiation	
	M	*SD*	*M*	*SD*
total conversations	15.43	4.16	5.67	3.01
contextualised & conflicted conversations	2.73	1.86	0.33	0.55
contextualised & non-conflicted conversations	4.93	2.36	2.67	1.77
decontextualised & conflicted conversations	1.27	1.42	0.30	0.65
decontextualised & non-conflicted conversations	6.50	4.29	2.37	2.08

Table 4. Pairwise comparison of the proportions of the four types of conversations.

conversational types (number, proportion)		z	p
1 *contextualised & conflicted* conversations (92, 14.5%)	1 < 2	15.36	.00
	1 > 3	−5.07	.00
	1 < 4	19.65	.00
2 *contextualised & non-conflicted* conversations (228, 36.0%)	2 > 3	−14/99	.00
	2 < 4	3.15	.00
3 *decontextualised & conflicted* conversations (47, 7.4%)	3 < 4	33.26	.00
4 *decontextualised & non-conflicted* conversations (266, 42.0%)	—	—	—

highest proportion, followed by *contextualised & non-conflicted* conversations (36.0%), which in turn had higher proportion than *contextualised & conflicted* conversations (14.75%). The *decontextualised & conflicted* conversations (7.4%) had the lowest proportion amongst the four types of conversations.

As to the distribution pattern of the four types of the conversations, the results of the 4 (conversational types) × 2 (initiation) cross-tabulation are presented in Table 5. The conversational types were significantly associated with the initiation ($\chi^2(3) = 21.26$, V = .18, $p < .01$). Specifically, the *contextualised & conflicted* conversations accounted for a significantly higher proportion in parent-initiated conversations (17.7%) than in child-initiated conversations (5.9%). The *contextualised & non-conflicted* conversations took up a significantly higher proportion in child-imitated conversations (47.1%) than in parent-initiated conversations (32.0%). For the other two types of conversations, no significant differences were found between the proportions that accounted for in parent- and child-initiated conversations.

Results of distribution patterns of the language expansions in total conversations and by initiation and conversational type

Table 6 shows the descriptive statistics of the three types of expansions by conversational type and by initiation. Altogether, there were 3,443 expanded messages in the total conversations. As shown in Table 7, for the distribution pattern of the language expansions in the total conversations, the results of one-sample proportion tests find that *extensions* took the highest proportion (67.1%), followed by the proportion of *enhancements* (19.1%), which were again higher than the proportion of *elaborations* (13.8%).

Table 5. Association between conversational types and initiation.

		initiation		
conversational types		parent	child	total
contextualised & conflicted conversations	Count	82$_a$	10$_b$	92
	% within initiation	17.7%	5.9%	14.5%
contextualised & non-conflicted conversations	Count	148$_a$	80$_b$	228
	% within initiation	32.0%	47.1%	36.0%
decontextualised & conflicted conversations	Count	38$_a$	9$_a$	47
	% within initiation	8.2%	5.3%	7.4%
decontextualised & non-conflicted conversations	Count	195$_a$	71$_a$	266
	% within initiation	42.1%	41.8%	42.0%
total conversations	Count	463	170	633
	% within initiation	100.0%	100.0%	100.0%

Note: Each subscript letter denotes a subset of categories whose column proportions do not differ significantly from each other at the .05 level.

Table 6. Descriptive statistics of the three types of expansions by conversational type and by initiation.

variables	parent-initiated		child-initiated		total	
	M	SD	M	SD	M	SD
elaborations in *contextualised & conflicted* conversations	0.95	0.99	0.60	0.84	0.91	0.98
elaborations in *contextualised & non-conflicted* conversations	0.61	0.89	0.67	0.90	0.64	0.89
elaborations in *decontextualised & conflicted* conversations	0.87	0.78	0.67	0.50	0.83	0.73
elaborations in *decontextualised & non-conflicted* conversations	0.81	1.01	0.69	0.86	0.77	0.97
extensions in *contextualised & conflicted* conversations	3.59	2.45	4.40	1.90	3.67	2.40
extensions in *contextualised & non-conflicted* conversations	2.85	2.08	3.05	2.52	2.92	2.24
extensions in *decontextualised & conflicted* conversations	5.11	4.56	6.22	2.22	5.32	4.21
extensions in *decontextualised & non-conflicted* conversations	4.10	3.15	3.62	2.53	3.97	3.00
enhancements in *contextualised & conflicted* conversations	1.26	1.54	0.60	1.27	1.18	1.52
enhancements in *contextualised & non-conflicted* conversations	0.78	1.19	0.93	1.23	0.83	1.20
enhancements in *decontextualised & conflicted* conversations	1.32	1.60	1.89	1.17	1.43	1.53
enhancements in *decontextualised & non-conflicted* conversations	1.05	1.53	1.24	1.52	1.10	1.53

The results of the 2×4 MANOVA showed that the main effect of initiation was not significant in all three types of language expansions. The main effect of conversational type, however, had significant effects on two out of three language expansions, namely *extensions* ($F(3, 625) = 9.96$, $p < .01$, partial $\eta^2 = .05$) and *enhancements* ($F(3, 625) = 3.17$, $p < .05$, partial $\eta^2 = .02$). There was no significant interaction effect between initiation × conversational type on all the three language expansions.

For the conversational type on *extensions*, the post-hoc pairwise comparisons reveal that the *decontextualised & conflicted* conversations generated the most *extensions* ($M = 5.32$, $SD = 4.21$), followed equally by *contextualised & conflicted* ($M = 3.67$, $SD = 2.40$) and *decontextualised & non-conflicted* ($M = 3.97$, $SD = 3.00$) conversations. The *contextualised & non-conflicted* produced the fewest *extensions* ($M = 2.92$, $SD = 2.24$). For *enhancements*, the pairwise comparisons show that *decontextualised & conflicted* ($M = 1.43$, $SD = 1.53$) and *decontextualised & non-conflicted* conversations ($M = 1.10$, $SD = 1.53$) generated significantly higher *enhancements* than *contextualised & non-conflicted* conversations ($M = 0.83$, $SD = 1.20$). However, *enhancements* did not differ between *contextualised & conflicted* conversations and the other three types. Nor did it differ between *decontextualised & conflicted* conversations. These results were visualised in Figure 1.

Discussion

This study explores the language expansions in parent–child conversations at the dinner table drawing on the stances of both parents and children' language use in a group of middle-class Chinese families. Previous research identified pedagogical

Table 7. Pairwise comparison of the proportions of the three types of language expansions in total conversations.

language expansion types (number, proportion)		z	p
1 *elaborations* (474, 13.8%)	1 < 2	90.68	.00
	1 < 3	9.02	.00
2 *extensions* (2310, 67.1%)	2 > 3	−59.95	.00
3 *enhancements* (659, 19.1%)	—	—	—

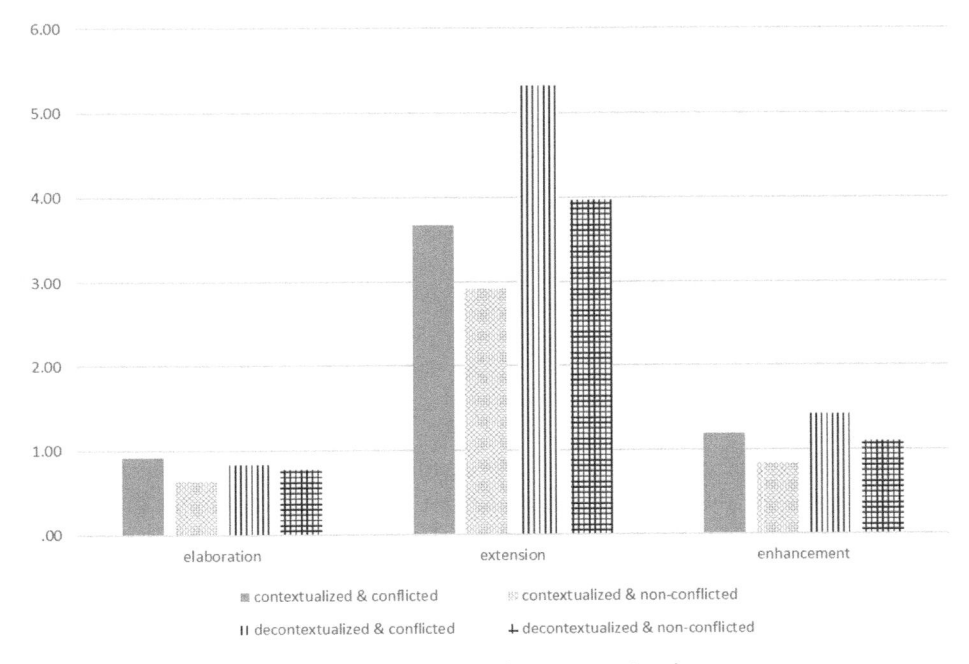

Figure 1. The distribution of language expansions by conversational types.

functions of expanded genres at the dinner table, yet the details about how such genres would offer language learning opportunities for children are less clear. Grounded in SFL theories, this study extends existing research in the field as it reveals the cohesive patterns in the expanded messages, which offer great potential for children to develop language skills of how to maintain language cohesion by constantly constructing meanings in conversations. The findings of this study also add to the literature of how Chinese children's language learning experiences are shaped in the family daily routine (at the dinner table) in Mainland China, which is an under-researched area.

The distribution of four types of conversations in Chinese parent–child mealtime conversations

The findings relating to the conversational types suggest that the parents dominated in all four types of the conversations and generated a significantly higher proportion of conversations than their children did. This finding corroborates the studies showing parents' leading position at the dinner table that create the conversations providing a supported and challenging situation for their children (Bova and Arcididacono 2014; Brumark 2006). However, children's contribution to the mealtime conversations was also noticeable in that they generated more than one-quarter of all the conversations, which demonstrates the young children's active role in creating the language environment at home.

The participating families' dinner table talk is presented with a range of conversations containing extensive language expansions, indicating the dynamic informational exchange among the family members on shared topics. Among the four types of conversations, *decontextualised & non-conflicted* conversations occurred most frequently and accounted for the highest proportion in the parent-initiated conversations. This result signifies the pedagogical functions and harmonious parent–child relationships embedded in these families' conversations. This finding may be attributable to the background of the participating parents, who are well-educated and professionals (middle-class). It is widely acknowledged that the well-educated middle-classed parents tend to use narrative or explanatory discourses which focus on decontextualised information (Bohanek et al. 2009; Busch 2017). Our results are also consistent with previous research on Chinese parent–child communication that well-educated younger generation of Chinese parents are reported to have warm and trusting relationships with their children and have open communication by significantly involving children in family communication.

The prevalence of *contextualised & non-conflicted* conversations, which ranks the second most among the four conversational types, takes a substantial proportion of more than one-third of total conversations. The proportion of this conversational type in child-initiated conversations amounted to almost half, which was significantly higher than that in parent-initiated conversations. In such conversations, the children showed positive attitudes or practices relating to food eating issues that were supported by the parents. Ranked as the third among the four conversational types, as the *contextualised & conflicted* conversations, however, showed completely opposite features (children's intense resistance) from those in *contextualised & non-conflicted* conversations. The proportion of *contextualised & conflicted* in the parent-initiated conversations (17.7%) was nearly three times than that in the child-initiated conversations. This result concurs with Bova's (2019) study that revealed parents' initiation of conflicting conversations often concerning contextualised issues (children's eating). Whilst the disputes between parents and children over food eating seem to be a common issue in many cultures (Arcidiacono and Bova 2015), Chinese parents are reported to demonstrate a high level of anxiety relating to their children health and eating habits (Guo 2015; Hu et al. 2019). This anxiety may be rooted in the Chinese cultural faith that parents should take full responsible for providing superb caring and learning experiences to their children so that children can grow physically, socially and academically well (Luo, Catherine, and Song 2013). The enforcement for children to take more food may reflect the Chinese parents' ideology of 'being responsible' for their children's wellbeing, however, this practice departs from parental authority rather than children's real physical needs and tends to trigger children's resistance. Hence, this practice seems not to be in line with educational principles for fostering children's wellbeing.

The least demonstrated conversational type is *decontextualised & conflicted,* in which the parents and the children argued for their standpoints for 'there and then' topics, such as *Can a princess join in dragon boat competition*? Considering the children of this study are only preschool aged, it is reasonable to see the low frequency of this type of conversations. Preschool-aged children's argumentative skills are limited, particularly in activity-unbound arguments, which the decontextualised information with reasoning discourse is often required (Arcidiacono and Bova

2015). It was very challenging for the preschool children to actively engage in such conversations.

The distribution of language expansion in Chinese parent–child mealtime conversations

In terms of language expansions in the conversations, *extensions* are used mostly in the total conversations, with *elaborations* and *enhancements* appearing much less. This finding indicates that the parents and the children generally expanded the topics with additional ideas on the previous messages. The findings of fewer *elaborations* and *enhancements* might be due to the small proportions of conflicted types (regardless of contextualised or decontextualised) in the total mealtime conversations, as the conflicted conversations were likely to trigger *elaborations* and *enhancements* through speakers' frequent use of justification discourses to reconcile the conflicts. This result is different from the findings in Bova and Arcidiacono's studies (2013, 2014), which reported frequent arguments occurred in parents and children's mealtime conversations in some Western families. The divergent results are likely to be related to differences in Western and Chinese culture. As Chinese culture values harmonious familial relationships and parental authorities (Luo, Catherine, and Song 2013), some arguments could be avoided between parents and the child.

Perhaps the most interesting point of this study relates to the effect of the conversational types on the expanded messages. The type of *decontextualised & conflicted* conversations occurred least, yet it contains the most *extensions* and also comparatively more *enhancements*. This finding is supported by the research on mealtime argument that identified the learning opportunities for children to co-construct the 'meaning making' with their parents over the conflicting topics through justification discourses (Bova 2019). Unlike the *contextualised & conflicted* conversations, which primarily focus on topics of food eating and often result in children's unpleasant experiences under parental authority, the arguments on 'then and there' topics had more logical reasoning language when the parents and the children tried to justify their ideas. For example, a child reasoned that a princess could eat Zongzi (a traditional Chinese food), because *princesses are rich and can afford yummy food like Zongzi*. In contrast, although the *contextualised & non-conflicted* conversations appeared as the second most frequently in all the conversations, they generated the fewest expanded messages, indicating quite limited conversational turns between the parents and the children. This finding is coincided with language research that suggests the limited pedagogical functions of contextualised conversations (Halliday and Matthiessen 2004). Our study further confirms the limitation of this type of conversations in the interactional situation of the participants having agreements on the topics.

In conclusion, this study presents the distributional patterns of conversations and language expansions in the conversations in Chinese parent–child mealtime talk by distinguishing parents' and children's contributions. The impact of the conversational types on the distribution of language expansions was apparent. While the *decontextualised & conflicted* conversations were the least occurring conversational type, they had more language expansions, which created extensive language learning opportunities for children in terms of exchanging information cohesively, hence being higher quality of language that merits more attention by both parents and early childhood educators.

The most language expansions in these mealtime conversations were *extensions*. This reflects the basic feature of these families' mealtime conversations characterised with the parents and the children's additional ideas for maintaining the conversations.

Limitations and implications

Before discussing the implications of the study, it is necessary to point out the limitations of the study, which may be addressed in future research. The participating families were all from well-educated professional backgrounds, thus do not cover all the patterns of mealtime conversations in Chinese families from diverse SES. Future studies should aim to collect mealtime conversations from Chinese families in different SES, so a more complete picture of Chinese parent–child mealtime talk can be captured. Another limitation concerned the video recording, which might affect the way the participants talked as they were aware of being filmed. It could be possible that sometimes the participants might not use the language which they normally use in more naturalistic settings without video recording. Nonetheless, the videos recorded by the participants themselves minimised the unnaturalistic effect than if the videos had been recorded by researchers.

Despite these limitations, the findings of this study have important implications as to how mealtime conversations could be better used as language learning occasions for children. Firstly, the *decontextualised & conflicted* conversations seemed to create more opportunities for the speakers to expand on each other's ideas constantly. This finding is consistent with the growing body of research that emphasise the didactic value in decontextualised talk or conflicting conversations at the dinner table (Bohanek et al. 2009; Busch 2017; Snow and Beals 2006). Raising parents' awareness of the educational affordance of different conversational types, especially the value of *decontextualised & conflicted* type is more likely to motivate them to adjust their language for improving the conversational quality. Secondly, the Chinese parents' initiation of around one-fifth of conversations as *contextualised & conflicted* type raises a concern about parents' attitudes and practices relating to their children's food intake issues. This finding suggests that these parents may need some support to develop constructive attitudes and strategies for encouraging children's positive eating habits, rather than using parental authority to enforce children to eat. Finally, although the research was undertaken in the context of Chinese families, the finding of children's active contributions to the family dinner table conversations may have value that goes beyond Chinese culture. Children's participation and contribution to the mealtime conversations create a constructive language learning and practice environment for themselves, hence, their participation should be encouraged by parents in order to promote 'learning about language' through spontaneous mutual conversations in daily mealtime routines.

Acknowledgements

We acknowledge the contributions of the participating families who generously shared their information with us and the organisations who assisted the data collection in collaboration with us.

Disclosure statement

No potential conflict of interest was reported by the author(s).

ORCID

Ling Sheng ⓘ http://orcid.org/0000-0002-0075-0077
Feifei Han ⓘ http://orcid.org/0000-0001-8464-0854
Jiangbo Hu ⓘ http://orcid.org/0000-0001-5471-7689

References

Arcidiacono, Francesco, and Bova Antonio. 2015. "Activity-Bound and Activity-Unbound Arguments in Response to Parental Eat-Directives at Mealtimes: Differences and Similarities in Children of 3-5 and 6-9 Years Old." *Learning, Culture and Social Interaction* 6: 40–55. doi:10.1016/j.lcsi.2015.03.002.

Aronsson, Karin, and Lucas GottAzén. 2011. "Generational Positions at a Family Dinner: Food Morality and Social Order." *Language in Society* 40 (4): 405–426. doi:10.1017/S0047404511000455.

Aukrust, Vibeke. 2002. "'What Did you Do in School Today?' Speech Genres and Talk Ability in Multiparty Family Mealtime Conversations in Two Cultures." In *Talking to Adult: The Contribution of Multiparty Discourse to Language Acquisition*, edited by S. Blum-Kulda, and C. Snow, 55–83. Mahwah, NJ: Lawrence Erlbaum.

Bohanek, Jennifer G., Robyn Fivush, Widaad Zaman, Caitlin E. Lepore, Shela Merchant, and Marshall P. Duke. 2009. "Narrative Interaction in Family Dinnertime Conversations." *Merrill-Palmer Quarterly* 55 (4): 488–515. doi:10.1353/mpq.0.0031.

Bova, Antonio 2019. "The Initial Phase of Argumentative Discussions Between Parents and Children." In *The Functions of Parent-Child Argumentation*, edited by Bova Antonio, 39–63. Springer International Publishing. doi:10.1007/978-3-030-20457-0-3.

Bova, Antonio, and Arcidiacono Francesco. 2013. "Investigating Children's Why-Questions: A Study Comparing Argumentative and Explanatory Function." *Discourse Studies* 15 (6): 713–734. doi:10.1177/1461445613490013.

Bova, Antonio, and Arcidiacono Francesco. 2014. "'You Must Eat the Salad Because It Is Nutritious '. Argumentative Strategies Adopted by Parents and Children in Food-Related Discussions at Mealtimes." *Appetite* 73: 81–94. doi:10.1016/j.appet.2013.10.0.

Brumark, Åsa. 2006. "Regulatory Talk and Politeness at the Family Dinner Table." *Pragmatics* 16 (2-3): 171–211. doi:10.1075/prag.16.2-3.06bru.

Busch, Gillian. 2017. "'What Does It Say About It?': Doing Reading and Doing Writing as Part of Family Mealtime." In *Children's Knowledge-In-Interaction*, edited by Amanda Bateman, and Amelia Church, 297–311. Singapore: Springer.

Dai, Qian, Catherine McMahon, and Ai Keow Lim. 2020. "Cross-Cultural Comparison of Maternal Mind-Mindedness among Australian and Chinese Mothers." *International Journal of Behavioral Development* 44 (4): 365–370. doi:10.1177/0165025419874133.

Demir, Özlem Ece, Meredith L. Rowe, Gabriella Heller, Susan Goldin-Meadow, and Susan C. Levine. 2015. "Vocabulary, Syntax, and Narrative Development in Typically Developing Children and Children with Early Unilateral Brain Injury: Early Parental Talk About the 'There-and-Then' Matters." *Developmental Psychology* 51 (2): 161–175. doi:10.1037/a0038476.

Doan, Stacey N, and Qi Wang. 2010. "Maternal Discussions of Mental States and Behaviors: Relations to Emotion Situation Knowledge in European American and Immigrant Chinese Children." *Child Development* 81 (5): 1490–1503. doi:10.1111/j.1467-8624.2010.01487.x.

Eggins, Suzanne. 2004. *Introduction to Systemic Functional Linguistics*. London: Continuum International Publishing Group.

Ferdous, Hasan Shahid, Bernd Ploderer, Hilary Davis, Frank Vetere, and Kenton O'Hara. 2016. "Commensality and the Social Use of Technology During Family Mealtime." *ACM Transactions on Computer-Human Interaction* 23 (6): 1–26. doi:10.1145/2994146.

Fiese, Barbara H, Kimberly P Foley, and Mary Spagnola. 2006. "Routine and Ritual Elements in Family Mealtimes: Contexts for Child Well-Being and Family Identity." *New Directions for Child and Adolescent Development* 2006 (111): 67–89. doi:10.1002/cad.

Fruh, Sharon M., Jayne A. Fulkerson, Madhuri S. Mulekar, Lee Ann J. Kendrick, and Clista Clanton. 2011. "The Surprising Benefits of the Family Meal." *Journal for Nurse Practitioners* 7 (1): 18–22. doi:10.1016/j.nurpra.2010.04.017.

Galatolo, Renata, and Letizia Caronia. 2018. "Morality at Dinnertime: The Sense of the Other as a Practical Accomplishment in Family Interaction." *Discourse and Society* 29 (1): 43–62. doi:10.1177/0957926517726110.

Guo, Karen. 2015. "Motivation, Responsibility and Anxiety: Parenting Dispositions of Chinese Mothers." *Asia-Pacific Journal of Research In Early Childhood Education* 10 (1): 1–19. doi:10.17206/apjrece.2016.10.1.1.

Halliday, Michael Alexander Kirkwood. (1980) 2004. "Three Aspects of Children's Language Development: Learning Language, Learning Through Language, Learning About Language." In *The Language of Early Childhood (the Collected Work of M. A. K. Halliday, Volume 4.)*, edited by Johnathan Webster, 308–326. London: Continuum.

Halliday, Michael Alexander Kirkwood, and Christian Matthiessen. 2004. *An Introduction to Functional Grammar*. London: Hodder Arnold.

Hasan, Ruqaiya. 1996. "Literacy, Everyday Talk and Society." In *Literacy in Society*, edited by Hasan Ruqaiya, and Geoffrey Williams, 377–424. London: Longman.

Hu, Jiangbo, and Jane Torr. 2016. "A Study of Reasoning Talk Between Australian Chinese Mothers and Their Preschool Children: What Messages Are Mothers Sending?" *Journal of Language, Identity & Education* 15 (3): 180–193. doi:10.1080/15348458.2016.1169801.

Hu, Jiangbo, Jane Torr, Yonggang Wei, and Changhua Jiang. 2019. "Mealtime Talk as a Language Learning Context: Australian Chinese Parents' Language Use in Interactions with Their Preschool-Aged Children at the Dinner Table Mealtime." *Early Child Development and Care* 191 (3): 415–430. doi:10.1080/03004430.2019.1621862.

Ji, Yan, and Yiran Zhang. 2020. "An Investigation of Parent-Child Communication in Families with Migrant Preschoolers." *Early Childhood Education* 27: 17–20. doi:CNKI:SUN:YEJY.0.2020-27-004. [In Chinese].

Li, Xuan. 2020. "Fathers' Involvement in Chinese Societies: Increasing Presence, Uneven Progress." *Child Development Perspective* 4 (3): 1–7. doi:10.1111/cdep.12375.

Luo, Rufan, Tamis-LeMonda Catherine, and Lulu Song. 2013. "Chinese Parents' Goals and Practices in Early Childhood." *Early Childhood Research Quarterly* 28 (4): 843–857. doi:10.1016/j.ecresq.2013.08.001.

McHugh, Mary. 2012. "Interrater Reliability: The Kappa Statistic." *Biochemia Medica* 22 (3): 276–282.

Rowe, Meredith. 2013. "Decontextualized Language Input and Preschoolers' Vocabulary Development." *Seminars in Speech and Language* 34 (4): 260–266. doi:10.1055/s-0033-1353444.

Rydstrom, Helle. 2003. *Embodying Morality: Growing up in Rural Northern Vietnam*. Honolulu, HI: University of Hawaii Press.

Snow, Catherine E, and Diane E Beals. 2006. "Mealtime Talk That Supports Literacy Development." *New Directions for Child and Adolescent Development* 2006 (111): 51–66. doi:10.1002/cad.

Wang, Qi. 2001. "Did You have Fun?' American and Chinese Mother-Child Conversations about Shared Emotional Experiences." *Cognitive Development* 16 (2): 693–715. doi:10.1016/S0885-2014(01)00055-7.

Zhang, Heyi. 2018. "Relations of Parent-Child Interaction to Chinese Young Children's Emotion Understanding." *Joural of Pacific Rim Psychology* 12 (22): 1–9. doi:10.1017/prp.2018.11.

'I'm a big boy, you're a baby': Negotiating labels, group boundaries and identities in an early childhood community of practice

Anna Strycharz-Banaś ⓘ, Carmen Dalli ⓘ and Miriam Meyerhoff ⓘ

ABSTRACT

'I'm a big boy, you're a baby': How do such phrases do the vital work of managing young children's peer interactions? We trace the function of such phrases as they were used over an 18-month period by young children (2; 6 - 4; 11) who attended a New Zealand an early childhood centre. Using interactional sociolinguistics methods of analysis we examine how children used particular phrases within their community of practice to manage their peer interactions and to mark out individual and group identities through inclusion and exclusion. The phrases we analyse are labels (big boys; baby); we document changes in the way they were used productively: there is 'ownership' of them; then they are re-purposed; and then some disappear. By viewing peer interactions as phenomena that include a temporal dimension, we trace how each phrase helped to establish individual and group identities that were constantly open to negotiation. We argue the need for greater attention to children's use of language to improve our understanding of children's lived experiences of peer interactions including inclusion and exclusion processes in early childhood settings.

Introduction

In-group membership and belonging are fundamental to who we are as human beings at any age; the social space of our friendships is tied up with our individual and group identities forged in the moment and over time (Puroila and Estola 2014; Stratigos 2016; Yuval-Davis 2006, 2011). Studies of children's peer interactions in early childhood have established that even in the first year of life, children orient to peers differently than to adults showing interest and affiliation through gaze and embodied responses long before they can express them verbally (e.g. Musatti and Panni 1981; Vandell, Wilson, and Buchanan 1980). In a study of 1–6-year olds in a Norwegian EC centre Engdahl (2012) reported that the 1-year olds not only demonstrated consistent interest in each other but used the same kind of actions to gain access to groups as were used by 3- to 6-year old children. By the third year of life notions of intergroup difference have been found to already be in place in toddlers' friendships, defined by Howes (1983, 1042) as relationships marked by 'mutual preference, mutual enjoyment, and the ability to engage in skilful interaction' that is complementary and reciprocal. Using their increasingly sophisticated language and social skills, children aged three years and over initiate advanced forms of play, including through the use of labels for inclusion and exclusion purposes (e.g. Corsaro 1986, 2009; Corsaro and Schwarz 1991; Greve 2008; Ladd 2005).

When in-group and out-group boundaries form, the labels that accompany them can be central to how we perceive ourselves as social actors, including in the early years. The process of naming and intergroup labelling has been quite widely studied in adolescent social networks (e.g. Eckert 2000) and to some extent in adult social interaction (e.g. Holmes and Woodhams 2013). However, research attention to the linguistic practices and skills that underpin the drawing of boundaries among very young children has been much more limited and largely as a secondary focus in studies seeking to understand how children construct a sense of belonging in EC group settings (Stratigos 2016; Skattebol 2005, 2006; Puroila and Estola 2014).

In this paper, we make young children's use of in-group and out-group phrases our primary focus using sociolinguistic methods to analyse how children's labelling and categorisations during peer interactions construct group boundaries, identities and friendship groups. Specifically, we focus on two structurally very simple labels – *big boy* and *baby*. The labels emerged in the interactions of a group of children aged 2; 6 - 4; 11 attending a multi-ethnic, multilingual, inner city EC centre in New Zealand. Although they are linguistically simple noun phrases, *big boy* and *baby* were used in socially complex ways. When *big boy* and *baby* were used together for the first time, their function was to establish and police in-group/out-group boundaries. Subsequently, however, they progressed to becoming resources available for self-reference and humour. Finally, as key members of the innovating group of users (the community of practice) moved to primary school, and as *baby* and *big boy* became more widely used outside the community of practice in which they originated, the labels disappeared. Their use over time demonstrates the multiple functions the labels performed in the children's positioning of themselves as having particular identities, and in relation to others as members of peer and friendship groups.

In using the terms 'peers' and 'friendship' we follow Corsaro's (1997, 95) distinction that peers are 'that cohort or group of children who spend time together on an everyday basis' while friends are those with whom children engage in observable shared activities, playing together, and protecting their play from other children. Friendship is collectively constructed by children through their active participation in activities and serves the primary function of building solidarity and mutual trust, and protecting interactive space (Corsaro 2009). Moreover, as Kantor, Elgas, and Fernie (1989) have also argued, access to a friendship group is often dependent on acquiring its in-group knowledge and applying it at appropriate times.

Theoretical and analytical framing

Communities of practice and membership categorisation devices (MCD)

A number of sociolinguist studies of labelling and social categorisation in the adult world have worked within the theoretical framework of 'communities of practice' (Lave and

Wenger 1991; Meyerhoff and Strycharz-Banaś 2013), a notion originally formulated as a theory of learning to explain how people are socialised into group norms, and grow new identities (Wenger-Traynor 2015). Communities of practice are social groupings unified by participants' mutual interest. They are a community (whether harmonious or adversarial) because they interact and learn from each other. Members of a community of practice develop a shared repertoire of practices, including linguistic ones. Among the shared linguistic practices are the ways participants negotiate how to refer to other people using category labels (such as *big boy* and *baby*) that: (a) have very local (community) relevance; and (b) have rules for application that enable or constrain possible roles, activities and social meanings. Sacks (1972) called these labels 'membership categorisation devices' (MCDs), where the use of one label evokes other dependent or related categories (see also Liu 2015).

When the notion of community of practice was introduced as a social theory of learning (Lave and Wenger 1991) it was rapidly adopted in some education circles. It also became widely used in sociolinguistics, where the focus on the negotiation of identities in action, and the emergent and fluid quality of identities, meshed well with the social constructionist turn in many social sciences. Many of the influential sociolinguistic studies of communities of practice focus on high school students, a social stage that is generally recognised as being characterised by extremely vibrant and active identity experimentation and identity formation (e.g. Moore 2006; Mendoza-Denton 2008; Drager 2015; but also among children, Eckert and McConnell-Ginet 1999; and adults, McElhinny 1993; Strycharz-Banaś 2016). The enormous work that young children need to do to establish social identities as an ontological category remains, however, under-studied.

As noted, a community of practice is characterised by mutual engagement (harmonious or adversarial), jointly negotiated enterprise(s), and a shared repertoire of language and behaviour (Wenger 1998). The interactions in the EC centre where we conducted our fieldwork easily satisfy these requirements. The EC centre itself can be argued to constitute a community of practice, but our focus is primarily on a friendship group of boys within the EC centre whose mutual engagement over time included harmonious and conflictual interactions. Each of the interactional sequences we analyse focusses on one occasion when the boys were engaged in some jointly negotiated activity, and our paper focusses on some of the linguistic features that constituted their shared repertoire. We refer to this friendship group as the *big-boys* community of practice.

Moreover, our concern is not merely to identify the labels that emerged as important parts of children's shared repertoire; we also explore those labels as membership categorisation devices that contributed to constructing children's identities. We understand identity both as a reputational construct within a social group as well as children's own self-concept of who they are. We follow Stokoe and Attenborough's (2013) methodology for membership categorisation analysis, in other words focusing on *how* the MCDs *big boy* and *baby* were used in these children's interactions with the aim of understanding the different types of local community knowledge carried in the category and how this positioned particular children within or outside the boundaries of that community. Identity theorists have long highlighted the relationship between identity and group inclusion and exclusions (Cerulo 1997; Chan and Spoonley 2017). By tapping into the social information of 'inference-rich' membership categories (Stokoe and Attenborough) used by the children, we explore the shifting social dynamics invoked through the use of the labels *big boy* and *baby* (Sacks 1992; Stokoe and Attenborough 2013), thus gaining a sense of the meaning that these identities held for the children in their day-to-day life in their EC centre. For example, 'big boys' do big boy work and, by implication, those who are not big boys, but 'babies', are bound to other activities – which are not big boys' work.

Interactional sociolinguistics

Our analysis of the children's interactions uses interactional sociolinguistics. Interactional sociolinguistics treats all communication as social action; its concern is with the contextual interpretation of communicative intent and its analysis is not limited to overtly verbal information. By exploring the different presuppositions and inferences made in speech, interactional sociolinguistics is useful for 'detecting systematic differences in interpretive practices' (Gumperz 2006, 728). It addresses global questions ('what is an exchange about?') and local ones ('what is intended by this particular move?'). A strength of interactional sociolinguistics is that it looks for contextualisation cues that include things like speaker stress, volume, and rhythm changes.

Children as active social agents

Our analysis is also grounded in a view of children's social world as a dynamic space of peer negotiations and meaning constructions that are best studied as they unfold in their natural settings. This position rests on the theoretical assumption that children are active social agents rather than passive recipients of socialisation forces (Corsaro 2003; James, Jenks, and Prout 1998). They interpret, negotiate, construct and reconstruct their understandings, identities, and practices (Strycharz-Banaś, Dalli and Meyerhoff 2020). They are agentic in negotiating their peer and friendship interactions, actively creating and re-inventing meanings and identities, and simultaneously reproducing and transforming their culture (Corsaro 1997, 2003, 2009; Greve 2008; Ladd 2005). To understand children's world from their perspective we gathered data through ethnographic non-participant observations (Hammersley and Atkinson 2007) using audio and video recording of naturally occurring interactions. Our analytical approach was informed by the phenomenological principle of seeking to describe phenomena as they are experienced (Husserl 2013/1931; Sixsmith and Sixsmith 1987).

Study site and methodology

The EC centre in our study is a small inner city community-based centre with a play-based curriculum located next to a primary school. At the time that we gathered our data, the centre had a roll of between 22 and 26 children aged two to five years and a staff of three qualified EC teachers and one untrained practitioner. Among the children, there were 11 different home languages, and three different languages (English, Mandarin, Samoan) were spoken by the centre adults. While our focus in this paper is not on the children's acquisition of English *per sé*, it is important to note the diversity within the centre as it speaks to (i) the ongoing work by children and centre staff to forge community across different cultural backgrounds, and (ii) the abbreviated English sentences in some of our examples. Fractured utterances are not necessarily a marker of interactional trouble among the children but may signify children operating at a wholly appropriate level given their multilingual status.

Our observations in the EC centre began in October 2017 and concluded in June 2019.[1] During this time, the lead author visited the EC centre regularly as a non-participant observer. For the entire time, she took fieldnotes, and between February 2018 and June 2019, she also video-recorded the children for two days a week, every week. Two recorders were placed strategically indoors in the centre and the lead author also moved in and out of doors with the children using a handheld camera. The children had multiple opportunities to familiarise themselves with the recording equipment and to handle it, and we have numerous recorded instances of interactions among them where it is very clear that they trusted the cameras as wholly impartial observers.[2]

Ethical considerations

Ethical approval for the project was gained through the Human Ethics Committee of the university of the principal investigator (Dalli) with ethical processes for the avoidance of harm to participants followed over a number of steps. In the first instance, informed consent for the research was sought from the management of the early childhood centre, the teachers at the centre, and parents of the children in the centre. Information sheets and consent forms were developed and translated as necessary into the different home languages of the children. All adult participants were informed of their right to withdraw themselves or their child from the study at any time, with no prejudice, and that no participants – children or teachers – would have their names revealed by the researchers. Teachers and parents were offered the option that faces and other identifying features would be blurred if photos or video data were used in presentations.

Following this initial step, we developed protocols for child consent starting with inviting parents to talk to their child at home about the project. With the teachers' assistance, a scheduled mat time was used by the main field researcher to meet with the children whose parents had consented to their child's participation, and to explain the activities of the project. A prepared script was used to tell the children that: they could say no to being recorded at any time; and that the researchers would write about what they recorded. An opportunity for the children to ask questions and to try out the video camera was also given, with the latter remaining an activity open to the children throughout the project.

Throughout the data-gathering the researchers remained continually mindful of the need to be attentive to any signals from the children that they were not comfortable with the cameras or the note-taking – including noticing any bodily signals or verbalised discomfort. At the commencement of each data-gathering session, before switching on the camera, the researcher would inform the children and teachers in the given area that the camera would now be on and that it would keep running. Protocols for stopping the filming and re-starting it were also put in place.

Data transcriptions

The video recordings were partially transcribed using ELAN (Wittenburg et al. 2006) and the extracts presented in this paper come from the approximately 270 hours of video recordings. Line numbering in the data extracts comes from our longer transcriptions; bolded text identifies the speaker and labelling phrases we focus on in the analysis. The extracts were selected through the interactional sociolinguistic process of identifying and tracing the emergence of labels that produced 'systematic differences in interpretive practice' (Gumperz 2006, 728). In this paper, the first extract signals the emergence of the labels *big boy* and *baby* as identity markers that carried an inclusion / exclusion function for a self-identified '*big boy*' friendship group which we are calling the *big-boy* community of practice. Extracts 2–6 illustrate how the use of the labels shifted over time (see Appendix for transcription conventions).

Labelling and boundary-work

The identity of being a *big boy* first emerged in the speech of the older boys in the centre as a self-reference to signal belonging to the *big-boys* friendship group, or community of practice ('we are big boys'), made up of the four oldest boys. The boys regularly played together and generally sought each other out for joint activities. As a label, *baby* was also in use among the children – invoked to tease or taunt others with the suggestion that they were behaving in a developmentally less competent manner. But the first time that the two labels emerged in our data positioned in contrast to each other was in Extract 1 where the labels became a mechanism for excluding others. In Extract 1, Rashid and Max, two of the oldest boys in the centre, attempt to exclude the younger Kareem from joining their play, digging a hole in the sandpit. Kareem had been eagerly working on joining Rashid's *big-boy* friendship group for some time. In Extract 1, we see Kareem adopting the labelling practices primarily associated with Rashid and Max as a way of protesting his exclusion from the joint play.

Extract 1: 'The sandpit fight: who can dig a hole in the sandpit?' (12/02/2018)

55	**Rashid:**	(looking down at the sand) **it's big boys' job**[3]
56	Teacher:	yeah maybe not now (directed at Kareem)
57	Teacher:	because Rashid re:ally really wants to finish the project by them all- by them two
	[...]	
145	Kareem:	Rashid baby
146	Rashid:	(angry grunt, turns back towards Kareem, makes an angry face)
147	Rashid:	**I'm not ba-by** (pulls at the stick Kareem is holding in his hand)
148	Teacher:	Rashid use your words first
149	Kareem:	baby Rashid baby
150	Max:	you're a baby Kareem
151	Kareem:	baby Rashid baby Rashid baby Rashid
152	Max:	no baby Rashid
153	Rashid:	Kareem baby Kareem baby
154	**Kareem:**	**Rashid baby Rashid baby**
155	Teacher:	Kareem-
156	Rashid:	(picks up spade) I'm gonna hit you with this spade
157	Teacher:	Rashid's really really angry when you call him baby
158	Kareem:	(smiles)

Rashid here invokes the label *big boys* to distinguish between himself and Max (who are digging together) and Kareem who is trying to insert himself into their play. Earlier that day Rashid and Max had already made several unsuccessful attempts to exclude Kareem: Max tried physically standing in Kareem's way, and then tried changing the subject to something he and Rashid were jointly attending to (discursively excluding Kareem). Rashid had told Kareem 'No!' eight times (at varying levels of volume), and Rashid tried other nonverbal forms of exclusion (growling in Kareem's face, banging his spade) as well as denying Kareem's assertion that Kareem could 'help' the older boys ('Kareem: I'm come help. Rashid: NO. No hel-ping' [emphasis on all Rashid's syllables], lines 33-35). The invocation of the intergroup difference between *big boys* and *babies* was therefore Rashid's final attempt at setting up a boundary around him and Max to exclude Kareem.

Notably, Rashid labelled himself and Max as *big boys*, and it was Kareem who invoked the implied opposite, *baby*, by accusing Rashid himself of being a baby. It appears that Kareem had learnt enough about the friendship group he aspired to join to know that *big boy* was part of a collective category and, in this community of practice, *big boy* formed a pair with *baby,* a label Rashid clearly was unhappy with. The category-bounded activities that Rashid invoked with *big boys* are: digging a hole with the spades, and deciding who is allowed to participate in this. The contrast between *big boy* and *baby* is inference-rich in multiple ways: because *big boy* made the contrast with *baby* relevant, *big boys' job* invites the inference that babies could not share in the digging.

By uttering the term *baby* and applying it to Rashid, we do not believe Kareem actually wanted to exclude Rashid from the group play – indeed, our fieldwork made it clear Kareem very much wanted to be friends with Rashid – and in line 158 we see evidence (Kareem's smile) that Kareem was using the label *baby* strategically rather than as an identity marker. Kareem's satisfied response to the teacher's evaluation that he was making Rashid angry suggests to us that Kareem may have been using the *baby* label to (i) demonstrate how angry he was when Rashid and Max excluded him from membership as a *big boy* in the earlier part of this interaction and (ii) to show Rashid that he understood the rules of this game (i.e. that *big boys* and *babies* are mutually exclusive), and that he was prepared (and able) to use this knowledge to try and beat Rashid at his own labelling and inclusion/exclusion game.

From Rashid's perspective, being categorised as *baby* by Kareem – an outsider to the *big-boy* community of practice – was not only a challenge to his identity of being a *big boy* but also to his membership status within the community of practice. In line 147, we see Rashid argue that he is 'not baby', but this is a not a particularly effective rebuttal for Kareem who persists with labelling Rashid as a baby (line 153). Since one of the rights of a *big boy* seems to be the ability to label others, by asserting Rashid is a baby, Kareem undermines Rashid's ability to assert his own label of himself as a *big boy,* an identity of which he was obviously very proud. The oldest boy Max intervenes verbally at line 150, invoking his own right as a *big boy* to explicitly label Kareem 'a baby', and to imply that Kareem is the only baby there.

The negotiation of labels and identities, activities and rights in these children's interactions demonstrates the richness of their social skills within their peer interactions. By using *baby* in this way and at this point in the sandpit fight, Kareem demonstrated his competence in mobilising understandings about the social structure of the EC centre in ways that would establish him as a potential core member of Rashid and Max's *big-boys* community of practice.

Max was the first of the older boys to move on to primary school, and this left Rashid with two younger boys, Kareem and Assad, as potential *big boys* with him; the original community of practice had dissolved and, with it, the regular invocation of the *big boy – baby* dichotomy whenever Kareem attempted to breach the group boundary around the *big-boys* community of practice. Our data show that Max's departure signalled a significant shift in Kareem and Rashid's interactions which became fundamentally amicable. The last time we heard the label *big boy* invoked between Rashid and Kareem was in the last week of February 2018 when, seeking a friend to accompany him on a library visit, Rashid invited Kareem and followed up with the suggestion that Rashid was a *big boy* and Kareem a *small boy*. Accepting Rashid's invitation, Kareem seemed content to also accept this re-labelling of his status vis-à-vis Rashid's *big-boy* friendship group and his new identity as not quite a *big boy* but not a *baby* either (Strycharz-Banaś, Dalli, and Meyerhoff 2020). The contrast between *big boy* and *small boy* was not reproduced again in our fieldwork.

Re-negotiating labels

Rashid, Assad and Kareem kept the labels *big boy* and *baby* alive within the EC centre for several months more, but as the community of practice that was centred around Max and Rashid broke up, the labels ceased to be used in contrast to each other. That is, they ceased to belong to the same collective category and developed associations with new activities and other categories (Stokoe and Attenborough 2013). In other words, the labels *big boy* and *baby* developed and acquired new significance within the wider communities of practice of the EC centre.

In Extract 2 and 3, we see the term *big boy* used as self-reference, first by Assad and then by Rashid.

Extract 2: 'Table play with magnets' (12/03/2018)

9	Teacher:	I can give you another one of these
10		(gets up, walks away and brings a different magnet)
11	Assad:	no I need this
12	Teacher:	have you tried this?
13		later you can have that
14	Assad:	no I'm a big boy
15	Teacher:	you want a taller one?
16	**Assad:**	**I'm a big boy**
17	Teacher:	yes
18		when Vince finishes tha-
19	Assad:	I want this
20		I want to be this (points to the magnet piece Vince is playing with)

Extract 3: 'Dressing-up and performing *Big Boy*' (07/04/2018) Assad and another child are sitting at a table playing with construction blocks. Rashid comes in with a big smile, wearing dress-up glasses and some fabric draped around his shoulders like a cape. He looks around.

1	Rashid:	hey hey
2	Assad:	(play-punches him in the stomach)
3	Rashid:	(laughs)
4	**Rashid:**	**I'm the biggest boy**
5	Rashid:	(moves around so everyone sees him)

While the label *big boy* in Extract 2 seems to be purely descriptive, in Extract 3, Rashid seems to feel he has special ownership of the term, proudly declaiming his identity as 'the biggest boy'. Not only does he invoke it as an assertion without asking for external validation (as Assad does in Extract 2), he also seems to feel free to manipulate it creatively (*the biggest boy*) and to use it in a stylised, dress-up performance. In Extract 4, we can see an example of how Rashid continued to negotiate the use of *big boy* as an in-group label with Assad, effectively teaching him how to use and invoke it appropriately. Extract 4: 'Catching the rope' (07/04/2018) Assad and Rashid are outside, Rashid is standing under a big rope that the teachers have tied across the outside play area. Assad is standing up on slightly higher ground and so is closer to the rope (he can touch it with his fingers) but he cannot take hold of it.

1	Rashid:	Assad
2	Rashid:	**big boy no go here** (pointing to where Assad is standing)
3	Rashid:	**big boy stand here** (pointing to his own feet)
4	Rashid:	(jumps up trying to reach the rope above his head)
5	**Rashid:**	**big boy here**
6	Rashid:	(comes close to Assad and puts his arms around his waist)
7	**Rashid:**	**you big boy?**
8	**Rashid:**	**you big boy?**
9	Assad:	uh huh Rashi:d
10	**Rashid:**	**you big boy?**
11	Assad:	yeah
12	Rashid:	here (pointing to the place below the rope)
13	Rashid:	(moves back to where he'd been standing before, under the rope)
14	**Rashid:**	**big boy do like this** (jumps up and tries to catch the rope)
15	Rashid:	(tries a few more times, fails, then both walk away)

Not only does Rashid teach Assad the type of behaviour appropriate for a *big boy* by physically aligning the term with their respective bodies (lines 2, 3, 5) and joint action (line 14), he also engages in three confirmation checks with Assad (lines 7, 8, 10). By framing the assignment of the label *big boy* as questions, Rashid cleverly brings Assad in as a co-owner of the term, and inducts him into new behaviours that befit his new identity as a *big boy* (lines 3, 5, 12, 14). Questions are known linguistically as 'adjacency pairs' (Sacks 1987). This means that a question expects to be paired with a response and there is a strong, cultural preference to provide affirmation to a question (Sacks 1987). By bringing Assad in as a participant in the labelling process, and by presupposing his agreement, Rashid allows Assad to see himself as co-constructing his group membership and the meaning and role performances that go with the label *big boy*. We note that in Extract 4, Rashid does not invoke the contrast between *big boys* and *babies* (as he did in Extract 1). At this point in the trajectory of the label, the two labels seem to have diverged from each other, and are now available for the children to use independently. In Extract 5, we see *baby* used as a label and (as with *big(gest) boy* in Extract 3) it is used self-referentially and as a humorous device. In Extract 6, from somewhat later in the year, we see *baby* being used by children well outside the core friendship group who originated the *big boy/baby* contrast, and among these children, the way to refute *baby*-status did not involve claiming that you are a *big boy*. Extract 5: 'Who is a stupid baby?' (10/05/2018) Rashid, Vince and Assad are playing with construction bricks. Assad is sitting at the table with his back to Vince and Rashid. Vince is crouching and Rashid has just got up. Facing Vince, Rashid is pretending that he is a baby and that one of the toys is a nappy 'on my bumbum'.

1	Vince:	you stupid baby
2	Vince:	stupid
3	Vince:	stupid
4	Assad:	(turning around to look at Vince, frowning)
5	**Assad:**	**[I'm not] BABY**
6	Vince:	[stupid] (smiling)
7	Rashid:	(coming closer to both boys, looks at Vince)
8	**Rashid:**	**he not a baby**
9	Vince:	no
10	**Rashid:**	**(to Assad) he wasn't saying you**
11	**Rashid:**	**he was saying me**

Extract 6: 'Call me Reza' (04/07/2018)

1	Reza:	I'm not the baby
2	Sara:	Reza is a BABY
3	Johnny:	(comes out of the enclosure)
4	**Johnny:**	**no he's Reza**
5	**Sara:**	**he is a BABY**
6	**Reza:**	(coming out from behind the scarves) **REZA**
7	**Sara:**	**you're a BABY**
8	**Reza:**	**Reza**
9	**Sara:**	**baby** (giggling)
10	**Reza:**	**REZA**
11	**Sara:**	**BABY**
12	Reza:	(starts walking away following Johnny)
13	**Reza:**	**Reza**
14	**Reza:**	**Reza**
15	**Reza:**	**[Reza]**
16	**Sara:**	**[baby]**

Extract 5 shows that *baby* continues to be seen as a derogatory label when used in the EC centre, but we also see that it is now being recognised as potentially being used as a label by children outside the *big-boy* friendship group that was started by Max and Rashid. Additionally, Extract 6 shows that where *baby* is invoked as a derogatory term, it seems to have undergone a diverging trajectory from *big boy*. Reza does not challenge Sara's labelling of him as a *baby* by claiming *big boy* status, rather, he invokes his proper name. The fact that he counters Sara's label *baby* with his name five times (and that he is backed up in this by Johnny) suggests that by now within the centre, an effective and appropriate contrast to being accused of being a *baby* is to assert one's identity through the use of one's proper name. The sense that *baby* implies in-group/out-group contrasts is considerably weakened in this exchange. When Vince used the label *baby* (directed at Rashid) and Assad thought Vince was talking to him, Assad was upset. As we saw in Extract 3, Rashid felt comfortable testing the boundaries of the labels that he helped to introduce into common usage in the EC centre. In Extract 5, he showed he was comfortable with testing the boundaries of his own status as a *baby*, including in referring to himself humorously as a baby when playing with Vince.

Shifts in meaning and concluding thoughts

The shifts in the way that Rashid used the word *baby* since his furious response to the label in Extract 1 are remarkable. In only three months, the labels appeared to move out of the control of the community of practice that introduced them, and to be used more widely by other children in the EC centre. As they made this move, the labels were inscribed with new meanings and this de-stabilised the original opposition between them. The person in the EC centre who had been using these labels the longest, Rashid, showed himself to be the most comfortable with treating them as performative resources. Rashid could perform 'being a baby' and perform 'being a big boy' apparently without too much threat to his social capital and standing. He did so with the ease of someone who fully understood their power and with what appeared to be a level of 'ownership' of these labels.

Other children in the EC centre also picked up the labels, but they did not appear to have translated all the social meaning that was associated with them in their original community of practice.[4] This is shown by the separation of the labels as opposites, and the emergence of new linguistic categories as the most salient contrasts. The original contrast was between *big boy* and *baby* as MCDs, whereas in the last extract an individual could reject the label *baby* by making salient their proper name.

As Stokoe and Attenborough (2013) point out, proper names can also be used as categorical phenomena, invoking a richness of inferences (when, for example, someone is referred to as 'Nigella of science'). When Reza repeatedly asserts his name in contrast to *baby,* he is not, we think, asserting a new categorial contrast between 'Reza-ness' and 'baby-hood'. In other words, he is not creating a new mutually exclusive category, like the previous contrast between *big boys* and *babies.* Using membership categorisation analysis allows for the use of categories (including proper names) to be potentially limitless – invoking, orienting to, and manipulating the meaning of categories like *baby* or the implied meanings here of self-hood. We can then see how the meanings attached to the label *baby* have shifted, so that in this example it appears to be used as potentially standing in opposition to a broader category of self, a notable and arguably agentic declaration of identity.

We have also shown the process by which aspiring or 'apprentice' members of a community of practice learned how to use the linguistic routines that characterised membership in that community of practice. We have seen them reverse the labels, implicitly disclaiming their own status as a *baby* by assigning it to others. We have also seen an expert member of the community of practice demonstrate the use of the positive term *big boy* through physical alignment, co-participation in an action, and co-construction of use of the term through question and answer pairs.

By tracing the two labels across time and across different speakers, we have shown how meanings attached to certain words change, sometimes quite rapidly. As children use labels and other linguistic devices for complex identity work, these labels do not remain static, but are creatively manipulated with consequent meaning shifts in different contexts. This points to the creativity and richness of children's peer interactions in EC settings and to the way that children's lived experiences and identities in EC centres can be impacted by the nuances of meaning generated in their peer interactions. A key implication from our analysis is that to understand the meanings attached to any words and phrases that can potentially be used for inclusion or exclusion, in-group or out-group boundary marking, EC researchers and teachers alike need to pay the same kind of attention to how labels and phrases are used in context and over time that the children themselves do.

Notes

1. Thanks to Marsden Fund for funding this research; our gratitude also goes to all parents, teacher and above all children.
2. The two lead authors also worked closely with the teachers in the childcare centre, sharing observations and occasionally jointly workshopping materials from our recordings. The applied outcomes of the partnership between researchers and the early childhood centre and the process are discussed in more detail in Strycharz-Banaś, Dalli and Meyerhoff (2020).
3. Bolded text identifies labelling.
4. Meyerhoff (2009) suggests that, when transferring social meaning to new linguistic forms, change in meaning should be entirely expected because social meaning is so complex and so situationally contingent.

Disclosure statement

No potential conflict of interest was reported by the author(s).

Funding

This work was supported by the Marsden Fund (Royal Society of New Zealand – Te Aparangi) [grant number VUW 1623].

Data availability statement

The data collected for this study are protected under the conditions set out in the Victoria University of Wellington Human Ethics Committee, approval 25333.

ORCID

Anna Strycharz-Banaś ⓘ http://orcid.org/0000-0001-9297-6868
Carmen Dalli ⓘ http://orcid.org/0000-0003-1979-2143
Miriam Meyerhoff ⓘ http://orcid.org/0000-0002-2599-1870

References

Cerulo, Karen A. 1997. "Identity Construction: New Issues, New Directions." *Annual Review of Sociology* 23: 385–409.
Chan, Angel, and Paul Spoonley. 2017. "The Politics and Construction of Identity and Childhood: Chinese Immigrant Families in New Zealand." *Global Studies of Childhood* 7 (1): 17–28.
Corsaro, William. 1986. "Routines in Peer Culture." In *Children's Worlds and Children's Language*, edited by J. Cook-Gumperz, W. Corsaro, and J. Streeck, 231–251. Berlin: Walter de Gruyter & Co.
Corsaro, William A. 1997. *The Sociology of Childhood*. Thousand Oaks, CA: Pine Forge Press.
Corsaro, William A. 2003. *We're Friends Right? Inside Kids' Culture*. Washington, DC: Joseph Henry Press.
Corsaro, William A. 2009. "Peer Culture." In *The Palgrave Handbook of Childhood Studies*, edited by J. Qvortrup, W. Corsaro, and M. Honig, 301–316. Basingstoke: Palgrave Macmillan.
Corsaro, William A., and Katherine Schwarz. 1991. "Peer Play and Socialization in two Cultures." In *Play and the Social Context of Development in Early Care and Education*, edited by B. Scales, M. Almy, A. Nicololpoulou, and S. Irvin Tripp, 234–254. New York: Teachers College Press.
Drager, Katie K. 2015. *Linguistic Variation, Identity Construction and Cognition*. Berlin: Language Science Press. http://langsci-press.org/catalog/book/75.

Eckert, Penelope. 2000. *Linguistic Variation as Social Practice*. Oxford: Basil Blackwell.

Eckert, Penelope, and Sally McConnell-Ginet. 1999. "New Generalizations and Explanations in Language and Gender Research." *Language in Society* 28 (2): 185–201.

Engdahl, Ingrid. 2012. "Doing Friendship During the Second Year of Life in a Swedish Preschool." *European Early Childhood Education Research Journal* 20 (1): 83–89.

Greve, Anna. 2008. "Friendships and Participation among Young Children in a Norwegian Kindergarten." In *Chapter 6: Participatory Learning in the Early Years*, edited by D. Berthelsen, J. Brownlee, and E. Johansson, 78–92. New York: Routledge.

Gumperz, John J. 2006. "Interactional Sociolinguistics." In *Encyclopaedia of Language and Linguistics*, edited by K. Brown, 2nd ed., 724–729. Boston: Elsevier. doi:10.1016/B0-08-044854-2/01284-0.

Hammersley, Martyn, and Paul Atkinson. 2007. *Ethnography: Principles in Practice*. London: Routledge.

Holmes, Janet, and Jay Woodhams. 2013. "Building Interaction: The Role of Talk in Joining a Community of Practice." *Discourse and Communication* 7 (3): 275–298.

Howes, Carollee. 1983. "Patterns of Friendship." *Child Development* 54 (4): 1041–1053.

Husserl, Edmund. 2013/1931. *Ideas: General Introduction to Pure Phenomenology*. London: Routledge; Taylor & Francis.

James, Alison, Chris Jenks, and Alan Prout. 1998. *Theorising Childhood*. Cambridge: Polity.

Kantor, Rebecca, Peggy M. Elgas, and David E. Fernie. 1989. "First the Look and Then the Sound: Creating Conversations at Circle Time." *Early Childhood Research Quarterly* 4 (4): 433–448. doi:10.1016/0885-2006(89)90002-1.

Ladd, Gary W. 2005. *Children's Peer Relations and Social Competence*. Yale: University Press.

Lave, Jean, and Etienne Wenger. 1991. *Situated Learning: Legitimate Peripheral Participation*. Cambridge: Cambridge University Press.

Liu, Ruey-Ying. 2015. "Invoking Membership Categories Through Marked Person Reference Forms in Parent-Child Interaction." *Working Papers in TESOL & Applied Linguistics* 15 (1): 1–13. https://eric.ed.gov/?id=EJ1176865.

McElhinny, Bonnie. 1993. "We All Wear the Blue: Language, Gender and Police Work." PhD diss., Stanford University.

Mendoza-Denton, Norma. 2008. *Homegirls: Language and Cultural Practice among Latina Youth Gangs*. London: Blackwell.

Meyerhoff, Miriam. 2009. "Replication, Transfer and Calquing: Using Variation as a Tool in the Study of Language Contact." *Language Variation and Change* 21: 297–317.

Meyerhoff, Miriam, and Anna Strycharz-Banaś. 2013. "Communities of Practice." In *Handbook of Language Variation and Change*, edited by J. K. Chambers, and Natalie Schilling, 2nd ed., 428–447. Oxford: Wiley-Blackwell.

Moore, Emma. 2006. "'You Tell All the Stories': Using Narrative to Explore Hierarchy Within a Community of Practice." *Journal of Sociolinguistics* 10 (5): 611–640.

Musatti, Tullia, and S. Panni. 1981. "Social Behavior and Interaction Among Day-Care Center Toddlers." *Early Child Development and Care* 7 (1): 5–27.

Puroila, Anna Maija, and Eila Estola. 2014. "Not Babies Anymore: Young Children's Narrative Identities in Finnish day Care Centers." *International Journal of Early Childhood* 46: 187–203.

Sacks, Harvey. 1972. "On the Analyzability of Stories by Children." In *Directions in Sociolinguistics: The Ethnography of Communication*, edited by John J. Gumperz, and Dell Hymes, 325–345. New York: Holt: Rinehart and Winston.

Sacks, Harvey. 1987. "On the Preferences for Agreement and Contiguity in Sequences in Conversation." In *Talk and Social Organisation*, edited by G. Button, and J. R. E. Lee, 54–69. Clevedon, England: Multilingual Matters.

Sacks, Harvey. 1992. *Lectures on Conversation* (Vols. I and II, Edited by Gail Jefferson). Oxford: Blackwell.

Sixsmith, Judith A., and Andrew J. Sixsmith. 1987. "Empirical Phenomenology: Principles and Method." *Quality and Quantity* 21: 313–333. https://link.springer.com/content/pdf/10.1007/BF00134526.pdf.

Skattebol, Jen. 2005. "Insider/Outsider Belongings: Traversing the Borders of Whiteness in Early Childhood." *Contemporary Issues in Early Childhood* 6 (2): 189–203.

Skattebol Jen. 2006. "Playing boys: Identity and Belonging in the Early Years." *Gender and Education* 18:507–522.

Stokoe, Elizabeth, and Frederick Attenborough. 2013. "Gender and Categorial Systematics." In *The Handbook of Language, Gender and Sexuality*, edited by Susan Ehrlich, Miriam Meyerhoff, and Janet Holmes, 2nd ed., 161–179. Oxford: Wiley-Blackwell.

Stratigos, Tina. 2016. "Babies and big Boys: Power, Desire and the Politics of Belonging in Early Childhood Education and Care." *Global Studies of Childhood* 6 (3): 268–282.

Strycharz-Banaś, Anna. 2016. "In-group Marker Going Out: Meaning-Making in a Community of Practice." *Language in Society* 45: 665–684.

Strycharz-Banaś, Anna, Carmen Dalli, and Miriam Meyerhoff. 2020. "A Trajectory of Belonging: Negotiating Conflict and Identity in an Early Childhood Centre." *Early Years*. doi:10.1080/09575146.2020.1817871.

Vandell, Deborah L., Kathy S. Wilson, and Nola R Buchanan. 1980. "Peer Interactions in the First Year of Life: An Examination of its Structure, Content, and Sensitivity to Toys." *Child Development* 51: 481–488.

Wenger-Traynor, Etienne. 2015. "Communities of Practice: A Brief Introduction." https://wenger-trayner.com/wp-content/uploads/2015/04/07-Brief-introduction-to-communities-of-practice.pdf.

Wenger, Etienne. 1998. *Communities of Practice: Learning, Meaning, and Identity*. Cambridge: Cambridge University Press.

Wittenburg, P., H. Brugman, A. Russel, A. Klassmann, and H. Sloetjes. 2006. "ELAN: A Professional Framework for Multimodality Research." Proceedings of LREC 2006, Fifth International Conference on Language Resources and Evaluation, Max Planck Institute for Psycholinguistics, The Language Archive, Nijmegen, The Netherlands. https://archive.mpi.nl/tla/elan.

Yuval-Davis, Nira. 2006. "Belonging and the Politics of Belonging." *Patterns of Prejudice* 40 (3): 197–214.

Yuval-Davis, Nira. 2011. *The Politics of Belonging: Intersectional Contestations*. Los Angeles, CA: Sage.

Appendix. Transcription conventions

tha-	hyphen indicates cut off word
(smiles)	brackets indicate paralinguistic and non-verbal features
CAPITALS	words spoken louder than surrounding speech
[words][words]	square brackets indicate overlapping speech
no:	colon indicates an extended vowel

Language as context: a case of early literacy practices in New Zealand and Sweden

Amanda Bateman and Asta Cekaite (ID)

ABSTRACT
Globally, there has been increasing adaptation of curricula frameworks in early childhood education, providing overarching principles of practice rather than subject specific templates for teaching and learning. While such a movement is to be commended as supporting a socio-cultural approach in meeting each child's unique social and cultural needs, the implementation of frameworks is not straightforward (Bateman 2022). By applying an ethnomethodological approach to child–teacher interactions, this article explores how early childhood curricula frameworks in Sweden and New Zealand are implemented in everyday talk-in-interaction between children and teachers. We use an ethnomethodological (EM) approach (Garfinkel 2002) and conversation analysis (CA) (Sacks, Schegloff, and Jefferson 1974) approach (EMCA) to situate language as context. This approach offers a move away from the broader perspective of context being a static environmental space, to context as co-constructed by the participants through their immediate interactions (Goodwin and Duranti 1992). Contextual resources involve the concrete social situations, background cultural knowledge, language, activity and situation types, participants' knowledge about topics talked about and about each other and their interactional biographies (Linell 2009, 17).

Swedish and New Zealand early childhood education curricula: a shared socio-cultural approach

This article focuses on language practices in children's and teachers' participation that relate to the development of children's early literacy skills. The analysis will be contextualised within the framework of the Swedish and New Zealand early childhood curricula where a holistic approach that emphasises values and viewing children as competent members of society is evident. The similarities and differences in pedagogical approaches in both countries will be considered where early literacy moments are engaged in outdoors in the New Zealand examples and indoors in the Swedish examples. We discuss language based early literacy practices using four transcripts of pedagogical interaction for 1–3, and 4–6-year-old children in both cultural contexts. We conclude by considering how social interactions can be attuned to the implementation of specific national curricula, whilst also addressing common global principles concerning the construction of positive learner identities.

To set out the context of the article and social interactions discussed here, we first introduce the early childhood education curricula of both Sweden and New Zealand. Although Sweden and New Zealand have published their own distinct early childhood curricula that represent the principles and goals relevant to their own country, there are many similarities found within the two international documents. One such commonality is the recognition that children provide valuable contributions to an evolving world, where the view of the child is one of being a competent and capable life-long learner. New Zealand's early childhood curricula *Te Whāriki* sets out the role of early childhood education and care in a 'rapidly changing society [where] [t]he curriculum provides an educational foundation that supports the full range of skills that children will need as life-long learners' (Ministry of Education [MoE] 1996, 18). Likewise, in Sweden, the national early childhood curriculum also presents children's learning as essential in an ever-changing world where' [t]he ability to communicate, seek new knowledge and collaborate is necessary in a society characterised by a high flow of information and continuous change' (Curriculum for the Preschool Lpfö 2018, 9).

The New Zealand early childhood curriculum *Te Whāriki* was first published in 1996 and revisited in 2017. *Te Whāriki* uses the metaphor of a woven mat (whāriki) which is created through the weaving of Strands and Principles (MoE 1996; 2017) where the Strands consist of Belonging – Mana Whenua, Communication – Mana Reo, Contribution – Mana Tangata, Exploration – Mana Aotūroa and Well-being – Mana Atua, and the Principles are Empowerment – Whakamana; Family and Community – Whānau Tangata; Holistic development – Kotahitanga; and Relationships – Ngā Hononga (see Figure 1).

Te Whāriki is a bicultural and bilingual document for children from birth to school entry (five years) that intentionally reflects the needs of New Zealand society. It was forward thinking and innovative in its design where a holistic approach to education for infants, toddlers and young children was conceptualised with the underpinning philosophical theory of Bronfenbrenner (see page 19 of MoE 1996; 2017) where the child is placed at the centre. Through promoting a socio-cultural approach to early childhood education, each child can be supported in ways that respond to their unique and changing interests and needs through the *social* network of people who are present at that time, as they co-construct the *culture* of that place through their verbal and non-verbal actions. Such a framework offers the weaving of the Strands and Principles of *Te Whāriki* in ways that are unique to each early childhood setting – creating meaningful social and cultural places through everyday practices that are distinct for the temporal needs of each centre.

There is an emphasis in *Te Whāriki* for early childhood teachers to provide opportunities for children to engage in Te Reo Māori to uphold the bicultural principles of the curriculum where 'The use of the Màori language and creative arts in the programme should be encouraged, and staff should be supported in learning the language and in understanding issues relating to being bilingual' (MoE 1996; 2017, 73).

In Sweden, the Curriculum for the Preschool (Lpfö 2018) offers guidelines for the holistic education of children. Written in 1998, it has been revised several times to reflect

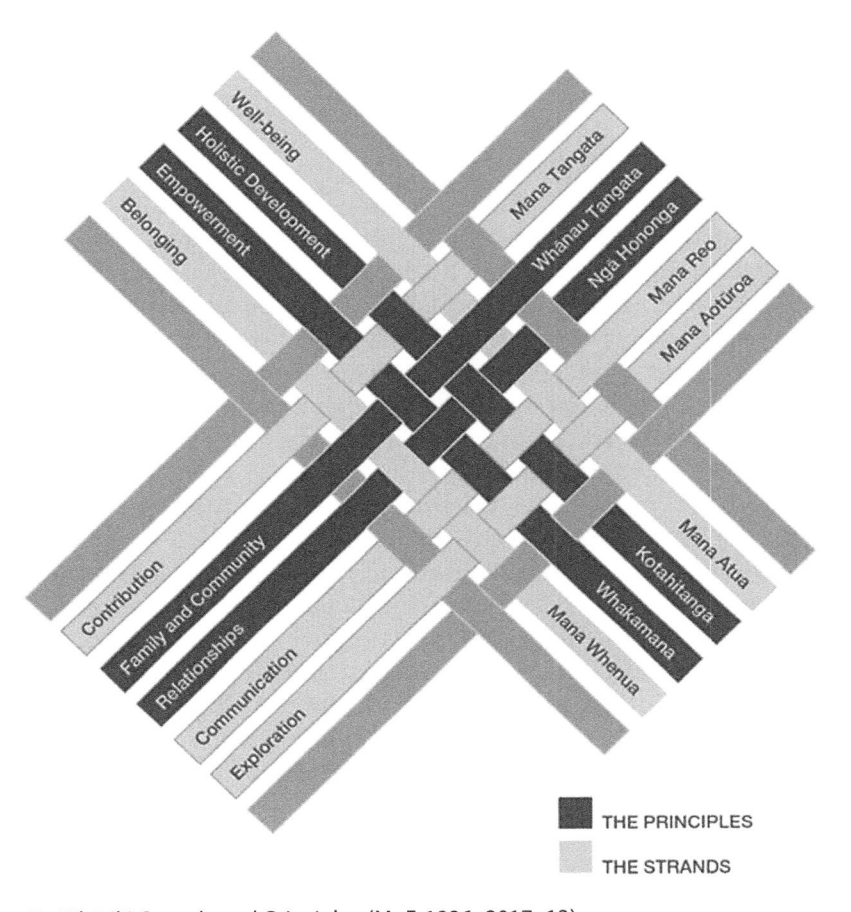

Figure 1. Te Whāriki Strands and Principles (MoE 1996; 2017, 13).

contemporary societal concerns and challenges. It outlines the fundamental values and tasks of the pre-school. The 'purpose of education in the preschool' is to 'ensure that children acquire knowledge and values'. Similar to the early childhood curriculum in New Zealand, pre-school should promote 'children's development and learning, and a life-long desire to learn' (Lpfö 2018, 5). 'Education should … convey and establish respect for human rights and the fundamental democratic values on which Swedish society is based' and 'lay foundation for a growing interest and responsibility among children for active participation in civic life and for sustainable development' (Lpfö 2018, 5), including fostering awareness of long-term and global future perspectives.

The commonality of children being viewed as essential participants in their ever-changing world demonstrates common global principles across both of these early childhood curricula, and the socio-cultural approach they both adopt. These are indeed commendable initiatives which position early childhood education as significant in proactively preparing a future society of adults who are innovative, confident and competent thinkers who can adapt to change in an unpredictable world. The big question for early childhood teachers then, is how exactly do we implement such curricula frameworks to ensure that each child receives context specific support and encouragement to fulfil these ambitious goals? Some investigation into specific areas and learning (language and literacy) and their implementation through specific language practices will now be discussed as a way of answering this question.

Language and literacy

Language learning and early literacy practices are often intertwined in both the Swedish and New Zealand curricula, where both documents identify a socio-cultural approach to the co-construction of learning in embedded and meaningful interactions with others, where neither curriculum have a specific definition of 'literacy'. Both curricula acknowledge that language, learning and the development of identity are closely linked. The preschool should therefore place great emphasis on stimulating children's language development by encouraging and taking into consideration curiosity and interest in communicating in different ways. Infants, toddlers and young children should be offered a stimulating environment where they are given the opportunity to develop their language by listening to reading aloud and discussing literature and other texts. Education should give children the opportunity to think, learn and communicate in different contexts and for different purposes. This will lay the foundation for children in due course to acquire the knowledge that everyone in society needs. The ability to communicate, seek new knowledge and collaborate is necessary in a society characterised by a high flow of information and continuous change (Lpfö 2018; MoE 1996; 2017).

In New Zealand, early childhood teachers are encouraged to support and extend children's early language and literacy development in multimodal ways where non-verbal communication such as sign and body language, dance and expressive actions to songs and poetry are highly valued. Teachers are also encouraged to provide opportunities for conversations with children, and to support children to initiate interactions with others.

The *Curriculum for preschool* in Sweden (Lpfö 2018) is formulated around the general factors and concepts rather than specific educational practices. Accordingly, early literacy and language goals of the pre-school are to provide each child with the conditions to develop skills in using nuanced spoken language and vocabulary, learn communication and argumentation and develop their interest in stories and texts in different media, and skills in using, discussing and interpreting them (Curriculum for the Preschool Lpfö 2018, 15).

Both curricula suggest a holistic approach to children's early literacy and language development and learning and emphasise spoken (oral) as well as written communication practices. This holistic, socio-cultural approach to learning places emphasis on knowledge being co-constructed by the members present, where the language used shapes the learning environment. Such an approach suggests early literacy and language development as both shaping and being shaped by the context.

Language as context

Within the current research, context is understood as the ever-changing co-construction of social order through verbal and non-verbal interactions. An ethnomethodological perspective views context as being co-constructed by the participants through their immediate interactions (Goodwin and Duranti 1992). This suggests a move away from the broader perspective of context as a static space, to a focus on how temporal inter-actions between the participants themselves work to co-construct the immediate context (Dupret and Ferrié 2008).

Through this perspective, context is viewed as being co-produced by each participant's turn taking interactions with one-another in systematic and organised ways. Each turn at talk and gesture prompts a specific response from the interlocutor in such a way as to build the immediate context as a collaborative and responsive activity. This involves how words are invoked by the members in their turn-by-turn co-production of utter-ances and their responses, referred to as 'context in action' (McHoul, Rapley, and Antaki 2008, 831). The perspective of the co-construction of social order actually being context is emphasised here where it is understood that in each individual social situation the context will be co-constructed through the turn taking of the members within (Garfinkel 1967; Sacks, Schegloff, and Jefferson 1974).

Schegloff (1992) argues that external or environmental surroundings should only be brought into analysis if the members themselves orient to them in their interactions. Where the environment is mentioned in analysis, but not oriented to by the participants, 'its status remains profoundly equivocal' (Schegloff 1992, 215). This offers an intra-inter-actional account of context where the wider aspects of the external environment are brought into play when the participants make references to them in situ. The physical environment is then made relevant by a person's acknowledgement of it though their talk, rather than the environment imposing on, and influencing peoples' conversation and interactions (Housley and Fitzgerald 2002). Through orientation to specific environ-mental features, they are made contextually relevant by the members and the context is established through this conduct (Schegloff 1992). Policy documents, societal and insti-tutional norms and regulations are enacted and made relevant through social interaction. Being able to take part, contribute to and interpret social interactional context necessi-tates participants'/members' knowledge about social practices (Duranti and Goodwin 1992). It is therefore understood that in each individual social situation the context will be co-constructed through the turn taking of the members present (Sacks, Schegloff, and Jefferson 1974).

Methodology

The Swedish and New Zealand footage discussed in this article belong to separate research projects – the New Zealand project focused on how the natural outdoor environment afforded pedagogical moments, and the Swedish project aimed to examine children's emotion and moral socialisation through pre-school practices.

The New Zealand project was initiated by two early childhood teachers who approached the researcher during one of her regular visits to assess early childhood stu-dents attending the centre as part of their teaching qualification. The teachers expressed an interest in exploring their pedagogical practice during their regular outdoor excur-sions with centre children, and so these teachers were the selected participant teachers for the project. Once the project idea was shared with other teachers in the centre, four other teachers also became interested and so they were also included in the study. The researcher gained ethical consent from the University of Waikato for the project, which included the drawing up and distribution of consent forms for videoing participants from the centre director, teachers, parents of the children and finally the children. The teachers chose moments of interest during the video collection which were then transcribed and analysed by the researcher; some of these moments are presented and analysed here.

The Swedish data was collected as a part of a research project 'Communicating emotions, embodying morality' on children's emotion and moral socialisation in preschool daily practices. The pre-school staff was contacted by the PI and upon showing their interest in the project, video-ethnographic data documenting common preschool practices during a six month period was collected by a team of researchers. The Regional Ethical Board has approved the project. Written and oral information was provided to the staff and parents. Participation was voluntary and they were informed of their right to withdraw from participation at any time. When approaching the children in order to record, the researcher recurrently asked the children about their willingness to be filmed. Data was viewed and pre-school practices that in various ways addressed emotions and everyday morality were identified. Storytelling and book reading and were identified as such focal practices. They were transcribed and analysed by the researchers.

There were commonalities between the projects in New Zealand and in Sweden as both research projects were framed by an ethnomethodological approach (Garfinkel 2002) where an investigation into everyday spontaneous interactions provided an inductive insight into the co-construction of social order between teachers and children of varying ages. Also, both research projects used video cameras to record participants' interactions, and the footage was analysed in a similar way with the researchers using 'unmotivated looking' to observe what the participants themselves oriented to as important; these moments were transcribed used conversation analysis transcription procedures (Sacks, Schegloff, and Jefferson 1974) (see Appendix for a list of transcriptions symbols used in this article).

Orientation to early literacy was a key finding in both projects – the ways in which these moments were co-constructed is now presented and discussed.

The footage

We will now demonstrate how early learning contexts in Sweden and New Zealand are co-produced by teachers and children through turns at talk and gesture in ways that implement the curricula principles of upholding and supporting a democratic society where children are perceived as competent and capable citizens. In our analysis and discussion that follows, we will explore how children and teachers – through their engagement in turns at talk and embodied actions – co-produce the context of early literacy practices. We will begin with the youngest children in our data – that of the toddler age group 1–3 years.

Sweden transcript 1:

In pre-schools in Sweden (attended by children from a very young age, starting from 1 year-old) book reading and storytelling constitute one of the main activities that aim to contribute to children's literacy (Curriculum for the preschool Lpfö 2018). Extract 1 concerns a narrative performance for three toddlers between 1.3 and 1.5 years. The teacher uses toy props to tell a story about three goats Bruse (a well-known children story in Sweden). The following is a transcript between the teacher (TCH) and a girl Lisa (LIS), 1.5 years old.

01 TCH:	de ja:g (.) den sto::ra bocken Bruse (.)
	Yes it is me:(.) the bi::g goat Bruse (.)
	((*moves toy goat*))
02 LIS:	sto::la.
	bi::k.
03 TCH:	då kommer jag och äter **u:**pp **dej** s[a trollet. (.)
	*then I come and eat **you u:**p. said the troll. (.)*
	((*moving toy troll*))
04 LIS:	[**dej *you***
05 TCH:	'ja ko::m du bara (.) jag inte rä:dd för dig.'
	'yes co::me here (.) I'm not afraid of you.'
	((*moving toy goat*))
06 TCH:	'nää:h' sa tro:llet.
	'noo:' said tro:ll.
	((*some reading omitted*))
07 TCH:	så nu kunde **bo**ckarna gå över bro:n (1.0)
	*so now the **go**ats could cross the bri:dge (1.0)*
08 och äta de **go**:	da gräset.
	*and eat the **goo:**d grass.*
09 LIS:	go:dä.
	goo:d.
10 TCH:	mm **go:**da gräset
	*mh **goo:**d grass ((pretends eating))*
11 LIS:	goda: gä:
	goo:d ge: ((smiling))
12 TCH:	snipp snapp snut så va (.) sa (.)gan (.)
	snipp snapp snut and (.) the fairy (.) tale is (.)
13 LIS:	slu::t.
	o::ver. ((rapidly raises her hands up-and-down))
14 TCH:	slu::t.
	o::ver.

Throughout the story telling, the teacher makes a performance by using expressive into-nation, elongated words and pauses. She also manipulates the props and emphasises the key words in the story: 'stora'/'big', 'dig'/'you' and 'goda gräset'/'good grass' (lines 01; 03; 07). The teacher's highlighting of the key concepts and the use of pauses contributes to the dramatisation and makes the meaning of the story more easily accessible to the lis-tening toddlers, thus contributing to literacy socialisation. With unwavering attention, the young children observe the story being enacted just in front of them; the teacher's embodied performance adds to the 'enchanting' ambience of the literacy activity (Cekaite and Björk-Wilén 2018).

A girl Lisa participates especially attentively and actively. She follows the teacher's telling, repeats the key lexical items (lines 02; 04; 09; 11) and shows her recognition of the key events in the story. The teacher confirms the girl's self-initiated repetitions and does not discipline her talk. At the end of the story telling the teacher uses a formu-laic expression in Swedish 'snipp snapp snut nu var sagan slut'/ *'snipp snapp snut and the fairy tale is'*, a rhyme that is performed as a conventional ending of a story for children (line 12). She does not finish the phrase; rather, she uses several dramatising pauses and allows the girl to finish the rhyme. The child enthusiastically finishes the phrase verbally and with gestures (line 13), thus showing her knowledge of the narrative and how the performance of story is traditionally enacted.

As demonstrated, the teacher and the child collaboratively co-construct the context of the literacy event as particularly relevant for fostering toddlers' interest in oral texts (see Curriculum for Preschool Lpfö 2018). This everyday activity concerns multiple literacy related dimensions: Recognisable story lines and visual information that is made available to the children through the use of props, enhances children's interest, curiosity and enchantment with the narrative. Through each participants' turn at talk and embodied gesture, the context is co-constructed as an early literacy one. The teacher, through her talk, addresses issues related to children's 'ability to create and ability to express and communicate ... in different forms of expression' (Curriculum for the preschool Lpfö 2018, 15). The teacher's emphasis on the key concepts allows the children to expand their passive and active vocabulary, contributing to the development of lexical concepts. Children's attentive participation can constitute a stepping-stone for children's development of literacy in terms of the child's investment into the plot and the storytelling activity (Cekaite and Björk-Wilén 2018). Such activities implement the curriculum goals of developing 'children's interest in stories ... and texts in different media and their ability' to use and interpret them (Curriculum for the preschool Lpfö 2018, 15).

NZ Transcription 1:

In a similar way to the prior Swedish example, we see a teacher 'performance' and use of rhyme in the following New Zealand transcript. As with the Swedish transcript, the prosodic rhythm and rhyme are used in specific ways here to encourage the child to contribute to mastering a specific event, using talk and gesture to frame the children as competent and capable of doing the activity.

In the following transcript we see a group of slightly older toddler aged children 2–3 years walking through very long grass with their teacher, as they engage in the collaborative activity of having a nature walk. All children are identified with (Boy 1; 2; and 3), and the teacher with (TCH).

01 Boy 1:	I'm gonna **stomp**. ((*stomps his feet in large steps*))
02 TCH:	>yeah< ♩ going on a <be¿ar> hunt. We're gonna catch a
	03 bi¿g one..hhh what a beautiful day. We're not scared ♩.
04 Boy 1:	uh oh?
05 Boy 2:	[grass.]
06 TCH:	[°uh oh.°] grass that's it what kind of grass is
	07 it?
08 Boy 2:	um [deep
09 Boy 1:	[(xxx)
10 TCH:	<lo::ng> wa:vey grass.
11 Boy 1:	stomp . stomp . stomp
12 TCH:	we can't go over it¿
13 Boy 1:	stomp . stomp
14 TCH:	we can't go under it¿
15 Boy 2:	**oh no we've got to go:?-**
16 Boy 3:	**through it.**
17 TCH:	through it. *swishy swoshy. . swishy swoshy*..hhh
18	*swishy swoshy*

| 19 Boy 1: | I found a piece of lo:ng grass |
| 20 TCH: | yeah. |

This playful culture of the interaction that is co-produced by each member's turn at talk and gesture links very closely to early literacy practices, where a popular rhyme from a book is spontaneously embedded in the interaction. The physical location of the children and teacher here is talked into the play activity, along with the book rhyme, where the children are making reference to the struggle of walking through the difficult grassy terrain.

The interaction begins with one of the children orienting to a physical tactic for manoeuvring through the grass by initially verbally articulating (with embodied physical actions) that he is going to 'stomp' (lines 01), as he talks the environment into significance (Schegloff 1992). The child's multimodal communications are displayed through talk and gesture and are shaped by the environment he is in and the difficulty of moving within it. His communication also initiates the shaping of the context, as his actions are immediately responded to by the teacher who begins singing the popular early childhood rhyme 'bear hunt' lyrics (lines 02–03), making the activity fun and playful. Through responding to the child by singing, the teacher offers a positive position that aligns with the child's 'stomping' approach to the situation, which frames it as more playful than stressful (Goffman 1974; Goodwin 2006). The song that the teacher chooses is one that has significant parallels with the current situation where children have to move through a difficult terrain in a specific way, and so has cultural significance. The child's stomping approach to mastering his environment and the teacher's singing a relevant context specific song both work together to co-construct the context as a playful and fun one, and one that presents a problem that will be overcome by their collective 'stomping' actions through orientation to early literacy.

In terms of early literacy practices, *Te Whāriki* suggests that children's 'developing literacy … abilities embrace new purposes, such as reasoning, verbal exploration, puzzling and finding out about the physical and social world' (MoE 1996; 2017, 15). Through embracing the opportunities for early literacy learning, as present in this specific situation, children and teachers collaboratively implement these curricula goals through their turns at talk, in meaningful ways that align with their national curriculum. The importance of education being fun in order to support children to become life-long learners is seen through how the role of the adult is implemented to encourage children to 'enjoy making music, and be developing a feeling for rhythm, singing, and improvisation' (MoE 1996; 2017, 73).

We now move on to our older age group of children, those aged 4–6 years.

Sweden Transcript 2:

A considerable goal of children's development and learning concerns their development of empathy, understanding of others' perspectives and solidarity (Curriculum for the preschool Lpfö 2018). Reading can involve socialisation into empathy and perspective taking in that emotions frequently feature narratives. Book reading and storytelling are therefore crucial activities where emotions (of the characters in the story) are implicated and presented for the child audience to note and explore; group reading constitutes an important feature of social literacy events in pre-school. This transcript exemplifies a story reading situation for 3–4 year olds in a regular Swedish pre-school. During a reading activity, performed on a daily basis for a small group of children in a cosy corner, the teacher and children (girls and boys, A, B, C, D) together choose stories from an I-pad. The stories comprise of narrative text and pictures, that the teacher displays for the child audience. The particular story is about a butterfly Fido who becomes sad because his friends fly away.

01	TCH:	ser ni va **led**sen Fido ser ut?
		*do you see how **sad** Fido looks? ((shows I-pad))*
02	D:	mh ((nods))
03	TCH:	man [blir ju **led**sen om kompisarna försvinner ifrån en?
		*one gets **sad** if friends dissapear from one?*
04	A:	[ledsen.
		sad.
05	D:	ja jag **vet** röda rosa och och lila.
		*yes I **know** red pink and and **purple**. ((points at the screen))*
06	TCH:	mh ((nods))
07	TCH:	'han blev helt förtvivlad och Fido började gråta.'
		*'he got very **sad** and Fido began to cry.'*
08	D:	inte gråta själv.
		not crying alone.
09	TCH:	ja han är så ledsen.
		yeah he is so sad.
10	D:	((moves her finger to her eye))
11	TCH:	((draws her finger from her eye along her cheek))
12	D:	ja han har **va**tten här.
		*yeah he has **water** here.*
13	TCH:	ja.
		yes.

In line 01 the teacher brings the children's attention to Fido's emotion – his sadness. She uses verbal means, an emotion label 'sad', and utilises a question to draw the children's attention to the illustration on an I-Pad. When the child audience demonstrate their agreement (line 02, 'mh') the teacher continues to elaborate on the story, telling 'one gets sad if one's friends disappear from one?'. She explains the situation of distress and clarifies the causal relation between social events in children's everyday life and the resulting negative emotion – sadness (line 03). One girl (A) responds to the emotional features of the story by repeating the key word 'sad' (line 04). In such a way, the teacher together with the child audience co-create a narrative context of the story, and the context for literacy and emotion socialisation, empathy and perspective taking.

Another child (girl D) orients to the story in a somewhat different way. She identifies illustrations of butterflies of various colours (line 05). The teacher confirms but does not expand on the girl's utterance. She immediately re-initiates her reading, demonstrating that the teacher is on track of the educational task (line 07). When the girl (D) again comments on the emotional aspects of the story (she mentions 'crying alone'), she yet again displays her perspective taking and investment in the story. The children's emotional interest is confirmed by the teacher as she expands on the child's utterance 'yes he is so sad' (line 09). When reading the story, the teacher closely observes children's emotional reactions and facial expressions towards the plot. She makes use of the text, dramatic talk, bodily and material resources. The collaborative characterisation of the protagonist's emotions, together with visual illustration on the I-Pad, constitutes a context for the child's further investigation of the protagonist's emotional expression as it is depicted: 'yes has water there' (on the face) (line 12).

The points that the teacher brings up concern the characters' emotional reactions and expressions, and the causal relation between one's actions and the recipient's emotional responses. In such ways, the teacher creates a storytelling context where the context of the curriculum, empathy, solidarity and understanding of social relations situation is indicated and can be fostered in children (Curriculum for the preschool Lpfö 2018). Our analysis of a reading sequence shows how the teacher uses language, bodily actions and socio-material features such as I-pad and pictures to create a specific institutional learning context that engages the children into the activity. Such daily reading activities constitutes an implementation of the pre-school curriculum, and more specifically the task to promote children's literacy.

NZ Transcript 2:

In contrast to the above Swedish example of reading inciting emotional connections for 3-year-old children, the below excerpt demonstrates how reading can be more centred as a way of acquiring factual information, as in the case of map reading.

The following interaction is co-constructed between an early childhood teacher and children aged between 4–5 years. The group is walking in a nearby bush reserve – a regular trip that they do at least a couple of times a week. There are many spontaneous learning moments within these walks, including opportunities for links to early literacy. In the following excerpt, the early childhood teacher (TCH) is reading a map of the reserve with 4 of the children including Hazel (HAZ). Opportunities to contribute knowledge of their surroundings and their map reading skills are given to the children here, and quickly taken up by Caleb (CLB). This interaction shows how verbal language and gesture are employed in orderly and sequential ways to co-construct the context of the map reading exercise.

01 TCH: Shall=we=have=a=look at the ma:p to see where=we=went st time?

02 la:

03 (1.3) ((organise themselves around the map))

04 TCH: oh Haze you weren't with ¿us last time were you¿

05 HAZ: oh yeah:.

06 TCH: oh yeah: you missed it. =

07 CLB: =yah=av=ta=walk- ((traces finger

08 on a pathway on the map)) over to the lunch tables.

09 ((*drops hand away from map*))

10 TCH: we did.

Some lines omitted as the attention of a child is called

11 TCH: so Haze wasn't here last week but Caleb just explained to

12 Haze where we went ((places finger on map and begins

13 tracing the pathway)) we went across the bridge. Alo:		ng
14 this one. Didn't stop at the gazebo last week. Then we		
15 came alo:		:ng here¿ went to the toilet. And then alo:ng
16 to:		:-
17 (0.8)		
18 CLB:		**the**re.
19 TCH:		the picnic table. Then we had our lunch there
20 and=turned=around=and=came back because we'd taken su:		ch
21 a long time along here¿ ((still tracing finger on map))		
22 (2.2) ((all looking at the map))		
23 CLB:		now let's go.

As with the prior excerpt from NZ, the opening of this interaction is initiated through verbal and gestural orientation to the immediate environment, talking it into importance for those people at that time (Schegloff 1992). In this situation, it is a large static wooden map that is situated in outdoors. The teacher speaks quickly as she turns to the map, using the collective pronoun 'we' prior to the words 'have a look at the map … ' to situate the specific activity of looking at the map as a collective one that involves all of those present. The indexical nature of the word 'we' holds different meanings depending on the context in which it is used (Bateman 2014). Here, 'we' refers to the group of children who were present the last time they visited that specific cite, as the teacher states ' … to see where we went last time' (lines 01–02) where the absence of one of the children is noted (lines 04–06 & 11–12). Placing the current learning situation in a historical situation means that the teacher can provide a continuity of learning for the children, as promoted in *Te Whāriki* (MoE 1996; 2017). Through the analysis of this very first utterance here, we can see how the teacher uses specific language to create a context that informs the children of the activity being initiated that ties with the implementation of the national early childhood curriculum.

Once the social order is organised as a group of people who are going to explore a map, and Hazel's absence from the prior visit has been noted, Caleb explores the map in multimodal ways, switching between communication modes of reading and tracing with his finger (lines 07–09), demonstrating a multimodal approach to 'reading'. Caleb finishes his self-elected reading of the map through interwoven verbal language and gesture as he traces a pathway, he shows that he has finished his turn by dropping his hand away from the map. The teacher orients to his action as a turn completion, as she then aligns with his reading to confirm that it is correct (line 10). The teacher responds by demonstrating the implementation of the overarching vision of *Te Whāriki* of children being competent and capable members who can contribute to society by orienting to his competence and knowledge by paraphrasing his contribution (lines 11–16). The teacher then uses a conversational strategy to invite further contribution from the children through offering an incomplete turn (line 16) and pause (line 17) to give the children an opportunity to contribute their knowledge to the map reading. As she has her finger on a specific place of the map – static at this time – the map is used as a prop for the children to read in order to gain the knowledge needed to fill in the incomplete turn, which Caleb does (line 18).

As well as offering opportunities for children to present themselves, and see themselves as competent and capable contributors to fulfil the overarching principles of *Te*

Whāriki, the teacher also addresses more specific goals such as offering the children opportunities to:

> experience an environment where they learn strategies for active exploration, thinking, and reasoning [where] suitable books, pictures, posters, and maps are easily available for children's reference. (MoE 1996; 2017, 88–89)

And

> spatial understandings, including an awareness of how two- and three-dimensional objects can be fitted together and moved in space and ways in which spatial information can be represented, such as in maps, diagrams, photographs, and drawings. (MoE 1996; 2017, 90)

Conclusion/Discussion

The detailed transcriptions presented and analysed in this article demonstrate how verbal actions and gesture are orderly and sequential co-constructed between teachers and children to create unique contexts that support early literacy practices. The co-construction of contexts of global overarching principles, values and visions of practice can be seen in both the New Zealand and Swedish data, suggesting that principles such as embracing and supporting opportunities for engagement in early literacy practices, and treating children as competent and capable citizens hold across countries. Further similarities are visible in the extracts of toddler interactions in both the New Zealand and Swedish data, where embodied storytelling through reference to props and linguistic strategies such as sing-song prosody created exciting and fun storylines to encourage the toddlers to engage with the literacy activity (Cekaite and Björk-Wilén 2018).

However, there were also some differences in early literacy practices between the New Zealand and Swedish data, where the New Zealand teachers utilised the outdoor environment in spontaneous ways by talking specific features into importance (Schegloff 1992) that stimulate exploration of their physical worlds for early literacy practices (MoE 2017). In contrast, the Swedish data analysed here could be perceived of as more formal, with the telling of children's stories. With the older children, the Swedish teachers took literacy opportunities to explore emotional teaching and the socialisation of empathy, whilst the New Zealand footage demonstrated a more pragmatic and factual exploration of map reading. Both teaching practices are essential for children's development, where teachers are encouraged to use their autonomy to teach in relevant context specific ways. Here we see the teachers prioritising specific learning goals which are different and dependant on the needs of the children present, which determines what teaching was important at that time. The differences in the pedagogical practice across Sweden and New Zealand demonstrate that teaching and learning is co-constructed in local and specific ways. For example, in the New Zealand footage, we see strong cultural connections to the land where 'Daily routines respond to individual circumstances and needs and allow for frequent outdoor experiences' (MoE 1996; 2017, 30) where spontaneous learning is frequent and responsive to children's interests, including that of early literacy. In Sweden, pre-school learning activities include both planned and spontaneous events, and although there is a strong interest to provide children with daily outdoor play activities, literacy events are part of daily routines that involve smaller groups of children in cosy environments inside the pre-school. Reading and storytelling are both educational, and also an activity related to building close social relations between the staff and the children.

Detailed interaction analysis of naturally occurring talk between teachers and children in the two cultural contexts allows to explore and document how multifaceted goals related to literacy and children's emotional development are co-constructed through the participants' social actions involving talk, bodily actions and their use of social space and material artefacts such as books, maps, digital texts and toy props (Curriculum for the preschool Lpfö 2018; MoE 1996; 2017). By looking at how the teachers and children attend to various features of literacy events we are able to demonstrate how the teachers create verbal, embodied and material context for meaning making and socialising children's emotional meaning making and reactions. The present theoretical paradigm and the associated methodology present a bottom–up view on how and which educational policies (e.g. pre-school curricula) are co-constructed and are made relevant in the social practices, rather than being taken for granted. Notably, when viewing language and social interaction as context for educational practices, children's development and learning, we can discover novel ways in which educational policies are interpreted by the teachers and how they are adapted to a variety of situations, where teachers respond to situational affordances when organising their teaching practices. Importantly, children's participation in the co-construction of these early literacy practices here demonstrates their willingness to contribute their knowledge and understanding in the co-construction of social contexts with others. Through the participants' co-construction of context in immediate, spontaneous interactions, we offer a shift away from perceiving the broader perspective of context being a static environmental space (Goodwin and Duranti 1992).

Limitations of the study

Although the footage presented and analysed here reports indoor literacy practices with books for the Swedish data and outdoor play experiences for the New Zealand data, this is of course limited to occurrences at the time of the data collection in each place. The authors have observed indoor book reading in New Zealand early childhood education and spontaneous literacy teaching in outdoor play in Sweden. Future research could span a greater number of contexts for early literacy practices in both the New Zealand and Sweden, and also include the early literacy practices of other countries, giving a broader perspective. The detailed analysis of such practices is a real strength of the research, and could be carried forward to future research as a way of exploring the sequential organisation of such practices, revealing strategies for early childhood teachers to support and extend early literacy practices.

Disclosure statement

No potential conflict of interest was reported by the author(s).

Funding

This work was supported by The Swedish Research Council (Vetenskapsrådet): [Grant Number 742-2013-7626].

ORCID

Asta Cekaite 🆔 http://orcid.org/0000-0003-4580-3002

References

Bateman, A. 2014. "Young Children's English use of *we* in a Primary School in Wales." In *Constructing Collectivity: We Across Languages and Contexts*, edited by Theodossia- Soula Pavlidou, 361–391. Philadelphia: John Benjamins.

Bateman, A. 2022. "Participation." In *Talking with Children: A Handbook for Early Childhood Education*, edited by A. Church and A. Bateman. Cambridge University Press.

Cekaite, A., and P. Björk-Wilén. 2018. "Enchantment in Storytelling: Co-operation and Participation in Children's Aesthetic Experience." *Linguistics and Education* 48: 52–60.

Curriculum for the Preschool Lpfö. 2018. *Läroplan för förskolan Lpfö 2018*. Stockholm: Skolverket.

Dupret, Baudouin, and Jean-Noël Ferrié. 2008. "Legislating at the Shopfloor Level: Background Knowledge and Relevant Context of Parliamentary Debates." *Journal of Pragmatics* 40: 960–978.

Duranti, Alessandro, and Charles Goodwin. 1992. *Rethinking Context: Language as an Interactive Phenomenon*. Cambridge: Cambridge University Press.

Garfinkel, Harold. 1967. *Studies in Ethnomethodology*. Oxford: Prentice-Hall.

Garfinkel, Harold. 2002. *Ethnomethodology's Program*. London: Rowman and Littlefield.

Goffman, Ervin. 1974. *Frame Analysis: An Essay on the Organisation of Experience*. Harvard: Harvard University Press.

Goodwin, Marjory H. 2006. "Participation, Affect, and Trajectory in Family Directive/ Response Sequences." *Text & Talk - An Interdisciplinary Journal of Language, Discourse Communication Studies* 26: 515–543.

Goodwin, Charles, and Alessandro Duranti. 1992. "Rethinking Context: An Introduction." In *Rethinking Context: Language as an Interactive Phenomenon*, edited by Alessandro Duranti and Charles Goodwin, 1–42. Cambridge: Cambridge University Press.

Housley, William, and Richard Fitzgerald. 2002. "The Reconsidered Model of Membership Categorization Analysis." *Qualitative Research* 2 (1): 59–83.

Linell, Per. 2009. *Rethinking Language, Mind, and World Dialogically: Interactional and Contextual Theories of Human Sense-making*. Charlotte, NC: Information Age Publishing.

McHoul, Alec, Mark Rapley, and Charles Antaki. 2008. "You Gotta Light? On the Luxury of Context for Understanding Talk in Interaction." *Journal of Pragmatics* 40: 827–839.

Ministry of Education. 1996; 2017. *Te Whāriki. He Whāriki Mātauranga mō ngā Mokopuna o Aotearoa. Early Childhood Curriculum.* Wellington: Learning Media.

Sacks, Harvey, Emanuel A Schegloff, and Gail Jefferson. 1974. "A Simplest Systematics for the Organisation of Turn-taking for Conversation." *Language* 50: 696–735.

Schegloff, Emanuel A. 1992. "In Another Context." In *Rethinking Context: Language as an Interactive Phenomenon*, edited by Alessandro Duranti and Charles Goodwin, 191–228. Cambridge: Cambridge University Press.

Appendix

Transcription conventions.

The conversation analysis symbols used to transcribe the data are adapted from Jefferson's conventions described in Sacks, Schegloff, and Jefferson (1974).

=	the equals sign at the end of one utterance and the beginning of the next utterance marks the latching of speech between the speakers. When used in-between words it marks the latching of the words spoken in an utterance with no break.
(0.4)	the time of a pause in seconds
::	lengthening of the prior sound. More or less colons are used to represent the longer or shorter lengthening.
?	a rising intonation in speech
.	a falling intonation in speech
↑	a sharp rise in tone
↓	a sharp lower in tone
<u>Underscore</u>	marks an emphasis placed on the underscored sound
<u>Bold</u>	words which are underscored and bold indicate heavy emphasis or shouting
°	degree sign either side of a word indicates that it is spoken in a quiet, soft tone
(brackets)	utterance could not be deciphered
((*brackets*))	double brackets with words in italics indicate unspoken actions
¿	a flat, or 'mid rising' contour at turn completion.
.hhh	audible in-breath
hhh	audible out-breath
♫	singing

When and why do early childhood educators reminisce with children about their past experiences?

Penny Van Bergen ⓘ and Rebecca Andrews ⓘ

ABSTRACT

When children reminisce with adults about their own past experiences, they are offered a rich forum in which to develop cognitive and socioemotional skills, build their sense of self, and form emotional bonds. Little attention has been directed to reminiscing in educational contexts, however. Our aim was to explore when, how often, and why early childhood educators engage young children in reminiscing conversations. Participants included 251 Australian educators with 1–45 years of experience. Educators completed an online survey asking them (i) the number of times per day they engaged children in reminiscing, relative to other types of talk, and (ii) the times and places these reminiscing conversations were most likely to occur. While individual differences were apparent, more than 85% of educators reporting engaging children in reminiscing multiple times per day. Popular times included arrival (67.7%), meals (65.7%) and group/circle time (58.2%). Educators' qualitative explanations suggested several important reasons to engage children in reminiscing, including to bond, establish home-centre connections, build children's socioemotional competence, reflect on 'centre life' and support intentional learning activities. Implications for research and practice are discussed.

Introduction

Reminiscing about the past is a rich, lifelong activity. Even before children can talk, they are told stories of their own past experiences and asked 'do you remember' questions (Nelson and Fivush 2004). As children develop the language to contribute to these conversations, in early childhood and beyond, they are increasingly offered opportunities to shape the emerging narrative themselves: first with closed questions and extensive scaffolding and later with more open prompts (Fivush, Haden, and Reese 2006; Salmon and Reese 2016). Research with parents highlights the value of these conversations as a way of scaffolding culturally significant traditions of storytelling and narrative and of supporting children's emerging sense of self as they move towards adolescence and adulthood (Habermas and Reese 2015; Waters et al. 2019). As adults, reminiscing about our past experiences helps us to further define who we are, to bond with others, and to guide and direct future actions (Bluck and Alea 2009; Pillemer 2003).

While adult–child reminiscing research has traditionally focused on parents, there have been recent calls to extend this work to early childhood educators (Neale and Pino-Pasternak 2017; Van Bergen and Sutton 2019). The majority of children in OECD member countries attend an Early Childhood Education and Care (ECEC) programme, with many enacting policies to increase this participation further (Balladares and Kankaraš 2020). Within these programmes, there is good reason to suggest that educators who engage children in language-based conversations about their own past experiences may further extend children's language skill, narrative and memory skill and 'sustained shared thinking' (blinded, Neale and Pino-Pasternak 2017). Reminiscing about the past is 'decontextualised', meaning there is the opportunity for children to think beyond their current experiences to make new connections between the past and present (Andrews et al. 2019 Test, Cunningham, and Lee 2010). Moreover, as early childhood education centres represent places of 'being and belonging' (e.g. Australian Government Department of Education, Employment and Workplace Relations 2009), reminiscing may help to scaffold children's sense of self and place. In the case of unshared experiences in particular, such as weekend activities, educator–child reminiscing may assist children in forging connections between home and centre. Building on these possibilities, the purpose of the current study was to determine how frequently educators report reminiscing with young children, when, and why.

Parent–child talk about the past

Over the past 30 years, there has been a wealth of sociocultural developmental research examining the ways that parents reminisce with their young children and the important implications of such talk for children's development (see Fivush, Haden, and Reese 2006; Salmon and Reese 2016; Wareham and Salmon 2006 for reviews). Parents who frequently discuss the past in rich and elaborative detail, using open-ended questions to encourage their child's contribution, have children who eventually come to adopt this same style themselves: showing stronger memory performance not just in shared parent–child conversations (Van Bergen et al. 2009) but also later when independently sharing their memories with an experimenter (Reese and Newcombe 2007). There are also benefits of rich parent–child reminiscing for children's understanding of self and emotion, particularly when these aspects of the narrative are explicitly scaffolded (Fivush 1994; Van Bergen et al. 2009; Wang 2007; Wareham and Salmon 2006).

Interestingly, although reminiscing has multiple developmental benefits for children, there are differences in the frequency with which parents report engaging children in such conversations. When European American mothers were asked how often they engaged in 'past talk' with their child, defined as shared talk about events the child has previously experienced, Kulkofsky and Koh (2009) found positive correlations with their frequency of reminiscing about their own lives. When asked to estimate the number of times per week reminiscing occurs, Kulkofsky, Wang, and Koh (2009) found wide individual and cultural differences. Although 40% of European American mothers reporting engaging their children in reminiscing 7+ times per week, 26% reported doing so 3–4 times per week and 11% just 1–2 times per week. For Chinese mothers, 28% reported engaging in past talk 5–6 times per week, and more than 50% reported doing so just 1–2 times per week.

There are also individual differences in the reasons parents reminisce with their children, including to support their children's emotion regulation, direct future behaviour, maintain positive emotionality, support children's sense of self, support conversation, teach cognitive skills and promote positive peer relationships (Kulkofsky and Koh 2009; Kulkofsky, Wang, and Koh 2009). We suggest that reminiscing might feature prominently in educator–child conversations, too, particularly given it is teaching function and connection to children's sense of self.

Educator–child talks about the past

While reminiscing has been under-researched in the early childhood context, a number of important similarities exist between educator–child reminiscing conversations and sustained shared thinking conversations (see Neale and Pino-Pasternak 2017 for review). Like reminiscing, for example, sustained shared thinking conversations offer educators and children the opportunities to co-construct and extend narrative dialogue together and to evaluate their everyday activities and experiences (Sylva et al. 2004). For educators, there is also the opportunity to provide formative feedback on children's responses in situ (Siraj-Blatchford and Sylva 2004): thus scaffolding and extending their development. Sustained shared thinking is an important element of early childhood pedagogy, suggesting similar possibilities and benefits for reminiscing too.

Sustained shared thinking between children and educators may be particularly important when discussing the past because reminiscing conversations are decontextualised: that is, removed from the here-and-now (Test, Cunningham, and Lee 2010). Decontextualised talk is more linguistically complex than other types of talk (Rowe 2012, 2013), more abstract and more likely to include cause-and-effect statements and relations (Rowe 2013). In the case of reminiscing, for example, there are opportunities to connect the past with the present and future, to connect the past to the self, and to reflect on the meaning of past episodes (Salmon and Reese 2016). Given the complexity and abstraction of conversations that are decontextualised, there is an important need for educators to scaffold and support children's participation (Test, Cunningham, and Lee 2010).

To our knowledge, only one study to date has considered patterns of reminiscing amongst early childhood educators and children. In our own study, in which we asked educator–child and mother–child dyads to talk about shared past events, we found that the individual differences in educator–child elaboration were even wider than those in mother–child elaboration (Andrews et al. 2019). Educators with diploma training were less elaborative on average than were degree-trained educators or mothers (blinded), but with higher mental state language (Andrews et al. 2019-). Because dyads in our previous work were asked to reminisce for us, however, we do not yet know how frequent these conversations are in everyday early childhood practice. This is particularly the case for one-on-one reminiscing conversations, given the frequent group interactions within the early childhood context (Test, Cunningham, and Lee 2010). Nor do we know how such conversations come about within the early childhood context, their function, or how they compare to other types of educator–child talk.

Given the educative nature of early childhood education, we consider it likely that some early childhood educators may be particularly likely to reminisce with children in order to support the development of key cognitive and socioemotional skills (Andrews et al. 2019, 2020, 2021). In addition, because reminiscing offers a valuable means of creating connections between children's home and centre lives (, Neale and Pino-Pasternak 2017), we also consider it likely that educators will reminisce about finding out more about children's experiences and to bond (see Test, Cunningham, and Lee 2010). In addition to understanding the frequency of educator–child reminiscing, therefore, and the times when it occurs most frequently, our present study also maps educators' explanations for reminiscing at these specific times.

The present study

In the present study, we aimed to determine when, how often and why early childhood educators report reminiscing with the children in their care. We focused our study on Australia, where long day-care is the most common type of care for children who do not yet attend school. Approximately 45% of 2- to 3-year-olds attend long day-care (Australian Institute of Family Studies 2018), for example, while 95% of 4–5-year-olds who are not yet in school also attend either a standalone pre-school or a pre-school programme in a long day-care centre (Australian Bureau of Statistics 2018). The vast majority of children, 95%, are enrolled for more than 15 h per week (Australian Bureau of Statistics 2018).

Given that early childhood classes have multiple children learning together, we also aimed to capture how patterns of educator–child reminiscing differ for individual children versus children in groups and for events that the educator has shared with the child or children versus those that the child has experienced separately, at home or in different parts of the centre. To do so, we used a mixed-methods explanatory design (Creswell 2009). In this design, quantitative data were collected to provide a broad understanding of when and how often reminiscing occurs in the early childhood context, how it differs for shared vs. unshared events and one-on-one vs. group discussions and how it compares to other kinds of talk. Rich qualitative data about why educators engage children in reminiscing at these times were then used to supplement, explain and extend the quantitative data (see Creswell 2009; Mertens 2010).

Materials and methods

Participants

Our initial sample included 251 early childhood educators from the state of New South Wales, Australia. Twenty-two educators commenced but did not complete the online survey: thus, the final sample included 229 educators. The majority of respondents reported that they currently taught children in the pre-school years, aged 3–5 (65%), with smaller numbers teaching toddlers, aged 2–3 (19%) or babies, aged 0–2 (16%).

Educators who took part in the study ranged in age from 21 to 70 years old ($M = 39.50$, $SD = 11.65$) and had between 1 and 45 years of experience ($M = 14.24$, $SD = 9.48$). The sample was also culturally diverse. While the majority of educators reported being

European Australian ($n = 175$), there were also educators who identified as being from Western Europe ($n = 25$), subcontinental Asia ($n = 25$), East or South-East Asia ($n = 16$) or other. No participants identified as Aboriginal or Torres Strait Islander. Consistent with sector trends, the vast majority (98.8%) were female.

In Australia, the early childhood educators responsible for delivering the education and care programme within long day centres can be tertiary degree qualified or have a non-degree qualification. Degree qualified educators are early childhood teachers with a four-year teaching degree, while non-degree qualified educators may have a Diploma in Children's Services, which is equivalent to one year of the four-year teaching degree or a Certificate III in Early Childhood Education and Care, which is the lowest level of qualification required (Australian Children's Education and Care Quality Authority 2019). Educators with Certificate III will possess some theoretical and practical knowledge and skills, although the certificate itself has no equivalency to a tertiary teaching degree.

Materials

The online survey completed by educators was hosted on the Qualtrics survey platform and included three sections.[1] In the first section, educators were asked to report a number of demographic variables, including their age, gender, cultural affiliation, country of birth, language/s, academic qualifications, years of experience teaching in the sector, the age of the children in their current room or class and the educator: child ratio in their current room or class.

In the second section, we administered a talk frequency questionnaire: asking educators the frequency with which they engaged children both in reminiscing and in other types of talk. Our questionnaire adapts and extends Kulkofsky et al.'s (2009) original memory sharing prompt. In the original prompt, parents were asked to record on a scale of 0–7+ how many *times per week* they estimate engaging with their child in the talk about past events. Although the prompt is sensitive to cultural and individual differences between mothers (Kulkofsky, Wang, and Koh 2009), pilot testing with four early childhood educators suggested that we may encounter ceiling effects. Indeed, all four educators with whom we spoke suggested that they would typically talk with children about events or activities they have experienced multiple times per day. These conversations included discussion about activities the educator and children had experienced together at the centre and unshared activities that the educator has knowledge of a particular child or group experiencing separately (e.g. at home, on non-rostered days). Following the advice of our pilot group, therefore, we revised our response rating scale to 0–7+ *times per day*.

To determine how reminiscing fit within educators' broader pedagogical strategies and to provide points of comparison, we also repeated the original memory sharing question for other kinds of talk. Our questionnaire, therefore, included eight items: (i) talk about past events the educator and child experienced together in the centre, (ii) talk about past events that the child experienced outside the centre, (iii) talk about the child's emotions, (iv) talk about others' emotions, (v) imaginative talk, (vi) talk about how things work, and (vii) talk about shared future events and (viii) talk about unshared future events. We administered this scale twice (in counterbalanced order): once for a one-on-one talk with individual children and once for a talk with children in a group.

Finally, in the third section of our survey, we asked educators to describe instances in the day when they were most likely to engage children in reminiscing. Participants were given the following prompt:

> We are interested in conversations that you have with children in your centre about events the children have previously experienced. We refer to these conversations as past talk. Past talk may include events you experienced together, as well as events that children experienced but you did not. In the box below, please describe when and where you usually engage in past talk with the children in your care. Please provide up to 5 instances.

Consistent with the exploratory nature of this research question, a large and expandable free recall box was provided in the survey for participants to enter as much or as little detail as they wished. All written responses were later extracted and analysed in light of: (i) the specific instances reported by educators and (ii) the justifications and explanations they provided alongside these instances, as below.

Procedure

Following institutional ethics approval, an invitation to participate in the research was emailed to Directors of early childhood education centres from Sydney and surrounding regional areas. Directors were invited to forward the invitation to educators in their centres. The invitation included a link to an information and consent form, and educators who agreed to participate were invited to then click a second link to the survey proper. The survey proper took no longer than 20 min to complete. Once complete, participants were invited to leave their email addresses in order to be entered into a draw to win a $150 gift voucher.

Analysis of qualitative data

To analyse educators' qualitative responses to the open-ended reminiscing prompt, we adopted an inductive thematic approach (Braun and Clarke 2006). First, the first author familiarised herself with the responses by reading and taking initial notes. Second, codes were created from the data. This process continued until all possible codes were exhausted. Two distinct types of codes emerged: specific locations or times of the day ('instances') when educators engaged children in reminiscings, such as 'mealtimes' and 'departure', and additional explanations or justifications that help contextualise their response, such as 'supporting home to centre transition'. The second author then reviewed all transcripts and codes and made suggestions where needed. Third, higher-level themes (i.e. sets of cohesive and patterned responses with multiple instances across the dataset; Braun and Clarke 2006) were drawn iteratively from the codes. For example, codes related to 'reflections on excursions' and to 'daily recaps' each contributed to a broader theme: 'reflections on centre life'. Infrequent codes that did not contribute to any larger patterns, such as 'at the playdough table', were discarded.

Results

To determine how often early childhood educators report engaging young children in reminiscing, alongside other types of talk, we present quantitative data from our talk frequency questionnaire. Next, to determine the instances during the day when educators were most likely to engage young children in reminiscing, we present reminiscing 'instances' from our open-ended exploratory reminiscing question. We ranked these instances in order of popularity. Finally, to explore educators' reasons for reminiscing in these instances, we present six qualitative themes and exemplar quotes that emerged as justifications in our exploratory reminiscing question. Taken together, these findings provide complementary quantitative and qualitative evidence from educators about how often, when, and why educator–child reminiscing occurs.

How often early childhood educators report engaging young children in reminiscing

Educators' self-reported talk frequency across all eight types of talk is presented in Figure 1. To test for differences in the frequency of talks reported by educators, we conducted a (2) × (8) repeated measures ANOVA. The first factor was talk partner (one-on-one vs. group), and the second was talk type (shared past events, unshared past events, child's emotions, others' emotions, imaginative talk, how things work, shared future events and unshared future events). There was a significant main effect of partner, showing that frequency scores for the one-on-one talk were slightly, yet consistently, higher than they were for group talk, $F = 107.21$, $p < .001$, partial eta = .30. There was also a significant main effect of talk type, $F = 48.49$, $p < .001$, partial eta = .16. As shown in Figure 1, reminiscing about shared or unshared past events was less frequent on average than talk about emotions, but as common as talk about imaginary scenarios, how things work, or the future.

Interestingly, and notwithstanding small but consistent differences in the frequency of one-on-one vs. group talk, large individual differences between educators emerged. As shown in Figure 2, approximately half of all participating educators reported engaging children in various types of reminiscing 5–7+ times per day. In contrast, more than one-third (37.3%) reported reminiscing with groups of children about unshared events just 0–2 times per day, and one in five (18.2%) reported reminiscing one-on-one about unshared events 0–2 times. Similar patterns emerged for reminiscing about shared events.

These findings suggest that reminiscing is a remarkably common way for educators to engage young children in talk. One-on-one reminiscing conversations were more

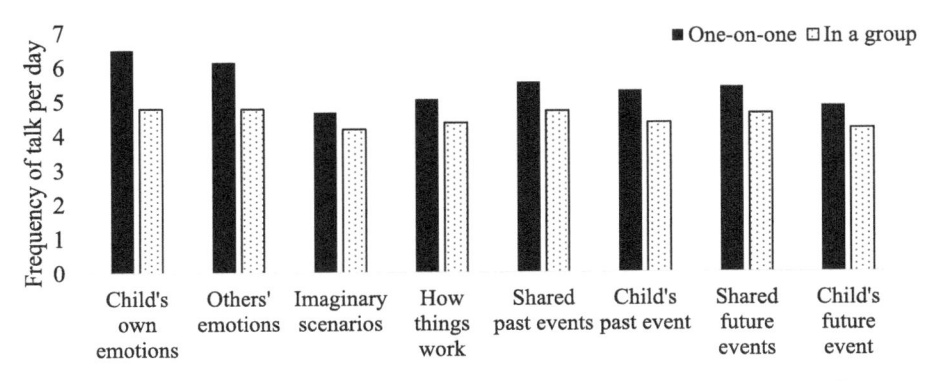

Figure 1. Educators' average frequency of talk each day with children one-on-one and in a group.

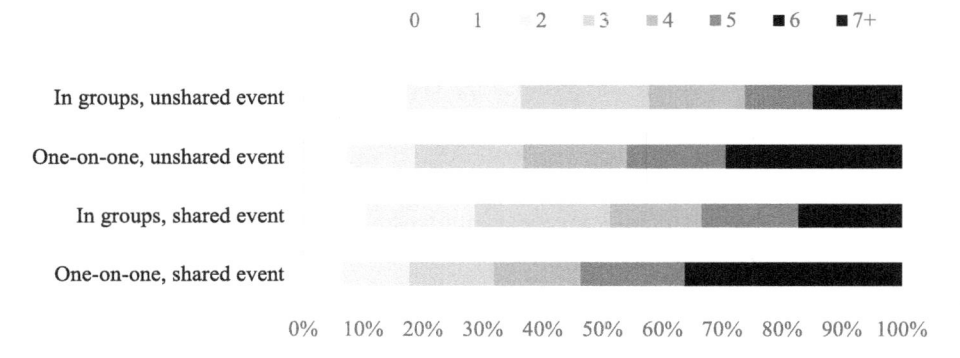

Figure 2. Individual differences in reminiscing frequencies for one-on-one vs. group conversations and shared vs. unshared events.

frequent than group conversations, as they were for other types of talk, and large individual differences in reported reminiscing frequency between educators also emerged. For the majority of educators, however, both are used to engage children in conversations about their past multiple times per day. This is true both for experiences the educator and child have shared together and those that the child has experienced separately, outside the early childhood education context.

When educators report reminiscing with young children

Drawing on our qualitative thematic coding, the most popular times for educators to engage children in reminiscing were as children arrive (e.g. 'on arrival … 'oh you went on the train to the city on the weekend? wow! What did you do?') and during meals (e.g. 'Meal times is always an area for discussion. We ask questions about both past and present events and what has happened and will happen during the day or week'). Approximately two-thirds of educators reported engaging children in reminiscing during these times (Figure 3). Reminiscing during group/circle time was also popular, being reported by more than half of the educators

> e.g. 'Each morning the group gathers for a "yarning circle". Children have the option of taking a "talking stone" indicating they would like to contribute to the circle. Topics of the circle vary daily as children openly discuss their weekend, events, families and how they are feeling'

Other relatively common instances for reminiscing reported by some educators included during departure, outdoor time, everyday chatting, change time, and rest time.[2] Each response was reported by at least 25 educators in the sample. Given the frequency of reminiscing among educators and children was relatively high, the wide diversity in other instances reported may suggest that reminiscing is common across multiple everyday early childhood activities.

Why early childhood educators report reminiscing with young children

Educators' qualitative explanations for why they engage children in reminiscing at various times fell into six broad themes: to settle children in; to support the formation

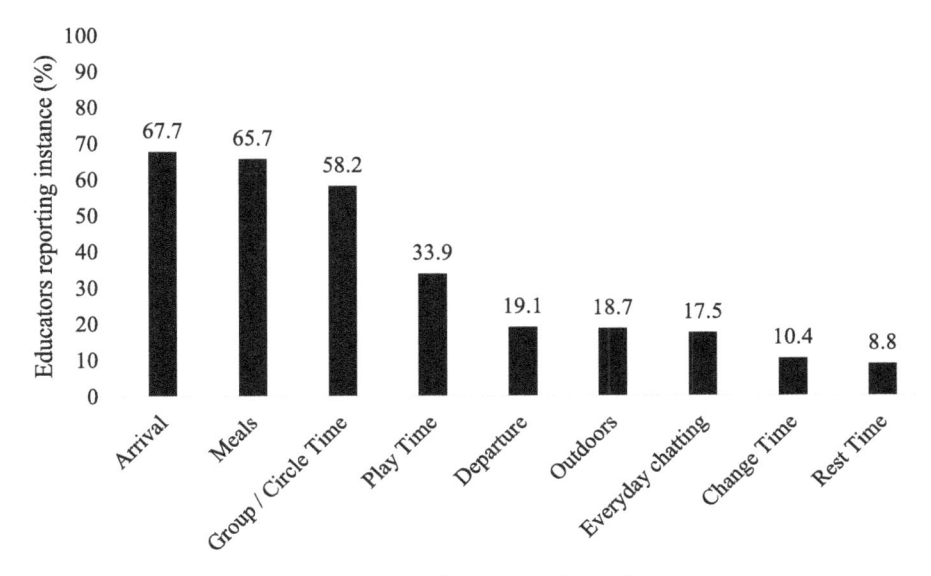

Figure 3. Instances of reminiscing in descending order of popularity.

of close home-centre connections; to support children's social and emotional competence; to support intentional learning activities; to support children's reflections on 'centre life'; and to bond. Note that pseudonyms are used for all educator quotes.

First, reminiscing conversations were considered by educators to be a useful tool for settling children in. Thus, there was an explicit preferencing of affective care. According to Stephanie (42 years old), a diploma trained educator in a babies' room, for example, 'I find this a good way to support children to transition from home to care. It helps them reflect, reset emotion and settle into the day'. Lily (45 years old), a degree trained teacher in a pre-school room, also used reminiscing 'during morning engagement to settle children', while Sam (43 years old), a degree trained teacher in a pre-school room, identified that reminiscing enabled children 'to settle on separation'.

Second, educators engaged children in reminiscing about supporting the formation of close connections between their home and centre lives. Billie (28 years old), a degree trained teacher in a babies' room, stated that reminiscing was useful 'when children are engaged in the activity that happened over the weekend, going to the farm, camping etc … ', while Terri (29 years old), a masters qualified teacher in a pre-school room, stated that:

> on Mondays we ask children what they did on their weekend as a show and tell group time in the morning/before lunch. Children usually describe going to swimming and parties, etc. … I talk to children about events in the community around them.

Like Terri, multiple educators reported being particularly likely to reminisce about children's home lives on the first day of the week ('Tuesday or Wednesday … their first day back').

Home-centre connections were also important at departure, with reminiscing used to share with parents what children have engaged in during the day. Avril (53 years old), a degree trained educator in a pre-school room, described 'assisting children in sharing information with their family at pickup'. Tammy (26 years old), also a degree trained educator in a pre-school room, encouraged children's reminiscing 'in conversations with their families', while Zali (29 years old), a degree trained teacher in a babies' room, scaffolded reminiscing 'on exit with their parents present'.

Third, educators engaged children in reminiscing about supporting their developing social and emotional competence. According to Stephanie (42 years old), a diploma trained educator in a babies' room, 'I use this as a social competence tool. Children find things easier to understand when they are reminded of a time they have been in the other persons shoes'. Janali (47 years old), a certificate-trained educator in a toddlers' room, reported using reminiscing 'when there is a dispute over a toy (angry, frustrated, sad)', while Tracey (41 years old), a degree trained teacher in a pre-school room, reported using reminiscing 'when a child is upset, using past knowledge to influence play – such as during role play'. Geraldine (63 years old), a degree trained teacher in a pre-school room, simply wrote 'during emotional upsets'. In all such cases, reminiscing was described as spontaneous, used to coach children's understanding of emotion and perspective-taking in moments of conflict or disturbance.

Fourth, educators engaged children in reminiscing during intentional learning activities. In these responses, explicit pedagogical intentions were clear ('during morning intentional teaching activities'; 'it is often related to what the children are doing, thinking about, challenged by'), with educators discussing how reminiscing about children's previous experiences could help reinforce new learning and create new connections. Mariella (45 years old), a degree trained teacher in a pre-school room, engaged children in reminiscing 'during experiences which can be linked to prior learning or events', while Zara (36 years old), also in a pre-school room, reported reminiscing ' … at intentional teaching periods, we often reflect on why we are exploring a topic or what we have already learned'. As highlighted in the following responses from Sal, Joanna, Ottie, Bethanie and Freida, reminiscing supported a wide range of intentional learning activities:

> During our unit of inquiry about how they have changed from babies to now. (Sal, 40 years old, degree trained teacher in a preschool room)

> During science activities to inquire about which experiences they have previously made. (Joanna, 53 years old, diploma trained educator in a preschool room)

> Reading books, making connections with children's relevant events. (Ottie, 50 years old, degree-trained teacher in a preschool room)

> When engaging in reflective drawing- children share thinking and recall shared experiences. (Bethany, 33 years old, degree trained teacher in a preschool room)

> If we're reading a book together, we may ask the children whether they've had the same or a similar experience … and get them to share their experiences and knowledge. (Freida, 21 years old, diploma trained educator in a toddler room)

Fifth, educators engaged children in reminiscing about reflecting on their 'centre life'. Yasmin (27 years old), a degree trained teacher in a babies room, explained how she reflects: 'when changing a child's nappy ("did you enjoy Emily's dance class this morning?"), when outside in the garden ("remember when the sun was out yesterday the ground got very hot, didn't it?") … ', while Bess (39 years old), a degree trained teacher in a pre-school room, explained how children's reflections across time might guide future centre activities: 'we talk regularly about where we have been and where we might want to go next, what we liked or didn't like'. Interestingly, when describing children's reflections on their centre life, several educators also mentioned the use of day-books and photos. Gabrielle (38 years old), a diploma trained educator in a babies' room, noted that she often engaged children in reminiscing when 'looking over a past project documentation book with photos of the children', while Jacqui (50 years old), a degree trained teacher in a pre-school room, engaged children in reminiscing 'when looking together through the children's portfolios and daybook – revisiting experiences, linking previous learning and exploration'. Alissa (36 years old), a masters' qualified teacher in a toddler room, described her use of photos: 'we will put photos on the wall and talk to children about the excursion during group time or whenever they are looking at the pictures'.

They were sixth, reminiscing provided educators and children with opportunities to bond. These bonding conversations were initiated by children as well as educators. Azalea (31 years old), a degree trained teacher in a pre-school room, reported reminiscing 'when a child initiates a conversation, … any time they unexpectedly come to me sharing of a past adventure or asking me where I was when not at the centre', while Mariam (32 years old), a degree trained teacher in a pre-school room, reported that 'during outside play, children approach me to share information or I see they need some support so I just sit and start a conversation with them'. In such cases, an educator's own approach is critical. Denise (24 years old), a certificate-trained educator in a toddler room, articulated how she initiates reminiscing conversations with shy children:

> I always engage myself in discussion all the time whether the child is responded or not, I find 9 times out of 10 the child is interested and will become comfortable about opening up with me as long as I am being open and patient with them.

Together, these six themes highlight the multifaceted nature of reminiscing in early childhood education contexts. They further illustrate an explicit acknowledgement and awareness among educators of the reasons they engage children in reminiscing and the expected outcomes of doing so.

Discussion

The aim of the current study was to determine when, how often and why early childhood educators report engaging children in reminiscing conversations. Drawing on sociocultural notions of development, these language-based interactions offer children an opportunity to reflect on and describe their everyday experiences and have important developmental benefits. A secondary aim was to capture how patterns of educator–child reminiscing differed for individual children versus children in groups and for events that the educator has shared with the child or children versus those that the child has experienced separately.

Reminiscing was a common and everyday activity for the vast majority of educators. Notwithstanding wide individual differences, nearly all educators reported engaging children in each form of reminiscing at least once per day. More than half engaged children in each form of reminiscing at least five times per day. In contrast, in Kulkofsky, Wang, and Koh (2009), just 40% of European American parents and no Chinese parents reported reminiscing with their children seven times or more per week. This finding is important: while rich developmental benefits have long been shown for parent–child reminiscing (Fivush, Haden, and Reese 2006; Salmon and Reese 2016; Wareham and Salmon 2006), and connections have been drawn between reminiscing, sustained shared thinking (Neale and Pino-Pasternak 2017) and decontextualised talk (Test, Cunningham, and Lee 2010), no research has yet considered the extent to which educator–child reminiscing occurs naturally in the early childhood context.

There are two possible explanations for the high rates of reminiscing reported by educators. First, because educators typically have multiple children under their care (ranging from 1:3 to 1:12 in the current study), the same educator may engage in multiple reminiscing conversations throughout the day to ensure each child has opportunities to contribute. Second, educators' professional qualifications may also make them more aware than parents of the positive benefits of decontextualised language-based interactions for children (see Test, Cunningham, and Lee 2010).

Interestingly, given the group-based nature of early childhood education and care, educators also reported that one-on-one talk was slightly, yet consistently, more frequent than group talk. This was true both for reminiscing and for other types of talk, suggesting that educators may be conscious of the need to scaffold each child's development in language-based interactions (see blinded-b). Further, and possibly also contributing to the higher frequency of one-on-one conversations, group discussions by definition include multiple children. Thus, several one-on-one conversations are needed to meet the same need for each individual child. The suggestion that educators were aware of the need for frequent one-on-one conversations with children was supported by their qualitative explanations for reminiscing, with high levels of intentionality and pedagogical reflection apparent.

Turning to educators' qualitative responses about when and why they engage children in reminiscing, the most frequently reported instances were during arrival and mealtimes. Group/circle time was also popular, while other instances included during outdoor play, departure and change time. Thus, reminiscing was common across numerous early childhood contexts throughout the day. Explanations for reminiscing were also varied and included not just to settle children in (thus supporting the home-centre transition) but to support the formation of close home-centre connections, to support children's development of social and emotional competence, to support children's intentional learning activities, to support children's reflections on 'centre life', and to bond. These explanations are similar to those reported by parents (Kulkofsky and Koh 2009), but extend further in supporting home-centre connections and settling in. Interestingly, several of these explanations are also predicted in early childhood literature. For example, Test and colleagues (2010) state that talk enabling children to share aspects of themselves with their educators will necessarily support bonding, while decontextualised talk should help to support the development of academic language and the formation of new learning connections. Importantly, however, our findings show that educators themselves are aware of these functions and use them with intentionality. Moreover, the findings provide a useful initial map of the different types of reminiscing most used by educators at different times.

Limitations and implications

Our study was limited by the use of educator self-report to measure opportunities for educator–child reminiscing in early childhood contexts. Although this approach enabled us to consider educators' own rationale for using different types of reminiscing in different ways and at different times of the day, we did not capture the length and style of these conversations. Future research might consider if more educators who report reminiscing more frequently with children also use a more elaborative style, as is the case for mothers (Kulkofsky and Koh 2009).

The study was also limited by not capturing data at the child level. Although educators frequently report engaging children in reminiscing, it is possible that this occurs more often with some children than others. To understand how frequently individual children are engaged each day in reminiscing with their educators, future research could consider the use of wearable recording equipment such as the Language Environment Analysis (LENA) system (e.g. Weisleder and Fernald 2013). By using this same system to also record children's language-based interactions with parents, educators, siblings, and others, there is potential to map multiple developmental pathways in the real world and determine how these pathways interact (see Van Bergen and Sutton 2019).

Notwithstanding these limitations, there are implications both for future research and for professional practice. First, we note the possibility for children's own contributions to the reminiscing to vary by instance, explanatory theme, and age. Educators in babies' rooms occasionally expressed that 'it's hard with the little ones', for example, and many of their descriptions of reminiscing appeared highly scaffolded. When reminiscing with older children about unshared events, such as weekend activities, educators instead reported using open prompts (see Fivush, Haden, and Reese 2006 for similar findings with mothers). While observational research is required to confirm these suggestive trends, a particularly interesting finding emerged with regards to intentional learning activities. Educators emphasised the importance of children themselves forming language-based connections between their past experiences and new learning, which in some cases may be unknown to the educator. In mother–child reminiscing, in contrast, fewer child contributions are sought. While bonding conversations are typically dialogic and co-constructed, mothers adopt a more didactic 'teaching' role in lesson-oriented reminiscing (Kulkofsky 2011). Future research is needed to consider how parents and educators differentially scaffold children's learning experiences with talk about the past for different reasons (i.e. drawing on our six themes).

Second, and related to our first implication, it is important that future research delineate the specific developmental benefits that are best conferred in specific types of reminiscing conversations and those conferred across all forms of reminiscing. Our research highlights the multifaceted reasons that early childhood educators engage children in reminiscing (see Kulkofsky and Koh 2009 for similar findings among parents). Across these instances, scaffolding may differ qualitatively. For example, educators who reminisced about supporting socioemotional competence described the spontaneous adoption of emotion coaching techniques in response to children's distress or conflict. Reminiscing in these instances is likely to offer a richer forum for the development of emotion knowledge and perspective-taking than is reminiscing for other purposes (see Van Bergen and Salmon 2010, Van Bergen, Salmon, and Dadds 2018). In contrast, the use of expansive and elaborative conversational cues should support children's development of vocabulary, narrative skill and self-understanding across all reminiscing contexts (Wareham and Salmon 2006).

Third, we highlight the potential to prompt and support reminiscing in a range of early childhood education contexts. Several educators in our study mentioned the use of daybooks to prompt children's reflections on centre life, for example, while others used reminiscing prompts during circle time. By introducing these techniques in curricula and planning documentation and by introducing physical reminiscing prompts in the environment, there are opportunities to address the wide individual differences in educators' reminiscing frequency and encourage the use of reminiscing for all children.

Finally, given the wide individual differences in educators' reminiscing frequency, we echo calls for professional learning that focuses on reminiscing quantity and quality (Andrews and Van Bergen 2020, Andrews, Van Bergen, and Wyver 2019; Neale and Pino-Pasternak 2017). Reminiscing interventions have been successful amongst mothers (Reese and Newcombe 2007; Van Bergen, Salmon, and Dadds 2018), and educators are already aware of the positive benefits of sustained shared thinking in other contexts (Siraj-Blatchford 2009). By encouraging language-based conversations about young children's own past experiences, using a high-quality elaborative style, we expect such interventions to offer significant developmental benefits.

Conclusion

Educator–child reminiscing engages young children in potentially rich, decontextualised conversations about their own past experiences. Educators in our study reported reminiscing with children multiple times per day, particularly on arrival and at mealtimes, but also in other contexts throughout the day. Multiple reasons for engaging young children in reminiscing were provided, including to bond, support the child in making home-centre connections, support the development of social and emotional competence and support children to form new knowledge connections during intentional learning activities. This study is the first to consider educators' views about reminiscing and has important implications for future research and practice.

Notes

1. A fourth section included two memory function scales (an adult scale and a child scale). These scales represented the first phase of longitudinal work considering the inter-relationships between adult and child memory functions. They are not the focus of the current analysis, however, and are not reported here.
2. Supplementary chi-squared analyses comparing responses by educators' teaching context showed that 'group/circle time' responses were more common among educators in pre-school rooms, $p < .05$, and 'change time' responses were more common among educators in babies' rooms, $p < .05$. No other differences were significant.

Disclosure statement

No potential conflict of interest was reported by the author(s).

ORCID

Penny Van Bergen ⓘ http://orcid.org/0000-0001-9542-812X
Rebecca Andrews ⓘ http://orcid.org/0000-0001-7560-5360

References

Andrews, Rebecca, and Penny Van Bergen. 2020. "Characteristics of educators' talk about decontextualised events." *Australasian Journal of Early Childhood* 45 (4): 362–376. https://doi.org/10.1177/1836939120966080.

Andrews, Rebecca, Penny Van Bergen, and Shirley Wyver. 2019. "Reminiscing and future talk conversations between young children, their early childhood educators and mothers." *Early Childhood Research Quarterly* 49: 254–268. https://doi.org/10.1016/j.ecresq.2019.07.005.

Andrews, Rebecca, Penny Van Bergen, and Shirley Wyver. 2020. "Use of Mental State Language during Educator-Child and Mother-Child Conversations about the Past and Future." *Early Education and Development* 31 (6): 838–853. https://doi.org/10.1080/10409289.2019.1689772.

Andrews, Rebecca, Penny Van Bergen, and Shirley Wyver. 2021. "Educators', children's and mothers' use of temporal language in reminiscing and future talk conversations." *Early Years*: 1–18. https://doi.org/10.1080/09575146.2021.1957780.

Australian Bureau of Statistics. 2018. "Childhood Education and Care, Australia." https://www.abs.gov.au/statistics/people/education/childhood-education-and-care-australia.

Australian Children's Education and Care Quality Authority. 2019. "Children Preschool Age or Under." https://www.acecqa.gov.au/qualifications/requirements/children-preschool-age-or-under.

Australian Government Department of Education, Employment and Workplace Relations. 2009. "Belonging, Being and Becoming: The Early Years Learning Framework for Australia." https://www.acecqa.gov.au/sites/default/files/2018-02/belonging_being_and_becoming_the_early_years_learning_framework_for_australia.pdf.

Australian Institute of Family Studies. 2018. "Childcare and Early Childhood Education." https://aifs.gov.au/publications/child-care-and-early-childhood-education-australia.

Balladares, Jaime, and Miloš Kankaraš. 2020. "Attendance in Early Childhood Education and Care Programmes and Academic Proficiencies at Age 15." OECD Education Working Paper No. 214. https://www.oecd.org/officialdocuments/publicdisplaydocumentpdf/?cote=EDU/WKP%282020%292&docLanguage=Eu.

Bluck, Susan, and Nicole Alea. 2009. "Thinking and Talking About the Past: Why Remember?" *Applied Cognitive Psychology* 23: 1089–1104.

Braun, Virginia, and Victoria Clarke. 2006. "Using Thematic Analysis in Psychology." *Qualitative Research in Psychology* 3 (2): 77–101.

Creswell, John W. 2009. *Research Design: Quantitative, Qualitative, and Mixed Methods Approaches.* Los Angeles: Sage.

Fivush, Robyn. 1994. "Constructing Narrative, Emotion, and Self in Parent-Child Conversations About the Past." In *The Remembering Self: Construction and Accuracy in the Self-narrative*, edited by Ulrich Neisser and Robyn Fivush, 136–157. New York, NY: Cambridge University Press.

Fivush, Robyn, Catherine Haden, and Elaine Reese. 2006. "Elaborating on Elaborations: Role of Maternal Reminiscing Style in Cognitive and Socioemotional Development." *Child Development* 77 (6): 1568–1588.

Habermas, Tilmann, and Elaine Reese. 2015. "Getting a Life Takes Time: The Development of the Life Story in Adolescence, Its Precursors and Consequences." *Human Development* 58: 172–201.

Kulkofsky, Sarah. 2011. "Characteristics of Functional Joint Reminiscence in Early Childhood." *Memory (Hove, England)* 19 (1): 45–55.

Kulkofsky, Sarah, and Jessie Bee Kim Koh. 2009. "Why They Reminisce: Caregiver Reports of the Functions of Joint Reminiscence in Early Childhood." *Memory (Hove, England)* 17 (4): 458–470.

Kulkofsky, Sarah, Qi Wang, and Jessie Bee Kim Koh. 2009. "Functions of Memory Sharing and Mother-Child Reminiscing Behaviors: Individual and Cultural Variations." *Journal of Cognition and Development* 10: 92–114.

Mertens, D. 2010. *Research and Evaluation in Education and Psychology: Integrating Diversity with Quantitative, Qualitative, and Mixed Methods.* Los Angeles: Sage.

Neale, Dave, and Deborah Pino-Pasternak. 2017. "A Review of Reminiscing in Early Childhood Settings and Links to Sustained Shared Thinking." *Educational Psychology Review* 29: 641–665.

Nelson, Katherine, and Robyn Fivush. 2004. "The Emergence of Autobiographical Memory: A Social Cultural Developmental Theory." *Psychological Review* 111 (2): 486–511.

Pillemer, David. 2003. "Directive Functions of Autobiographical Memory: The Guiding Power of the Specific Episode." *Memory (Hove, England)* 11 (2): 193–202.

Reese, Elaine, and Rhiannon Newcombe. 2007. "Training Mothers in Elaborative Reminiscing Enhances Children's Autobiographical Memory and Narrative." *Child Development* 78 (4): 1153–1170.

Rowe, Meredith. 2012. "A Longitudinal Investigation of the Role of Quantity and Quality of Child-directed Speech in Vocabulary Development." *Child Development* 83: 1762–1774.

Rowe, Meredith. 2013. "Decontextualized Language Input and Preschoolers' Vocabulary Development." *Seminars in Speech and Language* 34 (04): 260–266.

Salmon, Karen, and Elaine Reese. 2016. "The Benefits of Reminiscing with Young Children." *Current Directions in Psychological Science* 25 (4): 233–238.

Siraj-Blatchford, I. 2009. "Conceptualising Progression in the Pedagogy of Play and Sustained Shared Thinking in Early Childhood Education: A Vygotskian Perspective." *Education and Child Psychology* 26 (2): 77–89.

Siraj-Blatchford, Iram, and Kathy Sylva. 2004. "Researching Pedagogy in English Preschools." *British Educational Journal of Research* 30 (5): 712–730.

Sylva, Kathy, Edward Melhuish, Pam Sammons, Iram Siraj-Blatchford, and Brenda Taggart. 2004. "The Effective Provision of Pre-school Education (EPPE) project: Findings from Pre-school to end of Key Stage 1." http://eppe.ioe.ac.uk/eppe/eppefindings.htm.

Test, Joan E, Denise D. Cunningham, and Amanda C. Lee. 2010. "Talking With Young Children: How Teachers Encourage Learning." *Dimensions of Early Childhood* 38 (3): 3–10.

Van Bergen, P, and Karen Salmon. 2010. "The Association between Parent-Child Reminiscing and Children's Emotion Knowledge." *New Zealand Journal of Psychology* 39: 51–56.

Van Bergen, Penny, Karen Salmon, and Mark R Dadds. 2018. "Coaching Mothers of Typical and Conduct Problem Children in Elaborative Parent-Child Reminiscing: Influences of a Randomized Controlled Trial on Reminiscing Behaviour and Everyday Talk Preferences." *Behaviour Research and Therapy* 111: 9–18. https://doi.org/10.1016/j.brat.2018.09.004.

Van Bergen, Penny, Karen Salmon, Mark R. Dadds, and Jennifer Allen. 2009. "The Effects of Mother Training in Emotion-rich, Elaborative Reminiscing on Children's Shared Recall and Emotion Knowledge." *Journal of Cognition and Development* 10: 162–187.

Van Bergen, Penny, and John Sutton. 2019. "Sociocultural Memory Development Research Drives New Directions in Gadgetry Science. Commentry on Précis of Cognitive Gadgets: The Cultural Evolution of Thinking (Celia Heyes)." *Behavioral and Brain Sciences* 42 (e169): 1–58.

Wang, Qi. 2007. ""Remember When You Got The Big, Big Bulldozer?" Mother–Child Reminiscing Over Time and Across Cultures." *Social Cognition* 25 (4): 455–471.

Wareham, Penny, and Karen Salmon. 2006. "Mother-child Reminiscing About Everyday Experiences: Implications for Psychological Interventions in the Preschool Years." *Clinical Psychology Review* 26: 535–554.

Waters, Theodore E. A., Christin Camia, Christopher R. Facompré, and Robyn Fivush. 2019. "A Meta-analytic Examination of Maternal Reminiscing Style: Elaboration, Gender, and Children's Cognitive Development." *Psychological Bulletin* 145 (11): 1082–1102.

Weisleder, Adriana, and Anne Fernald. 2013. "Talking to Children Matters." *Psychological Science* 24 (11): 2143–2152.

Infant educators' use of mental-state talk in Australia and China: a cross-cultural comparative study

Sheila Degotardi ⓘ, Feifei Han ⓘ and Jiangbo Hu ⓘ

ABSTRACT

This study compares the mental-state talk of infant educators in Australia and China in order to determine the nuanced differences in the ways that they use this talk with the infants in their room. Participants are 44 native English-speaking Australian educators from centres in Sydney, Australia and 30 native Chinese-speaking infant educators recruited from centres in and around Hangzhou, China. Twenty-minute samples of each educators' naturally occurring play interactions with infants during play were coded to determine the frequency of their desire, emotion, perception, cognition and modulation of assertion talk. Each mental-state term was also coded according to the referent of that mental-state. We examined the extent to which Australian and Chinese educators' use mental-state talk and how the referents of such talk differed by mental-state talk type and culture. Australian educators used significantly more mental-state talk than their Chinese counterparts. Different patterns of referent use across cultural cohorts and mental-state talk types were identified. Findings have implications for the socialisation of very young children into culturally specific ways of talking and thinking about the mind.

Introduction

Caregiver's use of mental-state talk when interacting with young children has been shown to predict children's subsequent use of mental-state terms as well as their social-emotional, language and cognitive development (e.g. Ruffman, Slade, and Crowe 2002; Taumoepeau and Ruffman 2006; Symonds, Fossum, and Collins 2006; Hughes and Dunn 1998; Barnes and Dickenson 2018). When caregivers use words such as 'want', 'feel', 'see', 'know' and 'think' to describe desires, emotions, perceptions, cognitions and points of view, they explicit otherwise opaque mental states and processes, thus enabling children to acquire and use mental-state words and develop an understanding of their own and others' minds. A caregiver's use of mental-state talk when interacting with young children is argued to reflect their image of the child as a mental agent – one who possesses and acts on the basis of their own and others' desires, emotions, perceptions and cognitions (Degotardi 2015; Meins et al. 2003). For example, an educator who says to an infant 'Do you think we should go inside now?' as opposed to 'It's time to go inside' is using the mental-state term 'think' to frame the statement from the infants' point of view. This propensity to acknowledge the young child's perspective during interactions has been associated with levels of positivity, sensitivity and stimulation in both home and early childhood education and care (ECEC) contexts (Degotardi and Sweller 2012; Frampton, Perlman, and Jenkins 2009; King and La Paro 2015; Helmerhorst, Colonnesi, and Fukkink 2019; Laranjo, Bernier, and Meins 2008; Meins et al. 2001; Bernier and Dozier 2003). Because of its links to sensitive and stimulating interactions, an increasing body of multidisciplinary work therefore recognises that mental-state talk is an important relational support for young children's wellbeing and learning (Degotardi 2015; Barnes and Dickenson 2018; Grazzani, Ornaghi, and Brockmeier 2016).

Much of the existing research about mental-state talk has been undertaken in home and family contexts (e.g. Ruffman, Slade, and Crowe 2002; Taumoepeau and Ruffman 2006; Symonds, Fossum, and Collins 2006; Hughes and Dunn 1998; Meins et al. 2003). Across the world, young children are increasingly attending ECEC centres, so children's ECEC experiences contribute significantly to their learning and development (e.g. National Institute of Child Health and Human Development Early Child Care Research Network 2002; Li et al. 2013; Yazejian et al. 2017). Mental-state talk studies that have taken place in ECEC centres have observed that educators use mental-state talk more frequently than mothers in home contexts (Farkas et al. 2017; Degotardi and Sweller 2012; Frampton, Perlman, and Jenkins 2009). Because ECEC settings provide infants and young children with rich experiences with mental-state talk, they should be recognised as a valuable context for fostering young children's talk about, and understanding of the mind.

It is important, however, to acknowledge that most existing research on mental-state talk in both home and ECEC contexts has taken place in English-speaking countries and contexts. Yet cultural differences exist in the ways that caregivers talk to, and interact with young children (Bornstein and Cheah 2006). It is apparent that interaction styles reflect cultural conventions about self and other identity and about learning. While generalisations should be avoided, in independent-oriented cultures such as many English-speaking and European countries, caregiver-child interaction styles are often found to promote autonomy, agency and self-directed exploration and learning (Kagitcibasi 2007; Markus and Kitayama 1991). Other cultures promote inter-dependence, where values of social-connectedness and collective moral obligations are prioritised (Luo, Tamis Le Monda, and Song 2013). In these cultures, there may be less emphasis on individual perspectives and mental agency and more on conformity, group socialisation and information transmission (Markus and Kitayama 1991). This being the case, children's linguistic experience with mental-state talk may differ across cultures, and this raises questions about whether research undertaken in English-speaking contexts can necessarily be generalised universally.

The present study addresses the gaps in the current research base by conducting the first cross-cultural comparison of the mental-state talk of early childhood educators.[1] We compare the naturally occurring talk of native English-speaking infant educators from

Sydney, Australia and native Mandarin-speaking infant educators from Hangzhou, China in order to identify similarities and differences in the ways that they use mental-state talk with these very young children. These two cultural contexts are examples of the independent – interdependent orientations outlined above, and thus provide a valuable opportunity to examine how cultural orientations may shape educators' language use. Findings will contribute to understandings of the ways that the cultural context, through the language practices of early educators, fosters young children's self-identity and learning in culturally specific ways.

Prevalence and characteristics of mental-state talk in ECEC settings

A small, but increasing body of work has investigated the prevalence of mental-state talk in ECEC settings. Some studies have used a composite measure of all mental-state terms, and have reported that mental-state terms comprise four percent of all words used, and exists in around 11% of educators' utterances (Helmerhorst, Colonnesi, and Fukkink 2019; Barnes and Dickenson 2018). Other studies have described the relative frequency of specific categories of mental-state terms. When interacting with pre-schoolers in structured play or reading contexts, Colonnesi et al. (2017) and Misailidi, Papoudi, and Brouzos (2013) reported that educators most frequently used cognition terms, with desires, preferences and emotions referred to less frequently.

However, in data generated from naturalistic observations of normal classroom practice, King and La Paro (2015) found that educators of preschool-aged children used significantly more perception terms than desire and cognition terms, with emotions used least often. In contrast, observations of infant educators has shown that desire and emotion talk are more prevalent than talk about cognitions (Farkas et al. 2017; Degotardi and Sweller 2012). Young children begin to understand and use desire and emotion terms during infancy and toddlerhood, whereas cognitive terms tend to enter their vocabulary during their fourth and fifth year of life. The difference in relative frequency of educators' use of desire and emotion and cognitive terms in infancy and during the preschool years suggests that educators may adjust their mental-state talk to reflect the developmental levels of the children with whom they interact.

While educators' use of mental-state talk is widely argued to support young children's developmental outcomes, some ECEC studies have proposed that children's development may be further supported by the referent of, or the 'person doing', the mental state. For example, educators can ascribe a mental state directly to a child when they say 'Do you want the ball?', or 'You know where it is'. Alternatively, they can ascribe it to themselves 'I think it's time to go inside', or to another person 'Tilly feels sad now'. In an ECEC context, Barnes and Dickenson (2018) reported that, during instructional and book reading activities, educators most frequently ascribed mental-state terms to the child compared to themselves or others. They suggest that educators may adhere to the view that young children better understand talk about themselves than others. When more specific categories of mental-state terms were examined, King and La Paro (2015) found that when educators used perception, desire and cognitive terms, they were more likely to refer to the child's mental-state than to their own, other adult's or inanimate characters such as a doll or soft toy. In contrast, educators tended to refer to their own emotions rather than the child's or other people's. The researchers propose that these educators are thus de-emphasising preschool-aged children's emotional states while placing an emphasis on their cognitions, desires and perceptions.

Cultural differences in mental state talk

An emerging body of international research suggests cultural differences exist in parents' use of mental-state talk with young children. In a New Zealand study of mental-state talk used by mothers as they described pictures to their 15- to 26-month-old infants, Taumoepeau (2015) reported that mothers of Pacific Island heritage tended to use a lower proportion of mental-state terms than English-speaking mothers. The cultural differences were heightened by the strength of the Pacific Island cultural identity reported by the mother. On the basis of the differences in frequency of mental-state talk between these two cultural groups, the author suggests that mental-state talk may be less privileged in non-English-speaking cultures than in English-speaking ones.

This finding is supported by studies involving Chinese speaking parents. Analysing transcripts from Chinese ($n = 60$) and European American ($n = 71$) mothers' narration of a wordless picture book to their three-year-old children, Doan and Wang (2010) reported that Chinese mothers used significantly fewer mental-state words than their US counterparts. While both cohorts used cognitive terms most frequently and emotional terms least frequently, European American mothers used significantly more of these terms than their Chinese counterparts. They also more frequently drew attention to their own and others perspectives by modulating the certainty of their utterances using modal verbs and adjuncts such as 'might' and 'maybe'.

The frequency of particular types of mental-state talk appears to vary according to the age of the child being spoken to Dai, McMahon, and Lim (2020) compared the mental-state talk used by 50 Australian and 50 mainland Chinese parents as they played with their 18-month-old infants. Similar to findings in infant ECEC settings (Farkas et al. 2017), both cohorts used desire terms most frequently, followed by cognitive and then emotion terms. However, Australian mothers used significantly more mental-state talk than their Chinese counterparts, with the difference attributed to a greater frequency of desire, as opposed to cognitive and emotion terms. These findings are reflected in an interesting study by Cheng et al. (2020) in which bilingual mothers played with their 18-month-old infants twice – once interacting in English and once in Mandarin. Results again demonstrated that, in both languages, mothers used significantly more desire than cognitive terms. However, mothers used desire terms more frequently and cognitive terms less frequently when they spoke Mandarin compared with when they spoke English.

No known studies to date have analysed cultural differences in the referent of parents' mental-state talk. A suggestion that cultural differences may exist comes from a related study by Fujita and Hughes (2020) which analysed five-minute samples of Japanese ($n = 117$) and UK ($n = 119$) mothers when they were describing (as opposed to talking to) their three- to six-year old children. These researchers reported that the UK mothers used significantly more references to mental states than Japanese mothers and explicitly referred to the child's perspective more frequently than their Japanese counterparts, who used more references to their own or others' perspectives.

The present study

While an emerging body of research supports the argument that educators' mental-state talk comprises an important element of their classroom discourse, the literature cited above identified important gaps. First, despite findings from family based studies reinforcing the importance of experience with mental-state talk in infancy, there are few studies that explore this discourse type in the ECEC setting. Second, no infant ECEC studies to date have examined the referent of mental-state terms, and third, ECEC studies are yet to consider cross-cultural differences in educator's use of mental-state terms. Therefore, the present study aims to address these gaps by answering the two research questions:

(1) To what extent does the frequency of mental-state talk used by infant educators differ by type and by cultural-linguistic context (Australian English-speaking and Chinese Mandarin-speaking)?
(2) To what extent does the frequency of referents of mental-state talk used by infant educators differ by type and by cultural-linguistic context?

Method

Participants

Participants for this study comprised of 44 native English-speaking educators who worked in ECEC centres in and around Sydney, Australia, and 30 native Mandarin-speaking educators who worked in Hangzhou, Mainland China. All educators worked in rooms catering for infants aged birth to two years. The Australian cohort was derived from the participants of an Australian study on the language environment of infant ECEC rooms. Qualifications reflected those required in the Australian context, with 10 holding a specialised early childhood Bachelor degree, 20 holding a vocational diploma and 14 holding a vocational certificate in ECEC. Australian educator experience with infants ranged from 1 to 20 years, with a mean of approximately 10 years. The Chinese cohort was recruited specifically for this study. Qualification again reflected the requirements of the local context, 12 holding a specialised early childhood Bachelor degree, 15 possessing a vocational diploma, and three holding a non-early-childhood Bachelor degree. Chinese educators were less experienced than the Australian cohort, with experience working in infant rooms ranging from one month to 19 years with an average of approximately two years.

Data generation

Each educator was video-recorded as they conducted their normal activities and interactions with the infants in their room. Ethical approval for the study was gained from the [university's name] Human Ethics Research Committee. Prior to data collection, fully informed written consent was obtained from the focus educators, all other educators, and the parents of the infants in the room. Information letters explained that the researchers were interested in the naturally-occurring interactions that took place between educators and infants, and encouraged educators to interact as they normally would if the videographer was not in the room. The videographer who obtained the footage had early childhood qualifications and observed the infants' cues in a sensitive and responsive manner. She spent time at each research site prior to recording in order to become familiar with educators and infants. She ceased recording if an infant became upset, she removed herself temporarily if an infant was disturbed by their presence, seeking advice from room educators about the best way and time to recommence the recording. The participants were informed that they had the right to opt out of participation at any time, and educators were informed that they could request to cease the filming should they or any infant become upset or uncomfortable.

The data for the Australian cohort was extracted from three hours of video footage of normally occurring activities including play, mealtimes, and personal care. For this study, we extracted 20 min of play footage on the basis that the context of play has been observed to be rich in opportunities for mental-state talk (Degotardi and Sweller 2012). We used the following criteria to select the extracts: first, the focus educator needed to be present during the entire 20 min play activity from beginning to the end. Second, the focus educator needed to be actively interacting with the children. The first 20 min in the footage that met these criteria was selected for analysis. The Chinese data was extracted from 1.5 h of footage that captured the morning activities including free play and structured play in the infant rooms. The same criteria were used to select 20 min of free play footage for analysis.

Coding of the data

All educator talk directed at one or more infant in their room was transcribed in the native language. The transcriptions were then separated into *messages*, which is a semantic unit that is approximately equivalent to a clause (Hasan 1996). Each message was coded as follows:

Mental-state talk

Each message was coded as *mental-state* if it contained a mental-state term, or *non-mental-state* if it did not. Previous mental-state coding schemes (Ruffman, Slade, and Crowe 2002; Degotardi and Sweller 2012; Bretherton and Beeghly-Smith 1982) were used to categorise each mental-state term. *Desires* were references to motivations and preferences (e.g. want, like, love and hope). *Emotions* were references to emotional feeling states and processes (e.g. happy, sad, cranky, angry, frustrated, excited, and surprised). *Perceptions* were explicit references to perceptual states and processes (e.g. see, hear, taste, and smell). *Cognitions* were references to knowledge and epistemological states and processes (e.g. know, think, understand, remember, wonder, and pretend). *Modulations of assertion* were references that, through the use of a modal verb or adjunct, explicitly express a point of view (e.g. might, probably, maybe, should, and possibly).

Most mental-state messages only contained one mental-state term, but in rare instances, a message was coded in two categories (e.g. *I think you want the ball*). Table 1 provides examples from the data of Australian and Chinese educators' messages that contained each category of mental-state terms.

Table 1. Examples of mental state talk used by Australian and Chinese educators.

Mental-state category	Australian	Chinese
Desire	'Do you <u>want</u> to do it again?' '<u>Would you like</u> to help me fill up the teddy bear bucket?' 'Sophie <u>prefers</u> to use her hands'	'你还要玩这个吗?'(Do you still <u>want</u> to play with it?) 你喜欢这个鸭鸭?(You <u>prefer/like</u> this duck?) '你最喜欢这个火车了'(This train is your <u>favourite</u>)
Emotion	'I want to make sure that you're <u>not upset</u>' 'She's getting <u>frustrated</u>'	'你们在开心什么?'(What are you <u>excited</u> with?) '不要慌'(Don't <u>panic</u>)
Perception	'Did you <u>see</u> all of the fruit and vegetables?' 'How does it <u>feel</u> on your fingers?' 'That doesn't <u>taste</u> nice does it'	'我们玩吧, 听到音乐吗?'(Let's play, did you <u>hear</u> the music) 你见过这种冰激凌吗?(Have you even <u>seen</u> this ice-cream?) 你尝过它吗?(Have you ever <u>tasted</u> it?)
Cognitive	'<u>Remember</u> we were talking about it last week' 'I <u>wonder</u> where our big mixing stick went to' 'What else do you <u>think</u> a dinosaur would eat?'	'你能想想办法, 不让它倒下来吗?'(Can you <u>think</u> of a way to prevent it from falling down?) 你知道我手里的是什么形状吗?(Do you <u>know</u> the shape in my hand?) 你们记不记得长颈鹿怎样喝水?(Do you <u>remember</u> how giraffes drink water?)
Modulation of assertion	'<u>Maybe</u> it's in your bag' 'Mia, you <u>might</u> need to get a bucket'	'它好像没那个'(It <u>may</u> not have that (handle))' '我们应该出去了'(We <u>should</u> go out)

Mental-state referent

Each coded mental-state term was then further coded according to the mental-state referent. *Child* was coded when the referent was the child (e.g. *Do you remember when …*); *Educator* when the educator ascribed the term to herself (e.g. *I think it's in here*); Joint when the educator referred jointly to herself and one or more child (e.g. *We might play outside*); and *Other* when the educator referred to someone who she was not directly speaking to (e.g. *Tommy wants a turn now*) or to an inanimate object (e.g. *Teddy's feeling sad*).

Inter-coder reliability

We calculated Cohen's Kappa inter-coder reliability for Australian and Chinese cohorts separately (Table 2). We randomly selected 11 educators for Australian cohort (27.5%) and seven for Chinese cohort (23.3%). Our results are all above .70, which according to Cohen, represents substantial agreement (McHugh 2012).

Data analysis

As the number of the total messages varied widely among educators (range = 164–570, $M = 684.20$, $SD = 74.42$), we first calculated proportions of different types of mental-state talk in terms of the total messages. We also calculated proportions of the mental-state referent for different types of mental-state talk.

For the first research question, we performed a 5×2 MANOVA using the mental-state talk type (desire, emotion, perception, cognition, and modulation of assertion) as a within-subject independent variable and culture (Australia and China) as a between-subject independent variable. To answer the second research question, we conducted six separate 4×2 MANOVAs for the overall use of mental-state talk and for each type

Table 2. Inter-rater reliability.

variables	English	Chinese
total mental-state talk	.93	.96
desire	.97	.96
emotion	.74	1.00
perception	.83	1.00
cognition	.79	.81
modulation of assertion	.88	.94
referent	.91	.95

of mental-state talk using the mental-state referent type as a within-subject independent variable (i.e. Child, Educator, Joint, and Other) and culture as a between-subject independent variable (i.e. Australia and China). The data analyses were performed in IBM SPSS 25.

Results

Comparison of the proportions of mental-state talk by type x culture

Table 3 presents the descriptive statistics of the proportions of mental-state talk. The results of MANOVA show that there was a significant within-subject effect of mental-state talk type (F (4, 288) = 62.64, $p < .01$, partial $\eta^2 = .47$). Post-hoc pairwise comparison reveals that irrespective of the culture, educators used desires most and emotions least. There was no significant difference between perceptions and cognitions, both of which were more than modulations of assertion.

There was a significant between-subject effect for culture (F (1, 72) = 39.36, $p < .01$, partial $\eta^2 = .35$); and a significant interaction effect between mental-state talk type x culture (F (4, 288) = 3.93, $p < .01$, partial $\eta^2 = .05$). Overall, Australian educators ($M = 15.73\%$) used significantly more mental-state talk than Chinese educators ($M = 7.44\%$). Post-hoc analyses showed that, except for emotions (F (1, 72) = .24, $p = .63$, partial $\eta^2 = .00$), Australian educators used significantly more of each type of mental-state talk than Chinese educators: desires (F (1, 72) = 4.83, $p < .05$, partial $\eta^2 = .06$); perceptions (F (1, 72) = 39.97, $p < .01$, partial $\eta^2 = .36$); cognitions (F (1, 72) = 15.64, $p < .01$, partial $\eta^2 = .18$); and modulations of assertion: (F (1, 72) = 30.81, $p < .01$, partial $\eta^2 = .30$). To examine the interaction effect (Figure 1), we further conducted separate repeated ANOVAs for Australian and Chinese educators. We found that Chinese educators used desires most frequently, and modulations of assertion least frequently. The proportion of emotions used by Chinese educators did not differ from their use of

Table 3. Descriptive statistics of the proportions of mental-state talk.

variables (all figures are in %)	English (*n* = 44)		Chinese (*n* = 30)		Total (*n* = 74)	
	M	*SD*	*M*	*SD*	*M*	*SD*
total mental-state talk	15.73	6.50	7.44	3.85	12.37	6.90
desire	6.68	3.49	4.86	3.50	5.94	3.59
emotion	0.46	0.74	0.38	0.65	0.43	0.70
perception	3.21	2.14	0.67	0.62	2.18	2.10
cognition	3.15	2.42	1.27	1.14	2.39	2.19
modulation of assertion	2.24	1.90	0.26	0.47	1.44	1.78

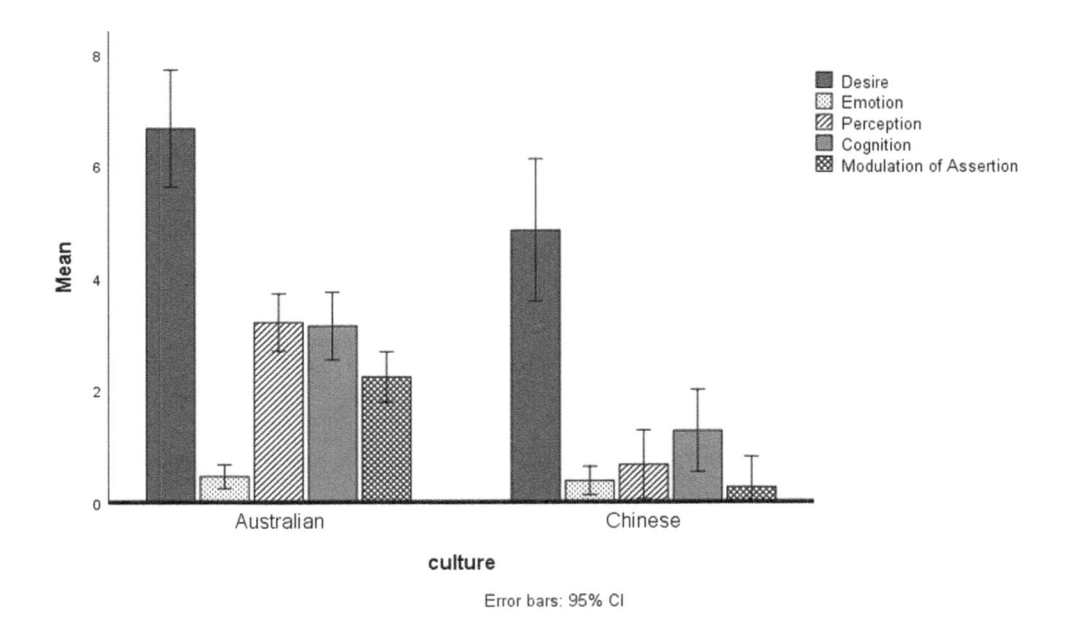

Error bars: 95% CI

Figure 1. Proportions of mental-state talk by mental-state talk type x culture.

perceptions and modulations of assertion. English educators also used desires the most, followed equally by perceptions and cognitions. However, emotion talk was used the least.

Comparison of proportions of mental-state talk referents by type x culture

Table 4 presents descriptive statistics of the proportions of the mental-state talk referents. For overall mental-state talk, the within-subject effect of the referent type was significant (F (3, 216) = 385.59, $p < .01$, partial $\eta^2 = .84$). The within-subject comparison shows that the Child referent was used most frequently, followed by the Educator, with Joint and Other referents used least frequently.

While the between-subject effect of culture was not significant (F (1, 72) = 0.23, $p = .64$, partial $\eta^2 = .00$), there was a significant interaction effect between referent type x culture (F (3, 216) = 22.69, $p < .01$, partial $\eta^2 = .24$) (Figure 2). The post-hoc univariate analyses show that Chinese educators used the Child referent significantly more than Australian educators (F (1, 72) = 33.37, $p < .01$, partial $\eta^2 = .32$) and used the Educator (F (1, 72) = 9.18, $p < .01$, partial $\eta^2 = .11$), the Other (F (1, 72) = 24.76, $p < .01$, partial $\eta^2 = .26$), and the Joint (F (1, 72) = 24.76, $p < .01$, partial $\eta^2 = .26$) significantly less often.

For desire talk, the within-subject effect (F (3, 216) = 273.71, $p < .01$, partial $\eta^2 = .79$), the between-subject effect (F (1, 72) = 19.51, $p < .01$, partial $\eta^2 = .21$), and the interaction effect (F (3, 216) = 10.97, $p < .01$, partial $\eta^2 = .13$) were all significant. The post-hoc pairwise comparison for the within-subject effect show that, consistent across the two cultures, educators attributed desires to the Child the most, followed by Educator and Other, which did not differ. Joint referent was used the least. As to the between-subject effect of culture, Australian and Chinese educators only differed in the Child

Table 4. Descriptive statistics of the proportions of the mental-state talk referents.

variables (all figures are in %)	English (n = 44)		Chinese (n = 30)		Total (n = 74)	
	M	SD	M	SD	M	SD
overall_Child	61.24	16.30	83.78	16.76	70.38	19.80
overall _Educator	18.84	14.37	9.04	12.56	14.87	14.42
overall _Joint	12.21	10.37	2.37	3.71	8.22	9.61
overall_Other	8.36	5.94	4.81	7.06	6.92	6.61
desire_Child	37.67	17.11	55.68	23.89	44.97	21.88
desire_Educator	2.78	6.64	4.27	7.24	3.39	6.88
desire_Joint	0.86	1.35	0.96	2.40	0.90	1.83
desire_Other	2.85	2.98	2.24	4.18	2.60	3.50
emotion_Child	1.26	2.44	3.60	6.76	2.21	4.79
emotion_Educator	0.22	0.76	1.11	3.95	0.58	2.60
emotion_Joint	0.09	0.39	0.13	0.70	0.11	0.53
emotion_Other	0.97	1.78	0.62	2.01	0.83	1.87
perception_Child	13.48	9.45	8.54	8.01	11.47	9.16
perception_Educator	3.48	3.90	1.33	3.95	2.61	4.04
perception_Joint	2.83	5.27	0.13	0.70	1.74	4.28
perception_Other	1.51	2.40	0.00	0.00	0.89	1.99
cognition_Child	7.02	5.11	12.86	11.86	9.39	8.92
cognition_Educator	10.24	7.49	1.50	3.55	6.70	7.53
cognition_Joint	0.93	3.17	0.83	2.15	0.89	2.79
cognition_Other	1.29	2.00	1.46	3.23	1.36	2.55
modulation_Child	1.82	2.67	3.11	5.33	2.34	3.99
modulation_Educator	2.12	2.51	0.82	3.72	1.59	3.10
modulation_Joint	7.50	6.99	0.33	1.83	4.59	6.53
modulation_Other	1.74	2.38	0.49	1.55	1.23	2.16

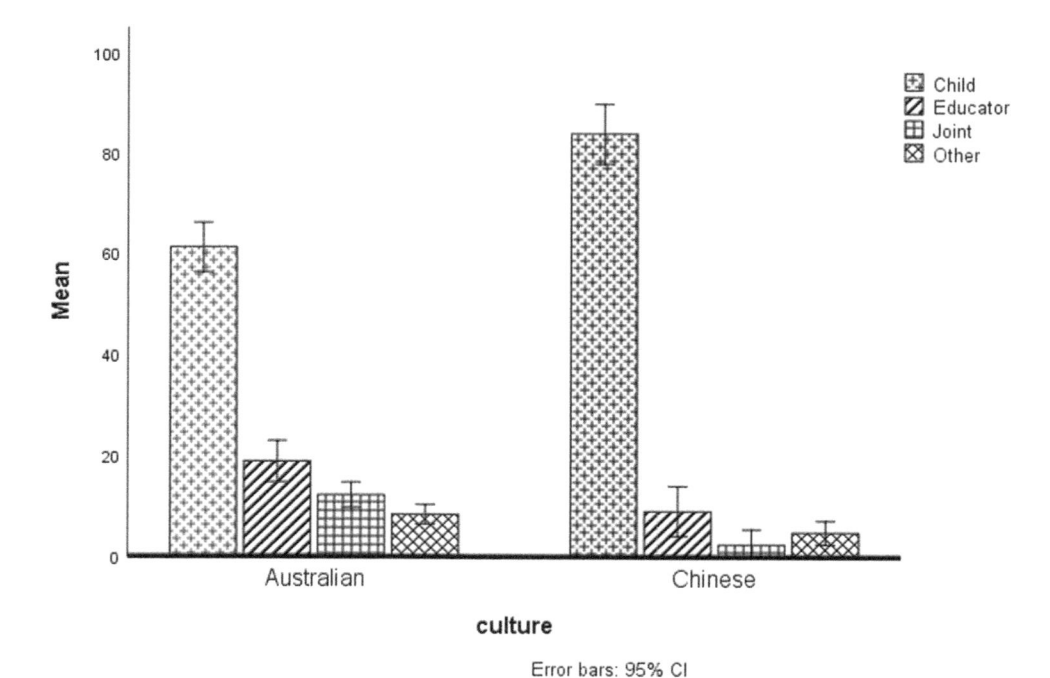

Figure 2. Proportions of referents used for overall mental-state talk by referent type x culture.

referent: (F (1, 72) = 14.30, $p < .01$, partial $\eta^2 = .17$), with Chinese educators using a significantly higher proportion than their Australian counterparts.

To examine the interaction effect (Figure 3), separate repeated ANOVAs were performed for Chinese and Australian educators. While Chinese educators used Child most frequently, the differences between Educator and Other, and between Joint and Other were not significant. Educator was found to be higher than Joint. However, for Australian educators, there was no difference between Educator and Joint. Australian educators used Other significantly more than Joint.

For emotion talk, the within-subject effect of the referent type (F (3, 216) = 9.89, $p < .01$, partial $\eta^2 = .12$), and the interaction effect (F (3, 216) = 3.51, $p < .05$, partial $\eta^2 = .05$) were significant. But the between-subject effect of culture was non-significant (F (1, 72) = 3.50, $p = .07$, partial $\eta^2 = .05$). The post-hoc pairwise comparison for the within-subject effect shows that the educators attributed emotions most frequently to the Child, followed by Other, which was higher than Joint. There were no significant differences either between Educator and Joint referents, or between Educator and Other referents.

For the interaction effect (Figure 4), the repeated ANOVA for Australian educators showed a similar use of Child and Other referents, both of which were used more frequently than Educator and Joint. In contrast, the Chinese educators' use of Child was significantly higher than Joint and Other, which were used equally. No pairwise differences between Educator and all the other three referent types.

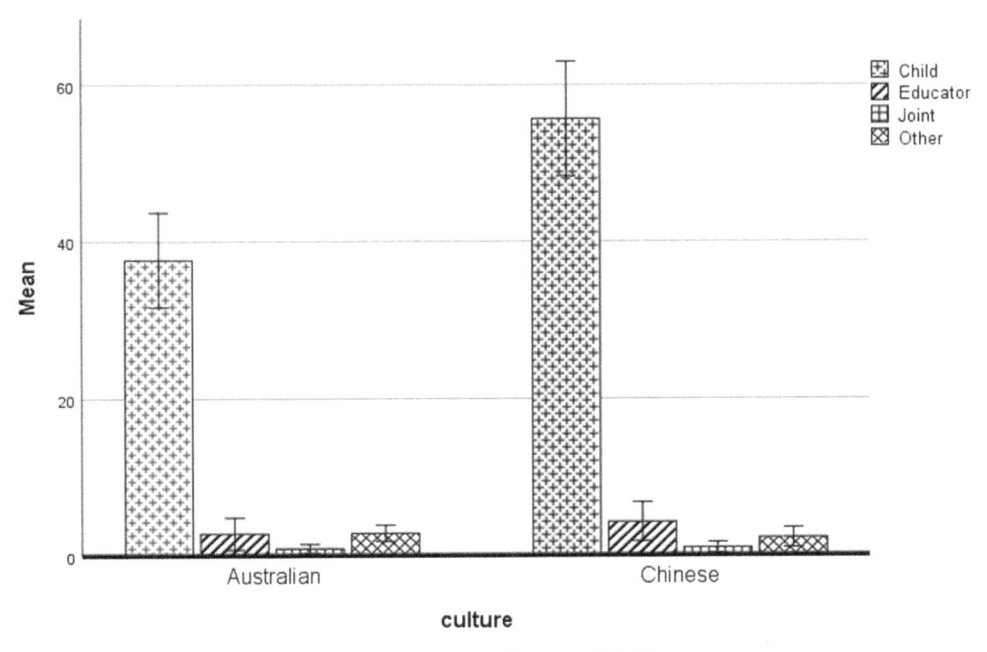

Figure 3. Proportions of referents used for desire talk referent type x culture.

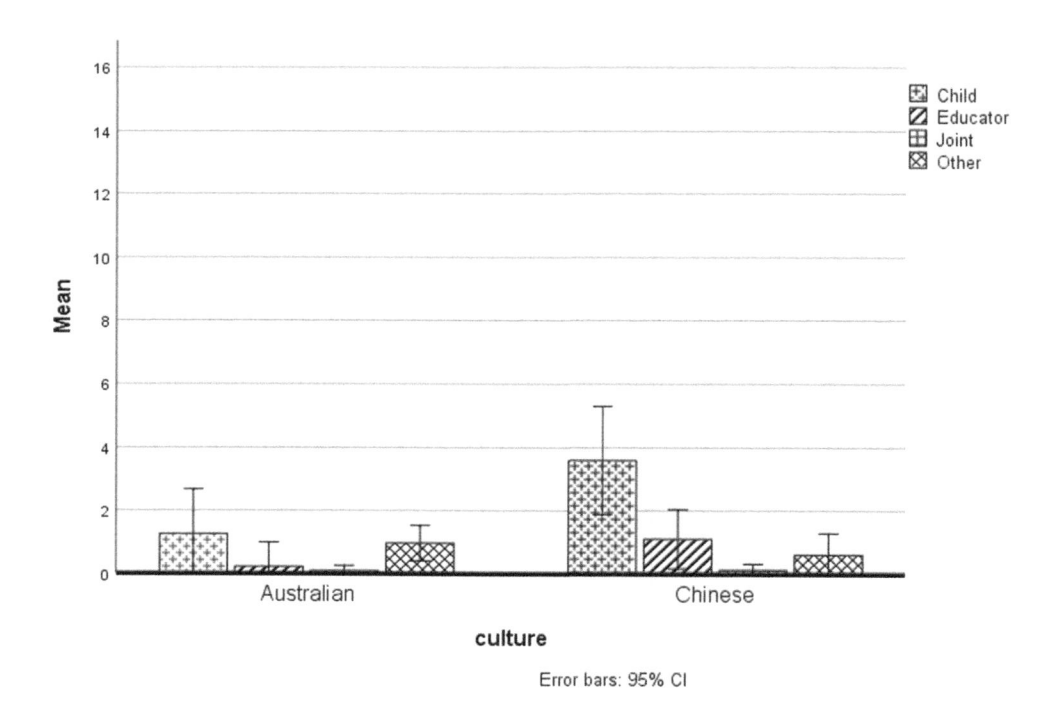

Error bars: 95% CI

Figure 4. Proportions of referents used for emotion talk by referent type x culture.

For perception talk, the effects of referent type (F (3, 216) = 58.86, $p < .01$, partial $\eta^2 = .45$) and culture (F (1, 72) = 17.96, $p < .01$, partial $\eta^2 = .20$) were significant, but the interaction (F (3, 216) = 1.43, $p = .23$, partial $\eta^2 = .02$) was not. The within-subject pairwise comparison shows that the educators ascribed perceptions to the Child the most, followed by Educator and Other. There were no significant differences between the Educator and Joint referents, or between Joint and Other referents. For the between-subject effect of the culture, Australian educators used each referent type significantly more than Chinese educators: Child (F (1, 72) = 5.50, $p < .05$, partial $\eta^2 = .07$), Educator (F (1, 72) = 5.35, $p < .05$, partial $\eta^2 = .07$), Joint (F (1, 72) = 7.79, $p < .01$, partial $\eta^2 = .10$), and Other (F (1, 72) = 11.73, $p < .01$, partial $\eta^2 = .14$).

For cognition talk, there was a significant effect of referent type (F (3, 216) = 47.27, $p < .01$, partial $\eta^2 = .40$), and an interaction effect (F (3, 216) = 23.59, $p < .01$, partial $\eta^2 = .25$). But the between-subject effect of culture was not significant (F (1, 72) = 0.83, $p = .37$, partial $\eta^2 = .01$). We performed repeated ANOVAs for Australian and Chinese educators separately to explicate the interaction effect (Figure 5). Australian educators used Educator most, followed by Child, which were then followed equally by Joint and Other referents. In contrast, Chinese educators used the Child referent the most, and rarely used the other three referent types (Educator, Joint and Other), which did not significantly differ from each other.

Finally, with regard to the referents of modulations of assertion, there were significant effects of referent type (F (3, 216) = 8.28, $p < .01$, partial $\eta^2 = .10$), culture (F (1, 72) = 16.42, $p < .01$, partial $\eta^2 = .19$), and the interaction (F (3, 216) = 16.92, $p < .01$, partial

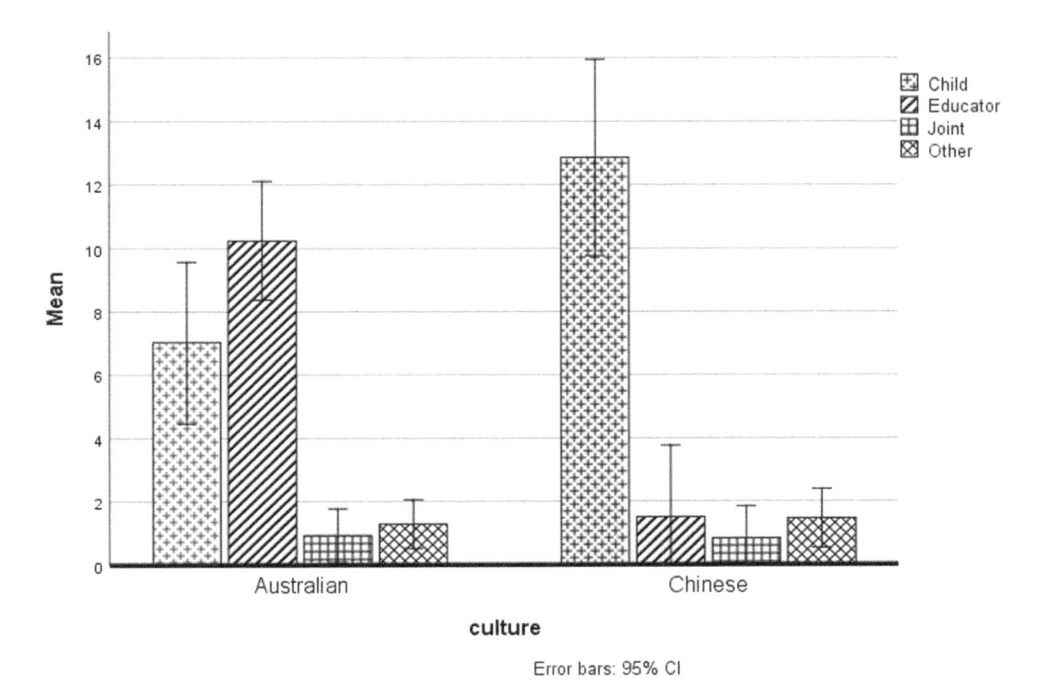

Error bars: 95% CI

Figure 5. Proportions of the referents used for cognition talk by referent type x culture.

$\eta^2 = .19$). For this mental-state talk type, while Joint had a higher proportion than both Educator and Other referents, there was no significant pairwise difference between Joint and Child. Neither were there significant pairwise differences between Child and Educator referents and between Educator and Other referents. Australian and Chinese educators differed only in their use of Joint (F (1, 72) = 29.99, $p < .01$, partial $\eta^2 = .29$) and Other (F (1, 72) = 6.40, $p < .05$, partial $\eta^2 = .08$) referents. The interaction effect (Figure 6) demonstrates that Joint was used most frequently by English educators, whereas Chinese educators most often ascribed modulations of assertion to the Child.

Discussion

This study is the first to compare the frequency of mental-state talk used by native English-speaking Australian and native Mandarin-speaking Chinese infant educators. Our findings concurred with those of other infant-educator studies (Degotardi and Sweller 2012; Farkas et al. 2017) to indicate that, regardless of cultural context, desire talk was the most frequently used mental-state talk type. Analyses of mothers talk to has also been found to privilege desire talk to infants while increasing the use of cognitive terms as children age (Cheng et al. 2020; Taumoepeau and Ruffman 2006; Degotardi and Torr 2007). Similarly, educators of older children have been found to preference talk about cognitions (Colonnesi et al. 2017). Together, these findings suggest that both Australian and Chinese educators and parents may respond linguistically to the developmental attributes of children by placing increasing emphasis on cognitive states and processes as children grow older.

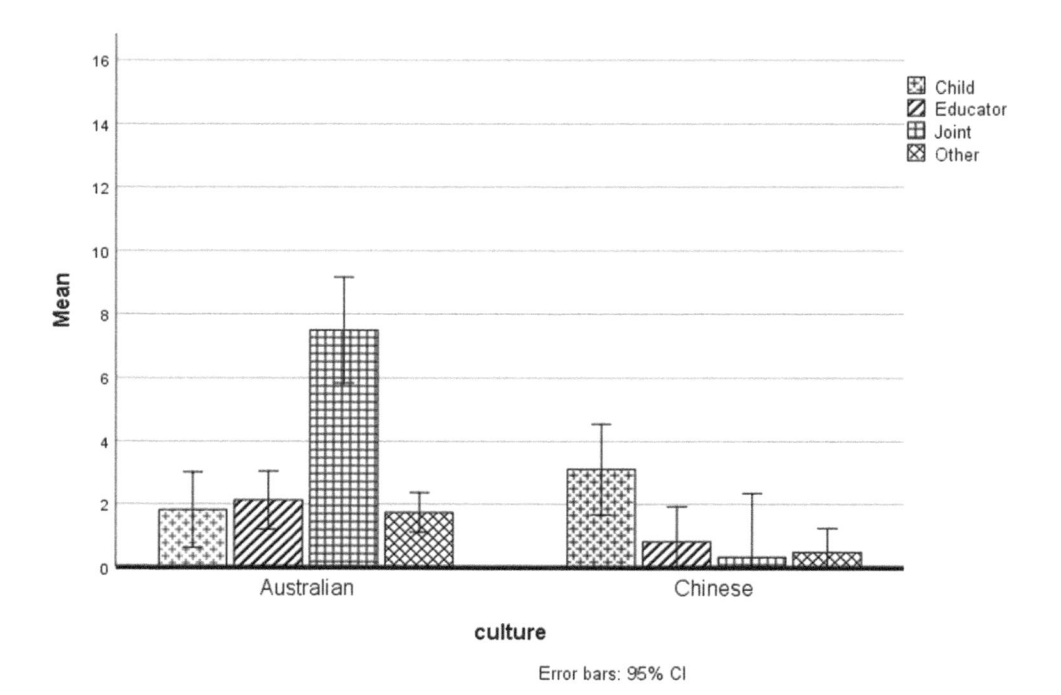

Figure 6. Proportions of referents used for modulation of assertion talk by referent type x culture.

Important differences in mental-state talk were also detected. Like family-based studies (Doan and Wang 2010; Dai, McMahon, and Lim 2020), we found that Chinese educators used significantly less mental-state talk than Australian educators. With the exception of emotion terms, the Australian cohort used all mental-state talk types significantly more frequently than their Chinese counterparts. The patterns of use also differed between cohorts. While both cohorts favoured desire talk, this talk made up nearly 65% of Chinese educators' mental-state talk with cognitive talk the next frequent (17%) and all other categories occurring infrequently. In contrast, Australian educators' desire talk comprised around 42% of their mental-state talk, with the remaining 58% largely made up of cognition talk and perception talk (20% each) and modulation of assertion talk (14%). Such differences may reflect cultural differences in emphases during adult–child interactions. A Western emphasis on subjective experiences and perspectives may be reflected in the Australian educators' incorporation of perception, cognition and modulation of assertion talk, while a Chinese motivation to use language to guide actions and social connectedness may result in their predominant use of desire talk (Luo, Tamis Le Monda, and Song 2013; Cheng et al. 2020).

This study is also one of the first to examine the referents that educators assigned to mental-state talk. Consistent with previous ECEC studies (King and La Paro 2015; Barnes and Dickenson 2018), we found that both cohorts predominantly used the Child referent, with educators ascribing desires, emotions and perceptions most often to the child. As young children start to develop an understanding of these three mental states during infancy, it may well be that educators are scaffolding this understanding by helping infants to make connection between these mental-state terms and their direct motivational, emotional or perceptual experience (Barnes and Dickenson 2018).

Cultural differences were also apparent. When compared with Australian educators, the Chinese educators were more likely to use the Child referent for all talk types. Most strikingly, while Chinese educators almost exclusively ascribed cognitions to the child, Australian educators used cognition talk to refer to their own and the child's cognitive states. For example, Chinese educators used phrases such as 'Think about it, put one of your feet in first' (想想看, 先放一只脚进去) or 'Did you forget our tissue paper?' (你是不是忘了我们的餐巾纸?), while Australian educators used phrases such as 'I think this one is pink' and 'I wonder where your shoes are' in addition to ascribing cognitions to child. Australian educators were also significantly more likely to use the Joint (e.g. *We forgot to do that, didn't we?*) and Other referents (e.g. *He thinks it's funny*) than Chinese educators. The more frequent inclusion of the Educator, Joint and Other referents by Australian educators could possibly reflect a Western focus on individual subjectivity as both the child's and others' perspectives are emphasised. The Chinese educators' predominant use of the Child referent may suggest a more direct and didactic interaction style, which emphasises information transmission and academic achievement (Doan and Wang 2010; Luo, Tamis Le Monda, and Song 2013).

Finally, Australian educators predominantly used the Joint referent 'we' when using modulation of assertion terms. In the context of giving directions to young children, the Joint referent is argued to introduce a tone of negotiation (Hu et al. 2019), so it is possible that Australian educators adopt a similar tone to emphasise the perspectival nature of modulation of assertion talk to infants. The inclusion of Joint referent was unique to our study, and the finding that over 16% of mental-state terms were assigned to a Joint referent suggests that this referent type should not be overlooked as an important pedagogical discourse feature in future research.

Limitations, future directions and implications

This study illustrated several significant differences in Australian and Chinese educators' use of mental-state talk during their interactions with infants. While demonstrating how language use cannot be separated from the cultural contexts in which it occurs, several considerations need to be kept in mind in order to avoid simplistic West–East dichotomies. First, the study methodology involved replicating, as closely as possible, the observations method used in the Australian study. Although both cohorts were observed during play, it is acknowledged that cultural differences not only occur in the ways that adults talk to infants, but also in the play styles that are promoted in Western and Chinese contexts (Bornstein and Cheah 2006). While independent-oriented Western approaches to play in both ECEC and home contexts emphasise child individuality, self-direction and expression, Chinese approaches tend to be more teacher-directed, structured and academically focussed (Liu et al. 2005; Rao, Ng, and Pearson 2009). With mental-state talk associated with the degree to which autonomy and individual agency is promoted during play (Degotardi 2013), it may be that the talk differences reported in this study are partially the product of different play styles rather than solely attributed to cultural linguistic differences. As play in Western cultures can also range from free to structured play (Edwards 2017), future studies are needed to examine how mental state talk is supported or constrained by qualitatively different play styles.

It should also be noted that the coding scheme used in this study was derived from those developed in English-speaking countries. This raises the question of whether the differences detected in this study resulted from the different linguistic encoding of mental states in the two languages. For example, the relative absence of modulation of assertion talk in the Chinese cohort may be a result of cultural differences in how individual perspectives are acknowledged in different languages. While English speakers explicitly modulate assertion by using modal verbs and adjuncts such as 'may', 'could', and probably' (Degotardi and Torr 2007), Chinese speakers do so less frequently. Instead, the phrase '好不好' (Is that OK?) is frequently used to indirectly suggest possibility to young children. Also noted by Dai, McMahon, and Lim (2020), this raises questions about how best to capture and code mental-state talk in different languages and cultures.

With its aim of determining differences between the two cultural cohorts, our study has not addressed the question of individual differences. Existing ECEC mental-state talk research has determined relationships between educators' mental-state talk and their qualification level (Farkas et al. 2017), years of experience (King and La Paro 2015), and the activity context of the interaction (Barnes and Dickenson 2018). While the present study is the first to report broadly on the prevalence of mental-state talk in a Chinese-speaking cohort, future research is needed to explore factors related to individual differences.

With the above cautions in mind, our findings provide a first glimpse of how children are socialised into an understanding of the mind in culturally specific ways by their early childhood educators in Australia and China. Our findings, as well as those showing cultural differences in home contexts (Cheng et al. 2020; Dai, McMahon, and Lim 2020; Doan and Wang 2010), caution against a universal approach to understanding how adults talk to infants about the mind. Findings also have implications for understanding different cultural developmental trajectories in children's understandings of the mind, such as why English-speaking children develop an understanding of subjective beliefs earlier than knowledge and ignorance, whereas the opposite developmental pattern is evident in Chinese children (Wellman et al. 2006). With increasing numbers of young children worldwide growing up in multilingual households (Langeloo et al. 2021; Verdon, McLeod, and Winsler 2014) findings also have implications for educators who have children from different language backgrounds than the majority language in their centres. With a clearer understanding of how children's home language experiences may be shaping their identities as thinkers and knowers, educators are better placed to work in partnership with parents to ensure that all children in their centres develop and use mental-state language in ways that will both enhance their cultural identify and support their learning.

Note

1. In this research, we adopt the term 'educator' to refer to any early childhood practitioner who works directly with children in ECEC settings, regardless of their qualification level.

Acknowledgements

We acknowledge the contributions of the educators, infants and research assistances who collaborated with us on this project.

Disclosure statement

No potential conflict of interest was reported by the author(s).

Funding

This work was funded by a Macquarie University Australia-China mobility scholarship.

Data availability statement

The de-identified quantitative dataset is held by the corresponding author and can be made available on reasonable request. The data supporting the findings of this study are available within the article.

ORCID

Sheila Degotardi ⓘ http://orcid.org/0000-0003-2066-2223
Feifei Han ⓘ http://orcid.org/0000-0001-8464-0854
Jiangbo Hu ⓘ http://orcid.org/0000-0001-5471-7689

References

Barnes, Erica M., and David K. Dickenson. 2018. "Relationships Among Teachers' Use of Mental State Verbs and Children's Vocabulary Growth." *Early Education & Development* 29 (3): 307–323. doi:10.1080/10409289.2018.1440844.

Bernier, Annie, and Mary Dozier. 2003. "Bridging the Attachment Transmission Gap: The Role of Maternal Mind-Mindedness." *International Journal of Behavioral Development* 27 (4): 355–366. doi:10.1080/01650250244000399.

Bornstein, Marc H., and Charissa S. L. Cheah. 2006. "The Place of "Culture and Parenting" in the Ecological Contextual Perspective on Developmental Science." In *Parenting Beliefs, Behaviors, and Parent-Child Relations*, edited by Kenneth H. Rubin, and Ock Boon Chung, 3–33. New York: Psychology Press.

Bretherton, Inge, and Marjorie Beeghly-Smith. 1982. "Talking About Internal States: The Acquisition of an Explicit Theory of Mind." *Developmental Psychology* 18 (6): 906–921. doi:10.1037/0012-1649.18.6.906.

Cheng, Michelle, Peipei Setoh, Marc H. Bornstein, and Gianluca Esposit. 2020. "She Thinks in English, But She Wants in Mandarin: Differences in Singaporean Bilingual English-Mandarin Maternal Mental State Talk." *Behavioral Sciences* 10 (7): 106–117. doi:10.3390/bs10070106.

Colonnesi, Cristina, Marleen van Polanen, Louis W. C. Tavecchio, and Ruben G. Fukkink. 2017. "Mind-mindedness of Male and Female Caregivers in Childcare and the Relation to Sensitivity and Attachment: An Exploratory Study." *Infant Behavior and Development* 48 (Pt B): 134–146. doi:10.1016/j.infbeh.2017.04.006.

Dai, Quian, Catherine McMahon, and Ai Keow Lim. 2020. "Cross-cultural Comparison of Maternal Mind-Mindedness Among Australian and Chines Mothers." *International Journal of Behavioural Development* 44 (4): 365–370. doi:10.1177/0165025419874133.

Degotardi, Sheila. 2013. ""I Think, I Can": Acknowledging and Promoting Agency During Educator-infant Play." In *Varied Perspectives on Play and Learning: Theory and Research on*

Early Years Education, edited by Ole Fredrik Lillemyr, Sue Dockett, and Bob Perry, 75–90. Charlotte, NC: Information Age Publishing.

Degotardi, Sheila. 2015. "Mind Mindedness: Forms, Features and Implications for Infant-toddler Pedagogy." In *Routledge International Handbook of Young Children's Thinking*, edited by S. Robson, and S. Flannery Quinn, 179–188. London: Routledge.

Degotardi, Sheila, and Naomi Sweller. 2012. "Mind-mindedness in Infant Child-Care: Associations with Early Childhood Practitioner Sensitivity and Stimulation." *Early Childhood Research Quarterly* 27: 253–265. doi:10.1016/j.ecresq.2011.09.002.

Degotardi, Sheila, and Jane Torr. 2007. "A Longitudinal Investigation of Mothers' Mind-related Talk to their 12- to 24-month-old Infants." *Early Child Development and Care* 177 (6 & 7): 767–780. doi:10.1080/03004430701379280.

Doan, Stacey N, and Qi Wang. 2010. "Maternal Discussion of Mental States and Behaviors: Relations to Emotion Situation Knowledge in European American and Immigrant Chinese Children." *Child Development* 81 (5): 1490–1503. doi:10.1111/j.1467-8624.2010.01487.x.

Edwards, Susan. 2017. "Play-based Learning and Intentional Teaching: Forever Different?" *Australasian Journal of Early Childhood* 42 (2): 4–11. doi:10.23965/AJEC.42.2.01.

Farkas, Chamarrita, Katherine Strasser, Maria Gabriela Badilla, and Maria Pia Santelices. 2017. "Mentalization in Chilean Educational Staff with 12-month-old Children: Does it Make a Difference in Relation to What Children Receive at Home?" *Early Education & Development* 28 (7): 839–857. doi:10.1080/10409289.2017.1287994.

Frampton, Kristen L, Michal Perlman, and Jennifer M Jenkins. 2009. "Caregivers' Use of Metacognitive Language in Child Care Centres: Prevalence and Predictors." *Early Childhood Research Quarterly* 24 (3): 248–262. doi:10.1016/j.ecresq.2009.04.004.

Fujita, Nao, and Claire Hughes. 2020. "Mind-mindedness and self-other distinction: Contrasts between Japanese and British mothers' speech samples." *Social Development* 1–16.

Grazzani, Ilaria, Veronica Ornaghi, and Jens Brockmeier. 2016. "Conversation on Mental States at Nursery: Promoting Social Cognition in Early Childhood." *European Journal of Psychology* 13 (5): 563–581. doi:10.1080/17405629.2015.1127803.

Hasan, Raqaiya. 1996. "Semantic Networks: A Tool for the Analysis of Meaning." In *Ways of Saying, Ways of Meaning. Selected Papers of Ruqaiya Hasan*, edited by C. Cloran, D. Butt, and G. Williams, 104–131. London: Cassell.

Helmerhorst, Katrien O. W., Cristina Colonnesi, and Ruben G Fukkink. 2019. "Caregiver's Mind-mindedness in Early Centre-based Childcare." *Early Education & Development* 30 (7): 754–871. doi:10.1080/10409289.2019.1593076.

Hu, Jiangbo, Sheila Degotardi, Jane Torr, and Feifei Han. 2019. "Reasoning as a Pedagogical Strategy in Infant-Addressed Talk in Early Childhood Education Centres: Relationships with Educators' Qualifications and Communicative Function." *Early Education and Development* 30 (7): 872–886. doi:10.1080/10409289.2019.1607449.

Hughes, Clare, and Judy Dunn. 1998. "Understanding Mind and Emotion: Longitudinal Associations with Mental-state Talk Between Young Friends." *Developmental Psychology* 34 (5): 1026–1037.

Kagitcibasi, Cigdem. 2007. *Family, Self and Human Development Across Cultures: Theory and Applications*. 2nd ed. Mahwah, NJ: Lawrence Erlbaum.

King, Elizabeth, and Karen La Paro. 2015. "Teachers' Language Interactions: An Exploratory Examination of Mental State Talk in Early Childhood Education Classrooms." *Early Education & Development* 26 (2): 245–263. doi:10.1080/10409289.2015.989029.

Langeloo, Annegien, Mayra Mascareno Lara, Marjolein I. Deunk, Jennifer LoCasale-Crouch, and Jan-Willem Strijbos. 2021. "Profiles of Learning Opportunities of Multilingual and Monolingual Children in Kindergarten." *European Journal of Psychology in Education* 36: 379–404. doi:10.1007/s10212-020-00487-0.

Laranjo, Jessica, Annie Bernier, and Elizabeth Meins. 2008. "Associations Between Maternal Mind-mindedness and Infant Attachment Security: Investigating the Mediating Role of Maternal Sensitivity." *Infant Behavior & Development* 31 (4): 688–695. doi:10.1016/j.infbeh.2008.04.008.

Li, Weilin, George Farkas, Greg Duncan, Margaret R Burchinal, and Deborah Vandell. 2013. "Timing of High Quality Child Care and Cognitive, Language, and Preacademic Development." *Developmental Psychology* 49 (8): 1440–1451. doi:10.1037/a0030613.

Liu, Mowei, Xinyin Chen, Kenneth H. Rubin, Shujie Zheng, Liying Cui, Dan Li, Huchang Chen, and Li Wang. 2005. "Autonomy- vs. Connectedness-oriented Parenting Behaviours in Chinese and Canadian Mothers." *International Journal of Behavioral Development* 29 (6): 489–495. doi:10.1080/01650250250500147063.

Luo, Rufan, Catherine S. Tamis Le Monda, and Lulu Song. 2013. "Chinese Parents' Goals and Practices in Early Childhood." *Early Childhood Research Quarterly* 28: 843–857. doi:10.1016/j.ecresq.2013.08.001.

Markus, Hazel R, and Shinobu Kitayama. 1991. "Culture and the Self: Implications for Cognition, Emotion, and Motivation." *Psychological Review* 98 (2): 224–253.

McHugh, Mary L. 2012. "Interrater Reliability: The Kappa Statistic." *Biochemia Medica* 22: 276–282.

Meins, Elizabeth, Charles Fernyhough, Emma Fradley, and Michelle Tuckey. 2001. "Rethinking Maternal Sensitivity: Mothers' Comments on Infants' Mental Processes Predict Security of Attachment at 12 Months." *Journal of Child Psychology & Psychiatry & Allied Disciplines* 42 (5): 637–648. doi:10.1111/1469-7610.00759.

Meins, Elizabeth, Charles Fernyhough, Rachel Wainwright, David Clark-Carter, Mani Das Gupta, Emma Fradley, and Michelle Tuckey. 2003. "Pathways to Understanding Mind: Construct Validity and Predictive Validity of Maternal Mind-Mindedness." *Child Development* 74 (4): 1194–1211. doi:10.1111/1467-8624.00601.

Misailidi, Plousia, Depsina Papoudi, and Andreas Brouzos. 2013. "Mind What Teachers Say: Kindergarten Teachers' Use of Mental State Language During Picture Story Narration." *Early Education and Development* 24 (8): 1161–1174. doi:10.1080/10409289.2013.765787.

National Institute of Child Health and Human Development Early Child Care Research Network. 2002. "Early Child Care and Children's Development Prior to School Entry: Results from the NICHD Study of Early Child Care." *American Educational Research Journal* 39 (1): 133–164. doi:10.3102/00028312039001133.

Rao, Nirmala, Sharon S. N. Ng, and Emma Pearson. 2009. "Preschool Pedagogy: A Fusion of Traditional Chinese Beliefs and Contemporary Notions of Appropriate Practice." In *Revisiting the Chinese Learner*, edited by C. Chan, and N. Rao, 255–279. Dordrecht: Springer.

Ruffman, Ted, Lance Slade, and Elena Crowe. 2002. "The Relation Between Children's and Mother's Mental State Language and Theory-of-mind Understanding." *Child Development* 73 (3): 734–751.

Symonds, Douglas K, Kristen-Lee M Fossum, and T. B. Kate Collins. 2006. "A Longitudinal Study of Belief and Desire State Discourse During Mother–Child Play and Later False Belief Understanding." *Social Development* 15 (4): 676–691. doi:10.1111/j.1467-9507.2006.00364.x.

Taumoepeau, Mele. 2015. "From Talk to Though: Strength of Ethnic Identity and Caregiver Mental State Talk Predict Social Understanding in Preschoolers." *Journal of Cross Cultural Psychology* 46 (9): 1169–1119. doi:10.1177/0022022115604393.

Taumoepeau, Mele, and Ted Ruffman. 2006. "Mother and Infant Talk About Mental State Relates to Desire Language and Emotion Understanding." *Child Development* 77 (2): 465–481. doi:10.1111/j.1467-8624.2006.00882.x.

Verdon, Sarah, Sharynne McLeod, and Adam Winsler. 2014. "Linguistic Diversity among Australian Children in the First 5 Years of Life." *Speech, Language and Hearing* 17 (4): 196–203. doi:10.1179/2050572814Y.0000000038.

Wellman, Henry M, Fuxi Fang, David Liu, and Guoxing Liu. 2006. "Scaling of Theory-of-mind Understandings in Chinese Children." *Psychological Science* 17 (12): 1075–1081. doi:10.1111/j.1467-9280.2006.01830.x.

Yazejian, Noreen, Donna M. Bryant, Sydney Hans, Diane Horm, Lisa St Clair, Nancy File, and Margaret Burchinal. 2017. "Child and Parenting Outcomes After 1 Year of Educare." *Child Development*, doi:10.1111/cdev.12688.

Viewing young children's drawing, talking, and writing through a 'language as context' lens: implications for literacy assessment

Shelley Stagg Peterson ⓘ and Nicola Friedrich ⓘ

ABSTRACT
We report on our analysis of talk during an assessment task where we asked children living in northern Canadian communities to draw and write about activities they share with family and friends in their daily lives. We introduce a language as context approach to assessing young children's (ages 4–6 years) literacy and sociocultural knowledge, defining context as understandings of the demands of creating texts through drawing and writing, the genre of classroom assessment, and the values and worldviews of their local community and family. From our inductive analysis of children's ($n = 64$) talk during the assessment tasks in the fall and spring of one school year ($n = 128$), we conceptualise relationships between children's oral language strategies and their understandings of the conventions of an adult-initiated, one-on-one classroom assessment, their strategies for carrying out the task, and of social meanings in everyday experiences with family and friends in their northern communities. We argue this form of assessment provides a comprehensive picture of children's meaning-making that encompasses social and cultural practices of a diversity of contexts, including school and community.

Introduction

Young children communicate meanings to others through the texts they create, using whatever tools they have at hand. To convey meaning through texts, children scribble, draw, make marks and letter-like forms, as well as print letters and words. Regardless of form, these texts are viewed as early writing because children intentionally use them as symbolic tools to achieve particular social purposes (Anning 1997; Kress 1997).

In the process of creating these texts, children construct understandings and hypotheses about print. They demonstrate knowledge of a foundational literacy principle – that graphic symbols communicate meaning and are used to carry out social purposes (Clay 1998; Vygotsky 1978). They also learn about social expectations for using written texts, such as the types of information being conveyed, the arrangement of text and images, and the signaling of intended relationships between author and audience (Kenner 2000), and that the social context and ways in which creators and readers/viewers of texts are positioned influence the perceived value of texts (Rowe 2008). The knowledge and skills developed through young children's early writing experiences provide a foundation for their overall literacy development and their later school achievement (e.g. Bourke et al. 2014; Clay 1998; Cutler and Graham 2008; Hall et al. 2015).

Building on this research, the purpose of this paper is to identify and describe children's oral language strategies and sociocultural understandings within an adult-initiated task in which researchers invited young children to draw and write about a personal experience. Our goal is to introduce what we and others in this special issue call a *language as context* approach to assessing young children's foundational literacy experiences. Our use of such an approach is apparent in the varied modes of communication (e.g. drawing, talking, writing) children take up within the one-on-one assessment context, in our consideration of the social situation and the accompanying social expectations for the texts that are assessed (Genishi and Dyson 2009), as well as our consideration of children's use of their lived experiences and background knowledge to create texts for assessment purposes (Yoon 2015). We are particularly interested in determining opportunities of this particular assessment for classroom teachers. The following questions guided our research:

(1) What oral language strategies do children and researchers use while carrying out an adult-initiated task involving drawing and writing?
(2) What sociocultural understandings are reflected in children's and researchers' talk regarding task demands and the one-on-one assessment context?

Given our focus on oral language strategies and sociocultural knowledge demonstrated in the talk, drawing, and writing of young children, we review relevant research on mediational roles of talk in children's drawing and writing, and on adults' roles in assessing early writing. After detailing our research methods, we present our analysis of interactions between one child and a researcher in a one-on-one assessment setting to contextualise our subsequent description of oral strategies and sociocultural knowledge demonstrated across the sample of young children and researchers.

Children's talk as a mediator of their drawing and writing

Viewed through a sociocultural lens (Vygotsky 1978), young children's talk serves a mediational function, guiding and assisting them in resolving problems in their drawing (Brooks 2017; Coates 2002; Frisch 2006) and in their writing (Parr, Jesson, and McNaughton 2009). Talk gives form to inchoate thoughts, bringing them to a conscious level (Vygotsky 1978). In the process, talk helps children clarify ideas, with the possibility of deepening and/or modifying understandings and perspectives (Myhill and Jones 2009).

Talk is especially important for more cognitively demanding tasks, such as creating texts. Through the use of language, children have access to the cultural knowledge of their society regarding text forms and designs, processes for creating texts, ways to get assistance in text creation, and audience expectations for particular texts. Children can employ the cultural knowledge to determine actions they might take to create texts that achieve intended social purposes, monitor the effectiveness of their actions, and generate alternatives when desired outcomes of actions are not achieved (Jesson, Fontich, and Myhill 2016; Myhill and Jones 2009).

Young children engage in self-talk to evaluate and manage their writing efforts (Dahl 1993), to spell individual words (Aram, Abiri, and Elad 2014), and to plan and monitor their storytelling while dictating to an adult (e.g. Fang and Cox 1999). In their review of the mediational role of talk on young children's writing, Parr, Jesson, and McNaughton (2009) propose that children's self-talk changes in relation to where they are in the writing process. Before writing, young writers use oral language to formulate a plan and rehearse what they intend to write. While writing, they use talk to problem solve and rehearse as they spell individual words, and say the completed text out loud in order to hear the language. Their use of oral language after writing allows them to evaluate their texts semantically and syntactically.

Assessment of young children's drawing and writing

Research on assessment of early writing has primarily involved assigning scores based on inferences about children's print-related knowledge reflected in their written symbols (e.g. Mackenzie, Scull, and Munsie 2013; Rowe and Wilson 2015). While recognising wide variation in children's writing development, researchers analyzed dictated messages and words to determine developmental patterns that progress from scribble marks to writing-like lines and shapes to conventional print symbols (Clay 1998; Molfese et al. 2011; Ouellette, Sénéchal, and Haley 2013; Puranik and Lonigan 2011) and spelling stages that reflect children's orthographic knowledge (Bear et al. 2012).

Researchers also made inferences about children's print knowledge (e.g. right-to-left and top-to-bottom directionality on the page, the assignment of meaning to graphic symbols, and the match between the task and content of the graphic text) as reflected in texts with print and images that were created for research purposes (Mackenzie, Scull, and Munsie 2013; Rowe and Wilson 2015). Researchers' formal prompts were designed to elicit texts that aligned more closely with daily classroom literacy practices. These texts included images with captions and writing in response to an open-ended prompt. Developmental patterns were identified as an outcome of researchers' analysis of the texts.

To sum up, although research has demonstrated how children's talk mediates their drawing and writing, early literacy researchers have inferred children's print-related knowledge by assigning scores to texts children create in response to researchers' formal prompts. Based on an assumption that teaching should be informed by information gathered through authentic assessments of children's learning (Heritage and Harrison 2019; Wiliam 2011), in this paper, we focus on what children show about their literacy learning in their talk before, during, and after engaging in researcher-initiated, drawing, talking, and writing tasks, providing implications for teaching practice.

Materials and methods

Participants and contexts

Data for this study were drawn from the Northern Oral Language and Writing through Play (NOW Play) project, a six-year collaborative action research project in which kindergarten and grade one teachers and we university researchers worked together to design, implement, and refine tools and practices for assessing and supporting the oral and written language development of young (ages 4–6 years) children. Participating teachers and the children in their kindergarten and grade one classes live in remote northern Indigenous and non-Indigenous communities in two Canadian provinces, Alberta and Ontario.

In Alberta, children begin kindergarten during the year they turn 5 years-old, and attend classes half-time, with some attending mornings or afternoon only and some attending two full-days per week. In Ontario, children begin junior kindergarten in the year they turn 4 years-old and senior kindergarten the following year. Children attend full-day classes, five days a week. Although kindergarten is not compulsory in any province and children begin grade one during the year that they turn six years-old across Canada, early childhood education policies and practices vary from province to province, as education is under provincial government jurisdiction.

The ethics protocol for our multimodal writing assessment study was approved by the Office of Research Ethics at our postsecondary institution. During the fall and spring of the fifth year of the project, the authors, along with a graduate research assistant (GRA), met one-on-one with the 64 children for whom we had received written parental consent. We asked each child for permission to video-record them as they carried out the assessment task: drawing something they like to do with their family or friends, telling us about their pictures, writing about their pictures, and then reading back their writing. If children requested assistance, we responded with the type of mediation that seemed appropriate to support the child in completing the tasks.

Table 1 displays the breakdown of the sample by grade, Indigeneity, and gender. The three English-speaking, female researchers who initiated the tasks had between one and eight years of experience teaching in primary classrooms and were well known to the children, as we were the researchers who conducted collaborative action research with the children's teachers.

Data collection and analysis

Data for this paper were comprised of: videos of the 64 students as they engaged in the drawing, talking, and writing tasks in the fall and spring (total of 128 videos); researchers' notes recorded during each task; children's pictures and printed texts; and transcripts of the 128 videos. The transcribers used the researcher notes and children's pictures and printed texts to ensure accuracy of the video transcripts.

Table 1. Grade, gender, and indigeneity of participating children (*n* values).

Grade (age when children enter grade) Gender	Indigenous		Non-indigenous	
	F	M	F	M
Junior Kindergarten (4 years)	4	1	2	1
Senior Kindergarten (5 years)	6	4	3	4
Kindergarten (5 years)	1	0	9	9
Grade 1 (6 years)	2	1	5	12
Totals	13	6	19	26
	19		45	
Total Number of Participating Children	64			

In phase one of our analysis, we used inductive analysis (Thomas 2006) of idea units within the children's talk before, during, and after drawing and writing. We define an idea unit as a unit of talk reflecting a single idea, within the children's self-initiated talk before, during, and after drawing and writing. Table 2 has illustrative examples of the codes created through this inductive process.

Working with four GRAs, over a two-month period, we identified and coded individual idea units within each of the 128 transcripts. Each GRA was given individual transcripts for coding as well as transcripts to code while paired with another GRA. In all, 66% of the transcripts were double-coded. Any discrepancies regarding the identification of idea units or the application of codes were reviewed and discussed, between pairs of coders or by the group as a whole, until agreement was reached. In all, we assigned codes to 1035 idea units from the drawing task and 931 idea units from the writing task, for a total 1966 idea units.

To identify sociocultural understandings reflected in the talk, in the second phase of our analysis, we applied a 'language as context' lens to our reading of the transcripts. We inferred what the interactions between child, researcher, and text revealed about their constructions of their roles in the conventions of the social context (an adult-initiated, one-on-one, multimodal classroom assessment). We did not engage in systematic coding of each idea unit, as the sociocultural knowledge was often reflected across a varying number of idea units within any child-researcher pairing. As such, our report of the findings of this branch of our analysis does not include frequencies. Instead, we narrate the interactions between child and researcher in illustrative examples from the data.

Discussion of the findings

In response to our research questions, we report the results of our analysis by describing oral language strategies and sociocultural knowledge demonstrated by one child, Tina (all

Table 2. Illustrative examples of children's oral language strategies.

Strategy	Definition	Example (Idea Unit)
Decoding	Assigning meaning to individual letters/words.	D. A. D. E. Y. Daddy.
Evaluating	Judging own abilities/texts.	That's a nice pony tail.
		I can spell 'Dad'.
Explaining	Labeling an individual symbol	That's my dad.
	Reporting an event by name.	This is me and my dad having a fire together.
	Elaborating on individual symbols/events.	Then there was a shiny rainbow coming in.
	Narrating the series of actions/events being represented symbolically.	One time, I hit my racket to Aiden and it broke right through. It, it was like a rocket.
	Rationalising the inclusion of a symbol/sign.	All of us like to play in the snow. That's why I drew snowballs.
Interacting	Initiating/maintaining social relationships.	Oh, he did! He's good at making things. He made the floor too.
Moving Along	Directing an ongoing action.	I'm finished.
Seeking Information	Asking another for information about what to do or how to do it.	How can I make a go kart? 'T' again?
Thinking	Reasoning out what to include in picture/text.	And now I have to make stairs. Because Grandma's house has stairs.
	Planning actions (present and/or future) while creating picture/text.	I'll draw the sun, and a happy face on the sun.
	Monitoring what needs to be changed, moved, added, or removed from picture/text.	Wait. I didn't draw everyone.

names are pseudonyms). This case contextualises our subsequent discussion of the language strategies and sociocultural knowledge of all children and researchers in the study.

Oral language strategies and sociocultural understandings: case of Tina and a researcher

Tina, an Indigenous girl who was five and in her second year of the 2-year kindergarten program at the time of the study, lived in a remote northern community in Ontario. The researcher was a postdoctoral fellow who had more than 20 years of teaching experience in southern urban primary classrooms.

Oral language strategies used in Tina's and a researcher's talk

In response to the researcher's prompt, Tina directed her actions by voicing her thoughts about a family activity she enjoyed: 'Watching a movie'. Throughout the drawing task, Tina periodically used talk to guide her drawing by describing what she would draw next: 'I'm gonna draw the stand', and later, 'Now I'm gonna draw a TV'.

Tina labelled the objects she had just drawn (e.g. 'This is dad'.). She also elaborated on these labels, both while she was drawing (e.g. 'He's smiling'.) and immediately after completing a part of her picture (e.g. 'You know my brother's nine years old. He's wearing a hat'). Tina also explained what individual characters were doing in her picture, saying, 'I'm doing a handstand on my mom's bed. My brother's doing a handstand. My whole family's doing a handstand'. On one occasion, the researcher responded to Tina's explanation of one of the images doing handstands, by seeking further information about the actions of characters in the picture: 'Oh, he is too?'

Later, Tina elaborated on various features of her picture, such as the hair on the figure representing her mother: 'My mom's hair is a mess'. She also elaborated on the actions of the characters: 'And they're just sleeping'; and on the setting: 'The TV's attached to the bed'.

Tina monitored her actions while drawing. For example, in her picture, she positioned the TV on top of the stand. Initially, her image of the TV was larger than her image of the stand. Tina's comment, 'Oh no, I have to erase this whole thing' suggests she recognised that the relationship between the TV and the stand that she was attempting to communicate graphically needed to be adjusted. The researcher used language to move the task along, asking questions such as: 'Are you going to draw more?' and later: 'Are you almost done?' Tina also moved the assessment along by signaling that she had completed the task: 'I'm done'.

In response to the researcher's prompt to write, Tina sought assistance, asking questions such as, 'How do you spell *am*?' The researcher responded with a statement that assessed and encouraged: 'Well, Tina, I have here that you are five-years-old, so I think you could try the sounds all by yourself'. Tina then used self-talk to sound out the next word she wanted to write: 'I … am … sleeeeeping'. The researcher assisted Tina in writing this word, sounding out the initial blend, *sl*. Tina then wrote the complete sentence found in Figure 1. After writing her text, Tina sought information by asking the researcher if she had spelled a word correctly: 'Sleeping?' The researcher used language to move the assessment along, asking Tina: 'Is there anything else you want to write?'

Sociocultural knowledge about task demands and the assessment context

Tina's response to the prompt to draw suggests she understood that the formal assessment context required her to demonstrate her best work: she revised her representation of certain images, even requesting a fresh sheet of paper. Additionally, during the writing task, she asked the researcher for confirmation that she had spelled a word correctly, suggesting that she constructed the assessment task as one requiring conventional spelling of words.

Initially, Tina said she would draw and write about her family watching movies. Because the picture better resembled the family sleeping on the bed, she revised both her verbal description of the actions and her written message, even though the activity did not actually take place in real life. It appears that Tina constructed the assessment task as one where consistency across verbal, written, and drawing modes was more important than fidelity to experience.

While Tina drew, the researcher appears to have constructed her role as that of objective observer, one who monitors the progress of the task and ensures that the assessment is carried out as intended. As such, apart from showing interest in what was happening in the picture by asking if Tina's brother was also doing handstands, the researcher's only oral language strategy involved moving the assessment along. She questioned Tina to see if she wanted to add detail to her picture before moving on to the writing task.

When the writing task began, Tina appears to have constructed the one-on-one context as a supportive interaction in which the researcher would provide information that Tina needed. The researcher's suggestion that Tina knew how to write the word indicates she recognised Tina as a capable writer. Her scaffolding of the initial blend in the word *sleeping* helped Tina recognise and draw on the tools she needed to write. As an experienced kindergarten and grade one teacher, the researcher may have used her

Figure 1. Tina's text. Note: Tina drew members of her family in a bed, facing the TV. She captioned her picture with the sentence, "I am sleping" (I am sleeping).

knowledge to determine what was developmentally appropriate for scaffolding Tina's writing.

In the following sections, we highlight patterns in the ways that children across the sample used talk to mediate their drawing and writing.

Children's oral language strategies in talk before, during, and after drawing and writing

Children used language more frequently before, during, and after drawing ($n = 910$) than when writing ($n = 630$). They did far more talking while they were drawing ($n = 545$) and writing ($n = 310$) than they did *before and after* carrying out the tasks. Children's use of oral language strategies varied, depending on whether they were verbalising before, during, or after completing the drawing task. One child's exclamation after hearing the prompt ('Go camping!') and Tina's pre-drawing planning about representing her family watching a movie are reflective of participating children's use of language to plan before they begin drawing ($n = 116$). Children's self-talk that included questions about how to carry out their intentions seemed to serve a guiding function, as well. For example, after one child considered, 'How can I make a go kart?' he paused, tapped the page with his pencil, drew some more, stopped, and then erased what he had drawn, saying, 'I messed up. My bad'. As was found in previous research, this talk guided the act of drawing, giving form to the children's thinking about possible family events and how to represent them in their pictures (Coates 2002; Frisch 2006).

While drawing, children explained what they were drawing ($n = 349$) using labels for the people and objects in their pictures. As shown in one child's elaborated description of a family member she had drawn: 'She's very big and tall', these explanations often included elaboration of particular characteristics of specific images. This talk seems to have supported children in refining their thinking about what meanings they would communicate through their drawing (Vygotsky 1978).

Children also used the oral strategy of explaining their pictures ($n = 111$) after they finished drawing and before being prompted to talk about it. For example, one child pointed to the smallest figure in the picture and explained how she had represented the youngest child in her family: 'Emma has little tiny arms'. The role of talk after the picture was completed appeared to clarify and consolidate the meanings that children intended to represent in their pictures (Coates and Coates 2006; Hopperstad 2008).

Children's use of oral language strategies associated with the writing task also varied depending on whether they were talking before, during, or after completing the writing. Before starting to write, children sought information about the task ($n = 49$), using language to get assistance in text creation (Myhill and Jones 2009). For example, after the researcher asked the child to write about what was happening in the picture, one child asked, 'Like write a sentence about it?' While writing their message ($n = 153$), children predominately voiced individual sounds or units of sounds within words (e.g. '/Ba/, /s/, /k/, /e/, /t/, /b/, /all/'), and isolated individual words in a sentence (e.g. 'Sleep. Sleeping. With. With. Mom'.) to guide their writing. This practice has been identified in past research (e.g. Aram, Abiri, and Elad 2014; Parr, Jesson, and McNaughton 2009; Rowe and Wilson 2015) and modelled and encouraged by classroom teachers to support emergent writers.

As was found in previous research (e.g. Coates and Coates 2006; Hopperstad 2008; Jesson, Fontich, and Myhill 2016; Myhill and Jones 2009), participating children used talk to monitor and revise their pictures ($n = 37$) and, to a lesser extent, their printed texts ($n = 14$). They monitored how closely the images matched their perceptions of the real-life people, objects, and other living things. One child's verbalised recognition, for example, that she had forgotten to draw her mother and little sister, guided her drawing of the missing family members. Another child expressed resignation that the image was 'as best as I can draw a birdie' and did not make changes, though her facial expression, as seen in the video, showed disappointment in the result of her best efforts. When writing, the children monitored the look of their printed text (Dyson 1983). For example, after reviewing his printed text, one child noticed he was missing a letter: 'And there's a 'y' at the end'. Another child commented on the quality of her print, saying 'Wait, I messed up on the 'm''.

The oral language strategies used by children help us understand how talk mediates their drawing and writing. In response to Research Question #2, using a *language as context* lens to view the data, we next discuss our interpretations of the socio-cultural knowledge reflected in child-researcher interactions.

Children's and researchers' constructions of their roles in a one-on-one drawing and writing assessment context

Children's talk while drawing and writing suggests they viewed the one-on-one context as an interactive opportunity to co-construct meaning, rather than as a formal assessment setting where children created texts independently. As we proposed earlier, children's explanations of what they were drawing may have served to guide their drawing (Coates 2002; Frisch 2006). Yet, they may also have been for the purpose of keeping the researcher updated on what they were doing and providing information about the picture that they felt the adult should know. Occasionally, researchers took up roles as conversational partners who were interested in the messages that children were communicating in their pictures and print. One researcher, for example, asked, 'Does your baby brother fall down sometimes when he walks?' The child responded with an explanation showing their cultural knowledge: 'Well, we have a gate to keep him from falling down the stairs'. This role is consistent with the interpersonal co-construction of meaning advocated by Kesler (2020) as supportive of young children's writing and their identities as writers.

In other cases, researchers took up the role of teacher, as in a dynamic assessment context, where mediational practices are intended to support children's learning so that they can complete the task at hand and apply what they have learned in future contexts where the adult is not present (Davin, Troyan, and Hellmann 2014). Researcher mediation included asking questions to make the generation of content for writing more manageable or to stimulate children to recognise and draw upon their background knowledge and experiences to write about their pictures. Many children narrated extensive stories when describing their pictures orally before informing the researcher that writing all that they had said was beyond their abilities (e.g. 'I don't know how to write all that thing'.). As a result, researchers provided suggestions through questions related to the children's verbalised stories, such as: 'What's your brother's name? Do you think you could write some of the letters?', or 'You said, 'I went fishing'. Can you write that?'

Researchers seem to have associated the need for adult mediation with children's writing far more than with children's drawing, as there were 301 idea units related to mediation of children's writing and 125 related to children's drawing. Mediation of the drawing consisted mainly of encouraging children to add to their pictures (e.g. 'What other games could you draw?') or inquiring whether the picture was complete, whereas mediation of the writing involved specific suggestions about potential content of the writing (e.g. 'How about you write the word 'camp'?') and ideas of approaches to resolving the challenges that young children face when creating print texts by hinting, as Matlew and Sorsby (1995) suggest, they could *draw* print (e.g. 'An 's'. It's like a curvy path'.). The children appear to have shared this perception of the adult role related to supporting the creation of print texts, as they asked questions about letters to write their intended messages, but did not ask researchers questions about how to draw individual images. For example, after the researchers repeated what the children had said about their picture (as potential content for the writing), children would ask if a particular letter would be appropriate for writing the first word of the phrase/sentence that the researcher had said.

However, in most cases, within the one-on-one assessments, researchers constructed roles of objective observers who prompted children to carry out tasks, but did not contribute to children's text creation. In this respect, the researchers' talk was consistent with a view of assessment as a measurement of children's independently-created texts and of assessment and teaching as unconnected practices (Calkins 2015; Puranik and Lonigan 2011).

Children's and researchers' constructions of early drawing and writing

Children's choice of topics for their drawing and writing and the way they talked about the topics suggest their perception that symbolic texts communicate special, out-of-the-ordinary, information. For example, one child who drew her family having a feast talked about how special the feast was – there was going to be 'cake with strawberries and blueberries and raspberries'. Topics of children's drawing, talking, and writing often included descriptions of special trips outside the local community, eventful local excursions, or unexpected happenings during typical family activities.

Children's use of talk while drawing reflects their knowledge about the object and activity they intended to draw (Dyson 1986). For example, one child, while planning her picture, talked about providing an appropriate context for dolls. She said she would draw the dolls 'in the stroller'. Children's talk also signifies their assumption that a picture should resemble as closely as possible the objects and relationships being represented (Watts 2010). One child's planning talk, for example, focused on a facial feature that needed to be represented in a particular way: 'And, I need the nose. So big'. Children's talk also demonstrated their understanding of ways to represent action in static pictures (Duncum 1993). For example, one child explained why a sibling's mouth was drawn as it was: 'His mouth is talking' and another explained a picture of his father on the trampoline with the boy and his siblings in this way: 'You can only see his head coming up'.

Researchers communicated an expectation that children could write something mean-ingful, regardless of whether the actual print on the page included one letter or multiple words (Clay 1998). Younger children's talk reflected a different view of early writing, as they explained to the researchers either that they were unable to write or that they were unable to spell particular words. In contrast, first-grade children were able to use invented spelling to write and did not tell researchers that they were unable to write. They seemed to construct writing as the use of conventional spellings, however, and recognised the difference between conventional and their invented spellings of words. For example, after 6-year-old Garrett wrote *tAPren*, he asked, 'I just spelled *trampoline*. That's it?' The researcher accepted the invented spelling because it reflected the print knowledge that she expected of emergent writers. However, Garrett's question and the doubtful look on his face (as seen on the video) showed that he knew this was not the conventional spelling (Gombert and Fayol 1992).

Conclusions, limitations, and implications

Children's oral language strategies mediating drawing and writing

Our analysis of children's oral language strategies before, during, and after the one-on-one assessment task enlarges the window into children's meaning-making through mul-tiple communicative modes. Participating children used language to plan the family interactions that they would draw and to identify notable features of the people, objects, and animals they could represent in their pictures. They explained what the family event would be before beginning to draw, and then while drawing, elaborated on characteristics of particular people, animals, objects, and settings that were part of the family story. In these ways, talk gave form to children's planning, and to their refining and elaborating of the message they intended to communicate through drawing. The potential of talk to support meaning-making throughout the creative process, found in many studies of older children's writing (e.g. Jesson, Fontich, and Myhill 2016; Myhill and Jones 2009), was in evidence in participating children's talk associated with their drawing.

Children also used talk to monitor how closely their picture resembled their percep-tions of the lived experience, identifying features of represented people and objects that needed to be modified or that were missing and needed to be included. As such, we suggest their talk served to mediate their mental representations (Coates and Coates 2006; Soundy 2015).

The function of revision in writing, to improve the text so that it more closely com-municates the intended message (Oliver 2019), appears to be inconsistent with the func-tion of the children's monitoring and revising of their print in the multimodal assessment context of our research. Most children used talk to monitor the appearance of individual letters and attend to their spelling of words, as letter fluency and knowledge of grapho-phonic relationships were nascent. As in previous research examining young children's talk while writing (e.g. Aram, Abiri, and Elad 2014; Rowe and Wilson 2015), children voiced sounds within words and said the words they intended to write. Thus, their talk served to guide the spelling of the words. A focus on lower-level writing skills and knowledge is consistent with research showing that working memory is freed-up to attend to the generating and organising of ideas in writing when children have a more developed spelling repertoire and letter-writing fluency (Berninger et al. 2010; Graham and Harris 2000).

Children's and researchers' constructions of drawing and writing and their roles in the one-on-one assessment context

The one-on-one assessment context created an interactive space for children to get immediate feedback on their interpretation of the adult-initiated tasks and to receive support in carrying out the tasks. Given that children communicated their need for support with writing and that the researchers were far more proficient in writing than in drawing, when researchers took up a mediational role, it was to support the children's writing, rather than their drawing. It is also possible that the notably greater amount and specificity of our mediation of children's creation of print texts reflects the well-documented differential valuing of the two types of texts in classroom teaching and assessment (e.g. Wohlwend 2009).

The one-on-one context provided opportunities for researchers to integrate assessment and teaching, taking up a role as mediator in a dynamic assessment context (Davin, Troyan, and Hellmann 2014). Despite the researchers' initial conceptualisation of the assessment as one meant to elicit children's independent performance, the one-on-one context offered rich opportunities for mediation that researchers came to see as being more important than fidelity to dominant assumptions about child-assessor relationships in assessments, such as their strict adherence to formal prompts within the assessment protocol.

The one-on-one context also provided opportunities for a sharing of perspectives on what counts as written texts and on what it means to be a writer. Children's questions and self-assessments reflected their perception of written texts as composed of conventional spelling and of their construction of their identities as non-writers. In the one-on-one setting, researchers provided alternative views of written texts as those that could be created by young children using invented spelling and of the open-ended task as a context for children to demonstrate that they were writers. Researchers' responses to children's questions and self-assessments reflects research on early writing showing that young children's developing knowledge of concepts of print supports symbolic communication through invented spelling and that invented spelling provides a foundation for conventional writing (Caravolas, Hulme, and Snowling 2001; Gerde, Bingham, and Wasik 2012).

Limitations and implications

Generalisability of the findings of our one-on-one assessment to classroom practice is limited because the assessments were carried out by researchers who were not in the classroom on a daily basis. Although the researchers were not strangers to the children, we had not developed the close relationships that classroom teachers shared with participating children. Additionally, we recognise that many teachers may not have the opportunities that researchers had to conduct one-on-one assessments. However, based on our observations of classrooms participating in the NOW Play project, we believe that the valuable information gained through one-on-one teaching/assessment experiences, such as the one we described in our paper, warrants consideration for setting up kindergarten classrooms. Our observations show that teachers may create space for one-on-one time with children for teaching that is responsive to children's immediate learning needs through the use of play centers or through sharing responsibility for working with groups of children with early childhood educators or educational assistants.

Our research contributes to the broader field of early literacy assessment by showing the value of one-on-one multimodal assessment contexts to support young children's literacy. Teachers who take up a *language as context* approach to assessing children's texts that include drawing and writing, take note of the ways in which children use talk to plan, to refine their goals for and to guide their drawing and writing, and to monitor and consolidate the meanings constructed in their drawing and writing. Using this approach, teachers are able to listen to children's talk before, during, and after drawing and writing to gather valuable information about their perspectives of what counts as writing and about their construction of their literate identities. The one-on-one context is viewed as a valuable part of classroom practice that allows teachers to learn more about each child as an individual learner, to teach to children's immediate needs, and to support children's construction of strong literate identities.

The focus of the assessment presented in this paper is on children's demonstration of their learning and development, rather than of standards imposed by authorities such as school districts and ministries of education (Yoon 2015). As such, we suggest the drawing, talk, and writing assessment provides specific information about children's thinking and literacy learning that teachers can use for documentation and for planning instruction (Ontario Ministry of Education 2020).

In this paper, we introduce an assessment that can be used in a wide range of contexts. Because the tasks are open-ended, children can take up diverse social and cultural practices in their written texts that extend beyond the remote northern communities of children participating in our study. In addition to providing a ready model for classroom practice, we hope that our research contributes to conversations about the potential for one-on-one assessment contexts to support children's multimodal literacy development and their construction of literate identities.

Acknowledgements

We acknowledge this research was conducted in the territories of: Treaty 3, Ojibwe First Nations; Treaty 8, Woodland Cree First Nation; and Treaty 9, Ojibway Nation. We are grateful to the communities for welcoming us to work and learn with them. We are thankful to the participating children and their teachers.

Disclosure statement

No potential conflict of interest was reported by the author(s).

Funding

This work was supported by Social Sciences and Humanities Research Council of Canada [grant number 895-2012-1007].

ORCID

Shelley Stagg Peterson ⓘD http://orcid.org/0000-0001-6985-5603
Nicola Friedrich ⓘD http://orcid.org/0000-0002-2914-9453

References

Anning, A. 1997. "Drawing Out Ideas: Graphicacy and Young Children." *International Journal of Technology and Design Education* 7: 219–239.

Aram, D., S. Abiri, and L. Elad. 2014. "Predicting Early Spelling: The Contribution of Children's Early Literacy, Private Speech During Spelling, Behavioral Regulation, and Parent Spelling Support." *Reading and Writing* 27: 685–707. doi:10.1007/s11145-013-9466-z.

Bear, D. R., M. Invernizzi, S. Templeton, and F. Johnston. 2012. *Words Their Way: Word Study for Phonics, Vocabulary, and Spelling Instruction.* Boston: Pearson.

Berninger, V. W., R. D. Abbott, W. Nagy, and J. Carlisle. 2010. "Growth in Phological, Orthogrpahic, and Morphological Awareness in Grades 1 to 6." *Journal of Psycholoinguistic Research* 39 (2): 141–163.

Bourke, L., S. J. Davies, E. Sumner, and C. Green. 2014. "Individual Differences in the Development of Early Writing Skills: Testing the Unique Contribution of Visuo-Spatial Working Memory." *Reading and Writing* 27 (2): 315–335.

Brooks, M. L. 2017. "Drawing to Learn." In *Multimodal Perspectives of Language, Literacy, and Learning in Early Childhood: The Creative and Critical "Art" of Making Meaning*, edited by M. J. Narey, 25–44. Cham: Springer International.

Calkins, L. 2015. *Writing Pathways: Performance Assessments and Learning Progressions.* Portsmouth, NH: Heinemann.

Caravolas, M., C. Hulme, and M. J. Snowling. 2001. "The Foundations of Spelling Ability: Evidence From a 3-Year Longitudinal Study." *Journal of Memory and Language* 45: 751–774. doi:10.1006/jmla.2000.2785.

Clay, M. M. 1998. *By Different Paths to Common Outcomes.* New York: Stenhouse.

Coates, E. 2002. "I Forgot the Sky! Children's Stories Contained Within Their Drawings." *International Journal of Early Years Education* 10 (1): 21–35. doi:10.1080/09669760220114827.

Coates, E., and A. Coates. 2006. "Young Children Talking and Drawing." *International Journal of Early Years Education* 14 (3): 221–241. doi:10.1080/09669760600879961.

Cutler, L., and S. Graham. 2008. "Primary Grade Writing Instruction: A National Survey." *Journal of Educational Psychology* 100 (4): 907–919. doi:10.1037/a0012656.

Dahl, K. L. 1993. "Children's Spontaneous Utterances During Early Reading and Writing Instruction in Whole-Language Classrooms." *Journal of Literacy Research* 25 (3): 279–294. doi:10.1080/10862969009547818.

Davin, K. J., F. J. Troyan, and A. L. Hellmann. 2014. "Classroom Dynamic Assessment of Reading Comprehension with English Language Learners." *Language and Sociocultural Theory* 1 (1): 1–23.

Duncum, P. 1993. "Ten Types of Narrative Drawing Among Children's Spontaneous Picture-Making." *Visual Arts Research* 19 (1): 20–29.

Dyson, A. H. 1983. "The Role of Oral Language in Early Writing Processes." *Research in the Teaching of English* 17 (1): 1–30.

Dyson, A. H. 1986. "Transitions and Tensions: Interrelationships Between Drawing, Talking, and Dictating of Young Children." *Research in the Teaching of English* 20 (4): 379–409.

Fang, Z., and B. W. Cox. 1999. "Emergent Metacognition: A Study of Preschoolers' Literate Behaviour." *Journal of Research in Childhood Education* 13 (2): 175–187. doi:10.1080/02568549909594738.

Frisch, N. 2006. "Drawing in Preschools: A Didactic Experience." *Journal of Art and Design Education* 25 (1): 74–85. doi:10.1111/j.1476-8070.2006.00470.x.

Genishi, C., and A. Dyson. 2009. *Children, Language, and Literacy: Diverse Learners in Diverse Times.* New York: Guilford.

Gerde, H. K., G. E. Bingham, and B. A. Wasik. 2012. "Writing in Early Childhood Classrooms: Guidance for Best Practices." *Early Childhood Education Journal* 40 (6): 351–359. doi:10.1007/s10643-012-0531-z.

Gombert, J. E., and M. Fayol. 1992. "Writing in Preliterate Children." *Learning and Instruction* 21: 23–41.

Graham, S., and K. Harris. 2000. "The Role of Self-Regulation and Transcription Skills in Writing and Writing Development." *Educational Psychologist* 35 (1): 3–12.

Hall, A. H., A. Simpson, Y. Guo, and S. Wang. 2015. "Examining the Effects of Preschool Writing Instruction on Emergent Literacy Skills: A Systematic Review of the Literature." *Literacy Research and Instruction* 54: 115–134. doi:10.1080/19388071.2014.991883.

Heritage, M., and C. Harrison. 2019. *The Power of Assessment for Learning: Twenty Years of Research and Practice in UK and US Classrooms.* London: Sage.

Hopperstad, M. H. 2008. "How Children Make Meaning Through Drawing and Play." *Visual Communication* 7 (1): 77–96. doi:10.1177/1470357207084866.

Jesson, R., X. Fontich, and D. Myhill. 2016. "Creating Dialogic Spaces: Talk as a Mediational Tool in Becoming a Writer." *International Journal of Educational Research* 80: 155–163.

Kenner, C. 2000. "Symbols Make Text: A Social Semiotic Analysis in a Multilingual Nursery." *Written Language and Literacy* 3 (2): 235–266. doi:10.1075/wll.3.02.03ken.

Kesler, T. 2020. "'Does it Have to be a Real Story?' A Social Semiotic Assessment of an Emergent Writer." *Language and Education* 5: 440–468. doi:10.1080/09500782.2020.1766060.

Kress, G. 1997. *Before Writing: Rethinking the Paths to Literacy.* London: Routledge.

Mackenzie, N. M., J. Scull, and L. Munsie. 2013. "Analysing Writing: The Development of a Tool for Use in the Early Years of Schooling." *Issues in Educational Research* 23 (3): 375–393.

Matlew, M., and A. Sorsby. 1995. "The Precursors of Writing: Graphic Representation in Preschool Children." *Learning and Instruction* 5: 1–19.

Molfese, V. J., J. L. Beswick, J. Jacobi-Vessels, N. E. Armstrong, B. L. Culver, J. M. White, M. C. Ferguson, K. M. Rudasill, and D. L. Molfese. 2011. "Evidence of Alphabetic Knowledge in Writing: Connections to Letter and Word Identification Skills in Preschool and Kindergarten." *Reading and Writing* 24 (2): 133–150. doi:10.1007/s11145-010-9265-8.

Myhill, D., and S. Jones. 2009. "How Talk Becomes Text: Investigating the Concept of Oral Rehearsal in Early Years' Classrooms." *British Journal of Educational Studies* 57 (3): 265–284. doi:10.111/1467-8527.2009.00438.x.

Oliver, L. 2019. "Nothing Too Major: How Poor Revision of Writing May Be an Adaptive Response to School Tasks." *Language and Education* 33 (4): 363–378. doi:10.1080/09500782.2018.1511728.

Ontario Ministry of Education. 2020. *Assessing and Learning in Kindergarten: Making Children's Learning Visible.* Toronto: Author. http://www.edu.gov.on.ca/eng/policyfunding/leadership/pdfs/issue15.pdf.

Ouellette, G., M. Sénéchal, and A. Haley. 2013. "Guiding Children's Invented Spellings: A Gateway into Literacy Learning." *The Journal of Experimental Education* 81 (2): 261–279.

Parr, J., R. Jesson, and S. McNaughton. 2009. "Agency and Platform: The Relationship Between Talk and Writing." In *The Sage Handbook of Writing Development*, edited by R. Beard, J. Riley, D. Myhill, and M. Nystrand, 246–259. London: Sage.

Puranik, C. S., and C. J. Lonigan. 2011. "From Scribbles to Scrabble: Preschool Children's Developing Knowledge of Written Language." *Reading and Writing* 24: 567–589. doi:10.1007/s11145-009-9220-8.

Rowe, D. W. 2008. "Social Contracts for Writing: Negotiating Shared Understandings About Text in the Preschool Years." *Reading Research Quarterly* 43 (1): 66–95. doi:10.1598/rrq.43.15.

Rowe, D. W., and S. J. Wilson. 2015. "The Development of a Descriptive Measure of Early Childhood Writing: Results from the Write Start! Writing Assessment." *Journal of Literacy Research* 47 (2): 245–292. doi:10.1177/1086296X15619723.

Soundy, C. S. 2015. "Making Sense of Children's Drawings and Semiotic Explorations." *Dimensions of Early Childhood* 43 (3): 39–46.

Thomas, D. R. 2006. "A General Inductive Approach for Analyzing Qualitative Evaluation Data." *American Journal of Evaluation* 27 (2): 237–246.

Vygotsky, L. 1978. *Mind in Society*. Cambridge, MA: Harvard University Press.

Watts, R. 2010. "Responding to Children's Drawings." *Education 3-13* 38 (2): 137–153. doi:10.1080/03004270903107877.

Wiliam, D. 2011. "What is Assessment for Learning?" *Educational Evaluation* 37 (1): 3–14.

Wohlwend, K. 2009. "Dilemmas and Discourses of Learning to Write: Assessments as a Contested Site." *Language Arts* 86: 341–351.

Yoon, H. S. 2015. "Assessing Children in Kindergarten: The Narrowing of Language, Culture and Identity in the Testing Era." *Journal of Early Childhood Literacy* 15 (3): 364–393.

Index

Note: Figures are indicated by *italics*. Tables are indicated by **bold**. Endnotes are indicated by the page number followed by 'n' and the endnote number e.g., 20n1 refers to endnote 1 on page 20.

Anderson, Daniel R. 15, 16
Anderson, Nina J. 8
Andrews, Rebecca 3
Attenborough, Frederick 43, 51
Aukrust, Vibeke 26
Australia 75; coding of data 92; cultural differences in 90; data generation 91–2; early childhood education and care (ECEC) context 88; infant educators' use of mental-state talk in 87, 89–90, **93**; infant-toddler educators in 3; inter-coder reliability 93–4; method 91; present study 91; results 94–9
Avineri, Netta 17

Barnes, Erica M. 89
Barr, Rachel 16
Barrett, Tyson S. 16
Bateman, Amanda 2
Beals, Diane E. 27
Blackwell, Anna K.M. 8
Bohanek, Jennifer G. 27
Bornstein, Marc H. 16
Bova, Antonio 36, 37
Brody, Gene H. 16
Brouzos, Andreas 89–90
Brown, Penelope 7

Calvert , Sandra L. 16
Cameron-Faulkner, Thea 15
Canada: kindergarten and Grade 1 practice in 3
Casillas, Marisa 7
Cekaite, Aste 2
Charney, Rosalind 13
Cheng, Michelle 90
Chesnick, Robert J. 14
child-educator interactions 2
childhood educators 72; in Australia 3; educator–child talks about past 73–4; parent–child talk about past 72; present study 74
Children as active social agents 44
China: communication in Chinese families 28; cultural differences in 90; early childhood

education and care (ECEC) context 88; infant educators' use of mental-state talk in 87, 89–90, 91–9; infant-toddler educators in 3; parent–child mealtime conversations 25, 29–38; participants and data generation 30–2; Peabody Picture Vocabulary Test 27
Chinese children's early language experiences (CCELE) 30
Chinese culture: in language learning 2
Choi, Soonja 13–14
Clugston, Lynn 14
Colonnesi, Cristina 89
Corsaro, William A. 42
Crago, Martha B. 7, 8
Crain-Thoreson, C. 13

Dahlin, M. P. 13
Dai, Quian 90, 102
Dalli, Carmel 2, 52n2
Degotardi, Sheila 3
Dickenson, David K. 89
Doan, Stacey N. 90
Doering, Elena 13, 17

early childhood community of practice 41; children as active social agents 44; interactional sociolinguistics 44; labelling and boundary-work 46–8; membership categorisation devices (MCD) 42–4
Early Childhood Education and Care (ECEC) 56, 72, 88
Elgas, Peggy M. 42
Engdahl, Ingrid 41
Ewin, Carrie A. 15

Farrar, Michael Jeffrey 14
Fernie, David E. 42
Flynn, Valerie 17
Forbes, James N. 14
Francesco, Arcidiacono 37
Fraser, Colin 14
Friedrich, Nicola 3

Friend, Margaret J. 14
Fujita, Nao 90

Gallimore, Ronald 18
Gattis, Merideth 15
Gelman, Susan A. 14
Goldenberg, Claude N. 18
Goldfield, Beverly A. 14
Gülgöz, Selin 14

Halliday, Michael Alexander Kirkwood 29
Han, Feifei 3
Hanson, Katherine G. 16
Hesketh, Anne 15
Howes, Carollee 42
Hu, Jiangbo 3, 28
Hughes, Claire 90

infant-toddler educators in: Australia 3; China 3

Jesson, R. 108
Jipson, Jennifer L. 14
Jones, Michael N. 4

Kantor, Rebecca 42
Kaye, Kenneth 13
Kertoy, Marilyn K. 13
Kesler, T. 114
King, Elizabeth 89
Kirkorian, Heather L. 15
Koh, Jessie Bee Kim 72, 81–2
Kuchirko, Yana 7
Kulkofsky, Sarah 72, 75, 81–2
Kwon, Kyong Ah 16

La Paro, Karen 89
Language Environment Analysis (LENA) system 83
language: in context 1; and culture 2; learning levels of 29; and literacy learning 1; and nonverbal communication modes 1
Larson, Anne L. 16
Lauricella, Alexis R. 16
Lavigne, Heather J. 16
Lawrence, Valerie W. 15
Levinson, Stephen C. 7
Lieven, Elena 15
Lim, Ai Keow 90, 102
Lucariello, Joan 14

Marcos, Haydée 14
Martlew, Margaret 14
Marvin, Christine A. 16
Masur, Elise Frank 17
Matlew, M. 115
Matthiessen, Christian 29
McConnell, Scott R. 16
McHugh, Mary 32
McMahon, Catherine 90, 102
McNaughton, S. 108

mealtime conversations for children: learning opportunities in 27
Melville, Joanna 15
membership categorisation devices (MCD): communities of practice and 42–4; interactional sociolinguistics 44
mental state talk: in Australia and China 87; coding of data 92; cognitions 92; cultural differences in 90; data generation 91–2; desires 92; emotions 92; infant educators' use of 87, 89–90; inter-coder reliability 93–4; method 91; modulations of assertion 92; perceptions 92; present study 91; results 94–9
Meyerhoff, Miriam 2, 52n2, n4
Misailidi, Plousia 89–90
Montag, Jessica L. 4
Muhinyi, Amber 15

Nelson, Katherine 14
New Zealand 2, 42; early childhood education curricula 55–8; footage 60–7; language and literacy 58; language as context 58–9; methodology 59–60; shared socio-cultural approach 55–8; Te Whāriki 56, 57, 63
Noble, Claire H. 15
Northern Oral Language and Writing through Play (NOW Play) project 108–9
Nyhout, Angela 14

O'Neill, Daniela K. 14
oral language strategies 107, 110–11, 113–14, 116

Painter, Kathleen M. 16
Papoudi, Depsina 89–90
parent–child communication: in Chinese families 28; language expansion in 29
parent–child interaction (PCI) 8
parent-child language: across activity contexts 6; activity context frequencies 12; activity contexts in early intervention 7–8; Joanna Briggs Institute (JBI) methodology 8; methods 8–9; PRISMA flowchart 10, 11; results 9–13; studying methods 7
Park, Jaihyun 16
Parr, J. 108
Pempek, Tiffany A. 15
Peterson, Shelley Stagg 3
Powell, T. A. 13
Privratsky, Amy J. 16

Raudsepp, Margit 15
Riordan, Jessica 15
Roberts, Naomi 14
Roopnarine, Jaipaul L. 17
Ryckebusch, Céline 14

Sacks, Harvey 43
Schegloff, Emanuel A. 59
Schluter, Kevin 13, 17
Shipley, Elizabeth F. 15

Simit, Linda B. 4
Snow, Catherine E. 4, 27
Socioeconomic status (SES) 26
Soderstrom, Melanie 15
Sorsby, Angela J. 14, 115
Stevenson, Marguerite B.16
Stokoe, Elizabeth 43, 51
Stoneman, Zolinda 16
Strycharz-Banaś, Anna 2, 52n2
Sweden 2; curriculum for preschool in 58; early
    childhood education curricula 55–8; footage
    60–7; language and literacy 58; language as
    context 58–9; methodology 59–60; shared
    socio-cultural approach 55–8
Systemic Functional Linguistics (SFL) 29

Tamis-LeMonda, Catherine S. 15, 16, 17
Taumoepeau, Mele 90
Te Whāriki 56, 57, 63

Test, Joan E. 82
Torr, Jane 14, 28
Tulviste, Tiia 15

Van Bergen, Penny 3
Vetter, Dolores Kluppel 13
von Suchodoletz, Antje 13, 17

Wang, Qi 28, 72, 81–2, 90
Waxman, Sandra R. 14
Weisner, Thomas S. 18
Wittebolle, Kelsey 15

young children: drawing 107–8; talking 107–8;
    writing 107–8; oral language strategies 110–11,
    113, 116; sociocultural knowledge 112;
    language and literacy learning 1

Zhang, Heyi 28